THE HIDDEN

NORTHUMBELAND AND DURHAM

By Peter Long

Published by:
Travel Publishing Ltd
Airport Business Centre, 10 Thornbury Road,
Estover, Plymouth PL6 7PP

ISBN13 9781907462085

First Published: 1992 Second Edition: 1995
Third Edition: 1998 Fourth Edition: 2001
Fifth Edition: 2003 Sixth Edition: 2005
Seventh Edition: 2008 Eighth Edition: 2011

Please Note:

All advertisements in this publication have been accepted in good faith by Travel Publishing.

All information is included by the publishers in good faith and is believed to be correct at the time of going to press. No responsibility can be accepted for errors.

Editor: Peter Long

Printing by: Latimer Trend, Plymouth

Location Maps: © Maps in Minutes ™ (2011)
© Collins Bartholomews 2011 All rights reserved.

Cover Photo: Remains of Lindisfarne Abbey on Holy Island.
© International Photobank / Alamy

Text Photos: See page 163

Foreword

This is the 8th edition of the *Hidden Places of Northumberland and Durham* which has an attractive new cover and redesigned page layouts. The changes will significantly improve the usefulness, accessibility and appeal of the guide. We do hope you like the new look.

Editorially, the new style continues Travel Publishing's commitment to exploring the more interesting, unusual or unique places of interest in Northumberland, County Durham and Tyne and Wear. In this respect we would like to thank the Tourist Information Centres who helped us update the editorial content of the book.

Northumberland offers the visitor plenty of picturesque places to visit such as the Kielder Forest, the Cheviot Hills, Holy Island, and the many miles of attractive coastline. Hadrian's Roman Wall also stretches across this largely unspoilt county. *County Durham* is blessed with an incredibly strong history that runs deep with industrial heritage. The landscape still shows evidence of coal mining traditions, but the spoil heaps and pit heads have now all but disappeared. The county encompasses the beautiful and historic City of Durham and, like its northern neighbour, has an impressive number of castles, churches and historic houses.

The Hidden Places of Northumberland and Durham contains a wealth of information on the history, culture and the hundreds of interesting places to be found within the two counties and island. But it also promotes the more secluded and little known visitor attractions and advertises places to stay, eat and drink many of which are easy to miss unless you know exactly where you are going. These are cross-referenced to more detailed information contained in a separate, easy-to-use section to the rear of the book. This section is also available as a free supplement from the local Tourist Information Offices.

We include hotels, bed & breakfasts, restaurants, pubs, bars, teashops and cafes as well as historic houses, museums, gardens and many other attractions throughout the area - all of which are comprehensively indexed. Many places are accompanied by an attractive photograph and are easily located by using the map at the beginning of each chapter. We do not award merit marks or rankings but concentrate on describing the more interesting, unusual or unique features of each place with the aim of making the reader's stay in the local area an enjoyable and stimulating experience.

Whether you are travelling around Northumberland, County Durham or Tyne and Wear on business or for pleasure we do hope that you enjoy reading and using this book. We are always interested in what readers think of places covered (or not covered) in our guides so please do not hesitate to use the reader reaction form provided to give us your considered comments. We also welcome any general comments which will help us improve the guides themselves. Finally if you are planning to visit any other corner of the British Isles we would like to refer you to the list of other *Hidden Places* titles to be found to the rear of the book and to the Travel Publishing website (see below).

Travel Publishing

Location Map

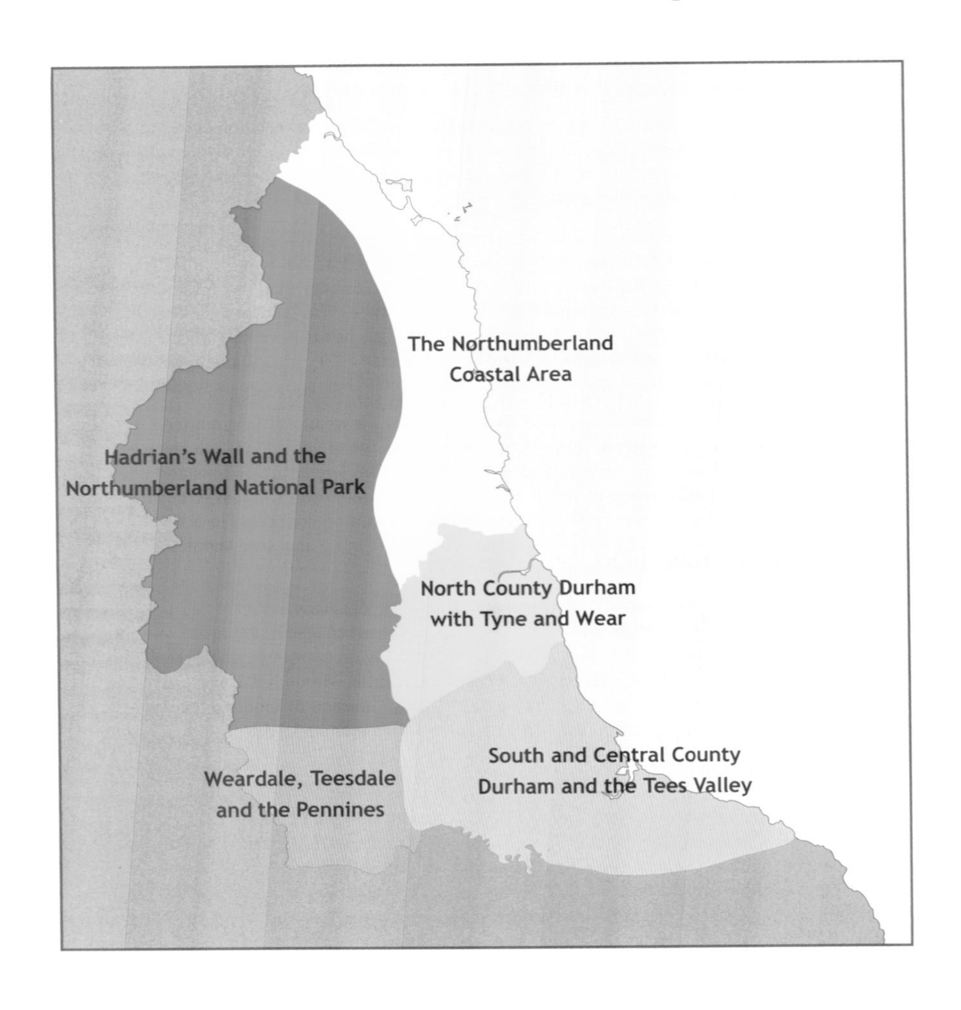

Contents

LOCATION MAP

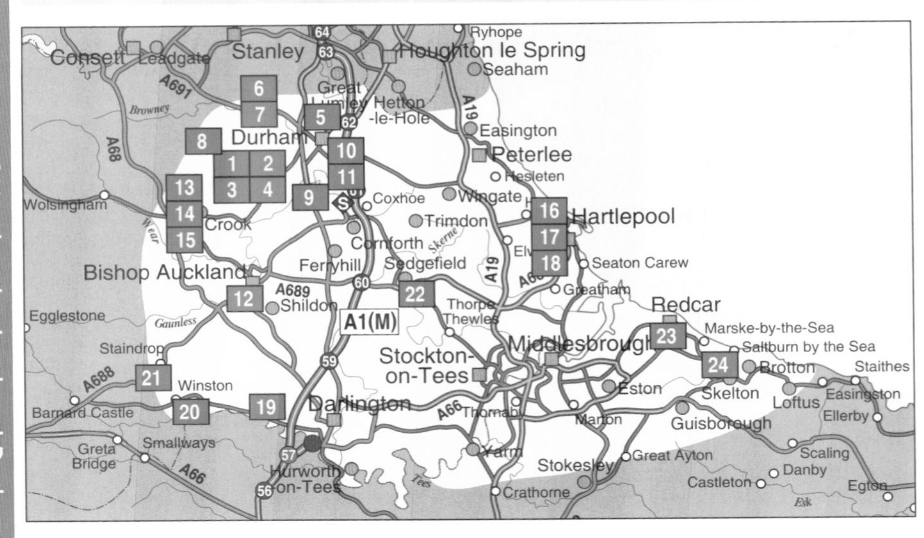

Accommodation

1	Moor End Guest House, Durham City	*pg 4, 82*
2	66 Claypath, Durham City	*pg 4, 82*
8	The Royal Oak, Cornsay Colliery	*pg 8, 85*
11	The Avenue Inn, Shincliffe, Durham	*pg 8, 87*
15	Dowfold House, Crook	*pg 10, 90*
22	Cross Hill Hotel & Salvo's Bistro, Sedgefield	*pg 16, 93*
23	The Clarendon Hotel, Redcar	*pg 19, 94*

Food & Drink

5	The Salutation , Framwellgate Moor, Durham City	*pg 7, 84*
6	The Travellers Rest, Witton Gilbert	*pg 7, 84*
7	Broom House Farm, Witton Gilbert	*pg 7, 86*
8	The Royal Oak, Cornsay Colliery	*pg 8, 85*
9	Coach and Horses, Croxdale	*pg 8, 86*
10	Brambles Coffee Shop, Shincliffe, Durham	*pg 8, 86*
11	The Avenue Inn, Shincliffe, Durham	*pg 8, 87*
12	Time For You Tea Rooms, Bishop Auckland	*pg 9, 87*
13	Colliery Inn, Crook	*pg 10, 88*
14	Cottons Cafe & Restaurant, Crook	*pg 10, 89*
16	The Causeway, Hartlepool	*pg 11, 90*
18	Nip In Cafe, Hartlepool	*pg 11, 91*
19	The Carlbury Arms, Piercebridge, Darlington	*pg 14, 91*
20	The Bridgewater Arms, Winston, Teesdale	*pg 14, 92*
21	The Black Swan, Staindrop, Darlington	*pg 15, 93*
22	Cross Hill Hotel & Salvo's Bistro, Sedgefield	*pg 16, 93*
23	The Clarendon Hotel, Redcar	*pg 19, 94*
24	Rapp's Cafe & The Kings Grill, Saltburn By The Sea	*pg 19, 95*

Places of Interest

3	Durham Castle, Durham City	*pg 5, 83*
4	Crook Hall and Gardens, Durham City	*pg 7, 83*
7	Broom House Farm, Witton Gilbert	*pg 7, 86*
17	Hartlepool Historic Quay and Museum, Hartlepool	*pg 11, 90*

SOUTH AND CENTRAL COUNTY DURHAM AND THE TEES VALLEY

County Durham's prosperity was founded on coal mining, and nowhere is this more apparent than in the central and southern parts of the county. Coal had been mined here for centuries, but it wasn't until the 18th century that the industry was established on a commercial basis. When the railways arrived in the early 19th century, the industry prospered, creating great wealth for the landowners, and frequently great danger and misery for the miners. Now that the industry has all but disappeared, the scars it created are being swept away. Spoil heaps have been cleared or grassed over, pitheads demolished and old industrial sites tidied up. Colliery villages such as Pity Me, Shiney Row, Bearpark, Sunniside and Quebec still exist - tight-knit communities that retain an old-style sense of belonging and sharing, and even in the most unprepossessing of villages there are delightful surprises to be discovered, such as the near-perfect Saxon church at Escomb. Other notable religious buildings in the region include St Brandon's at Brancepeth, St Andrew's in Bishop Auckland, St Cuthbert's in Billingham, St Edmund's in Sedgefield and, of course, the magnificent Cathedral in Durham.

Coal may have been king, but County Durham's countryside has always supported an important farming industry, and Central and South Durham still retain a gentle landscape of fields, woodland, streams and narrow country lanes. This area stretches from the East Coast to the Pennines in the west, and from the old border with Yorkshire in the south to the edge of the Tyne and the Wear conurbations in the north. Within this area there are picturesque villages, cottages, grand houses, museums, snug pubs, old churches and castles aplenty.

The coastline too has been cleaned up. An 11-mile coastal footpath snakes through the district of Easington from Seaham Hall Beach in the north to Crimdon Park in the south. Much of it is along clifftops with spectacular views down onto the beaches. This coastal area has recently been designated as a National Nature Reserve and is blessed with many reminders of a rich maritime heritage. Captain Cook was born in Middlesbrough in 1728, and his story is told in the Captain Cook Birthplace Museum in that town. In nearby Stockton is a replica of his ship HM Bark Endeavour. At Hartlepool lies HMS Trincomalee, the oldest warship afloat. Saltburn's coast is a recognised part of the 36 miles of Heritage Coast, and Redcar is home to the oldest lifeboat in the world, housed in the Zetland Lifeboat Museum. Saltburn is the only place in the region which still has its own pier, this one built in 1870.

Travelling around the region the visitor is also constantly reminded of its rich social, industrial and Christian heritage. The Romans marched along Dere Street in County Durham, and in the 9th and 10th centuries holy men carried the body of St Cuthbert with them as they sought a place of refuge from the marauding Vikings. The railways were born in the county in 1825, with the opening of the famous Stockton and Darlington Railway.

Dominating the whole area is the city of Durham - one of Europe's finest small cities. It was here, in 1832, that England's third great university was established. The towns of Darlington, Stockton-on-Tees, Hartlepool and Bishop Auckland are all worthy of exploration.

River Wear, Durham City

DURHAM CITY

'A perfect little city' with 'the best cathedral on Planet Earth' - the words of travel writer Bill Bryson in his book *Notes from a Small Island*.

Arriving in Durham by train, the visitor is presented with what must be one of the most breathtaking urban views in Europe. Towering over the tumbling roofs of the city are the magnificent Durham Cathedral and Castle.

The **Cathedral** is third only to Canterbury and York in ecclesiastical significance, but excels them in architectural splendour, and is the finest and grandest example of Norman architecture in Europe. This was the power base of the wealthy Prince Bishops of Durham who once exercised king-like powers in an area known as the Palatinate of Durham. The powers vested in them by William I permitted them to administer civil and criminal law, issue pardons, hold their own parliament, mint their own money, create baronetcies, and give market charters. They could even raise their own army. Though these powers were never exercised in later years, they continued in theory right up until 1836, when the last of the Prince Bishops, Bishop William Van Mildert, died. The Palatinate Courts, however, were only abolished in 1971. It is little wonder that the County Council now proudly presents the county to visitors as 'the Land of the Prince Bishops'.

The Cathedral owes its origin to the monks of Lindisfarne, who, in AD 875, ffled from Viking attacks, taking with them the coffin of St Cuthbert, shepherd saint of Northumbria. In AD 883 they settled at Chester-le-Street. However, further Viking raids in AD 980 caused them to move once more, and they eventually arrived at a more easily defended site about ten miles to the south, where the River Wear makes a wide loop round a rocky outcrop. Here, in Durham, they built the 'White Church', where St Cuthbert's remains were finally laid to rest.

The present building was begun by William de St Carileph or St Calais, Bishop of Durham from 1081 to 1096. William arrived at the White Church, bringing with him holy relics and a group of monks and scholars from Monkwearmouth and Jarrow. Forced to flee to Normandy in 1088, having been accused of plotting against William Rufus, William returned in 1091 after a pardon, determined to replace the little church with a building of the size and style of the splendid new churches he saw being built in France at that time. In August 1093 the foundation stones were laid, witnessed by King Malcolm III of Scotland, famed as the soldier who slew

Durham Cathedral

Macbeth in battle.

The main part of the great building was erected in a mere 40 years, but over ensuing centuries each generation has added magnificent work and detail of its own, such as the 14th century Episcopal Throne, said to be the highest in Christendom, and the Neville Screen made from creamy marble. On the North Door is a replica of the 12th century Sanctuary knocker used by fugitives seeking a haven. They were allowed to remain within the church for 37 days, after which time, if they had failed to settle their affairs, they were given a safe passage to the coast carrying a cross and wearing a distinctive costume.

Nothing is more moving, however, than the simple fragments of carved wood which survive from St Cuthbert's coffin, made for the saint's body in AD 698 and carried around the North of England by his devoted followers before being laid to rest in the mighty Cathedral. The fragments are now kept in the **Treasures of St Cuthbert Exhibition**, within the Cathedral, with examples of the Prince Bishops' own silver coins. Also here is an exhibition describing the crafts and skills used in the building of the church.In recognition of the renewed interest in the life of St Cuthbert, the Cathedral is now officially called the Cathedral Church of Christ, the Blessed Mary the Virgin and St Cuthbert of Durham. **Sacred Journey**, at the Gala Theatre in Millennium Place, is a spectacular Giant Screen tourist attraction telling the story of the city and the life and death of St Cuthbert. Durham Cathedral contains the tomb of the Venerable bede (673-735), saint, scholar-monk and Britain's first pre-eminent historian. Bede spent most of his life teaching at Jarrow (qv) and was originally buried there. His body was moved from Jarrow in 1020 and to the southern side of the Galilee Chapel in 1370.

The Cathedral and its neighbour Durham Castle are now a World Heritage Site. **Durham Castle**, sharing the same rocky peninsula and standing close to the cathedral, was founded in 1072 and belonged to the Prince Bishops. Such was the impregnability of the site that Durham was one of the few towns in Northumbria that was never captured by the Scots. Among the motte-and-bailey castle's most impressive features are the Chapel, dating from 1080, and the Great Hall, which was built in the middle of the 13th century. The 18th century gatehouse has a Norman core, as does the massive keep, which was rebuilt in Victorian times.

Only open to the public at limited times, the Castle is now used as a hall of residence for the students of Durham University, and The Great Hall serves as the Dining Hall of University College. But students and visitors should beware - the castle is reputedly

3 DURHAM CASTLE

Durham City

Experience the atmosphere of the steam railway age as you step back in time in the history of North Road Passenger Station of 1842.

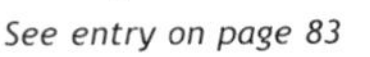

See entry on page 83

haunted by no less than three ghosts. One is said to be of Jane, wife of Bishop Van Mildert, and takes the form of the top half of a woman in 19th-century dress. She glides along the Norman Gallery, leaving the scent of apple blossom in her wake. A second spirit is of university tutor Frederick Copeman, who, in 1880, threw himself off the tower of the Cathedral. His ghost is said to haunt his former room off the Norman Gallery. A further apparition, who has been seen at various locations within the castle, is a cowled monk.

The university, England's third oldest after Oxford and Cambridge - was founded in 1832 by Bishop Van Mildert. In 1837 it moved into Durham Castle, though today its many buildings are scattered throughout the south of the city. The importance of the whole area surrounding the Cathedral and Castle was recognised in 1987, when it was designated a UNESCO World Heritage Site.

A favourite walk past the site starts at Framwellgate Bridge or Elvet Bridge and follows the footpaths that run through the woodlands on each bank of the River Wear, around the great loop. The path along the inside of the loop goes past The Old Fulling Mill, situated below the Cathedral, which now houses the **University of Durham Museum of Archaeology** containing material from excavations in and around the city, the northeast and far beyond. Prebends Bridge offers spectacular views of the Cathedral. At the southern end of this bridge is an inscription of words by Sir Walter Scott about the town:

'Grey towers of Durham,
Yet well I love thy mixed and massive piles,
Half Church of God, half Castle
'gainst the Scot,
And long to roam those venerable aisles,
With records stored of deeds
long since forgot.'

If walking isn't to your taste you can take a cruise along the river from Elvet Bridge.

The rest of Durham reflects the long history of the Castle and Cathedral it served. There are winding streets, such as Saddler Street and Silver Street (whose names attest to their medieval origin), the ancient Market Place, elegant Georgian houses - particularly around South Bailey, and quiet courtyards and alleyways. Much of Durham's shopping area is closed to traffic, making for a more relaxed atmosphere (in October 2001 Durham introduced the UK's first congestion charge). There are several churches worth visiting, including St Nicholas's Church in the Market Place, St Mary le Bow Church in North Bailey, which houses the **Durham Heritage Centre and Museum** (with a brass rubbing centre), and St Oswald's Church in Church Street. Their presence highlights the fact that in medieval times this was a great place of pilgrimage.

The **Durham Light Infantry Museum and Durham Art Gallery** at Aykley Heads tells the story of the county's own regiment, which was founded in 1758 and lasted right up until 1968. The horrors of the First World War are shown, as is a reconstruction of a Durham street during the Second World War. Individual acts of bravery are also remembered, such as the story of Adam Wakenshaw, the youngest of a family of 13, who refused to leave his comrades after his arm was blown off. He died in action, and was awarded a Victoria Cross. The art gallery has a changing exhibition of paintings and sculpture.

The **Durham University Oriental Museum** houses a collection of Oriental art of great importance, with exhibits from ancient Egypt, Tibet, India, China, Persia and Japan and many family activities. Located in parkland off Elvet Hill Road to the south of the city, the museum entrance is guarded by two stately Chinese lion-dogs.

The university also runs the 18-acre **Botanical Garden**, on Hollingside Lane (off the A167) on the south side of the city. Presenting a whistle-stop world plant tour, the gardens house rare and exotic plants from North America, Japan, South Africa, Australia and the Himalayas. A large collection of North American trees includes junior-sized giant redwoods, and in the fossil fern bed ferns and horsetails grow around the 310-year-old fossilized stem of their local ancestor *Cordaites*. Two display greenhouses

Durham Botanical Gardens

with trees and plants from all over the world feature cacti and a tropical 'jungle'. The Botanic Garden is filled with some sensations of the gardening world; the Japanese Katsura tree smells of burnt sugar or candyfloss for a week every autumn, after the leaves turn yellow. The gardens, visitor centre, plant sales and glasshouses are open all year.

Crook Hall and its Gardens in Frankland Lane, close to the River Wear, offer many delights, including the Secret Walled Gardens, the Shakespeare Gardens, the Cathedral Garden and the Silver & White Garden, an orchard and a maze. The gardens have been described by Alan Titchmarsh as 'a tapestry of colourful blooms'.The medieval manor house, one of the oldest inhabited houses in Durham City, has a Jacobean Room haunted by the White Lady. Call 0191 384 8028 for opening times.

On the western outskirts of Durham, straddling the A167, is the site of the Battle of Neville's croos, fought in 1346 between Scotland and England. The Scottish army was heavily defeated and the Scottish king, David II, was taken prisoner.

4 CROOK HALL AND GARDENS

Durham City

Owned by the Percy family since 1309, Alnwick is one of the finest castles in the British Isles.

See entry on page 83

AROUND DURHAM CITY

FINCHALE PRIORY

4 miles NE of Durham off the A167

On a minor road off the A167 lies 13th century **Finchale Priory** (pronounced Finkle). It was built by the monks of Durham Cathedral as a holiday retreat on the site of a hermitage founded by St Godric in about 1115. The ruins sit on a loop of the Wear in a beautiful location, across the river from Cocken Wood Picnic Area, which is linked to the Priory by a bridge.

LANCHESTER

8 miles NW of Durham on the A691

Lanchester owes its name to the Roman fort of Longovicium ('The Long Fort'), which

5 THE SALUTATION

Framwellgate Moor

Inviting pub popular with locals and tourists alike for its good beer, lively atmosphere and fantastic entertainment at the weekends

See entry on page 84

6 THE TRAVELLERS REST

Witton Gilbert

Both a traditional pub atmosphere with blessed near-rural setting and a small modern-design restaurant.

See entry on page 84

7 BROOM HOUSE FARM

nr Witton Gilbert

Farm shop selling home-reared meat, a coffee shop serving delicious treats and an exciting Adventure Trail - all on a large family-run organic farm.

See entry on page 86

stood on a hilltop half a mile to the southwest. The fort was built to guard Dere Street, the Roman road that linked York and the north. The scant remains sit on private land, however, and can't be visited. Stone from the fort was used in the mostly-Norman All Saints Church, and Roman pillars can be seen supporting the north aisle. There is also a Roman altar in the south porch and some superb 12th century carvings over the vestry door in the chancel.

The area to the south of Lanchester was a typical County Durham mining area, with several small colliery villages such as Quebec, Esh Winning, Tow Law and Cornsay Colliery. A place definitely worth visiting near Lanchester is **Hall Hill Farm**, on the B6296 four miles southwest of the village. It's a real working farm, open all year to the public, and voted Farm Attraction of the Year 2010.

BRANCEPETH

4 miles SW of Durham on the A690

Brancepeth is a small estate village built by Matthew Russell in the early 19th century, with picturesque Georgian cottages and an 18th century rectory. To the south, in parkland, is the imposing Brancepeth Castle. The original 13th century castle was owned by the Nevills, Earls of Westmorland, and was for many years the headquarters of the Durham Light Infantry.

Close to the castle are the remains of **St Brandon's Church**. In 1998 a fire destroyed everything but the four walls and tower of what was once a beautiful and historic building. The church's magnificent woodwork, commissioned by its rector John Cosin in the early 17th century, was completely destroyed. Cosin went on to become Bishop of Durham, and restored many churches in the county. Thanks to an appeal, work is under way to restore the church.

PITTINGTON

3 miles E of Durham off the B1283

A small village, Pittington contains one of County Durham's hidden gems - the Saxon-Norman St Laurence's Church at Hallgarth. The present church dates from the 11th century, on the site of what is believed to be an even earlier Saxon church. The 12th century paintings of St Cuthbert are well worth seeing.

BISHOP AUCKLAND

Bishop Auckland is an ancient town, standing on what was Dere Street - an old Roman

8 THE ROYAL OAK

Cornsay Colliery

Fine hospitality, excellent cooking and comfortable accommodation in a friendly family-run pub.

See entry on page 85

10 BRAMBLES COFFEE SHOP

Shincliffe

Whilst you're here for lunch or dinner, why not browse around the Poplar Tree Garden Centre, a great day out for all the family.

See entry on page 86

9 COACH AND HORSES

Croxdale

A fine drinking spot renowned for its reasonably priced food and real ales.

See entry on page 86

11 THE AVENUE INN

High Shincliffe

An outstanding village inn well known for its friendly atmosphere, traditional food and real ales.

See entry on page 87

Bishop Auckland Castle

road. Like many County Durham towns, it owed its later prosperity to coal mining. When the surrounding pits closed, the town went into decline, but it is now gradually rediscovering itself as new industries are established. As its name implies, this was part of the territory of the Prince Bishops of Durham, who controlled what was then a scattering of small villages. Rapid expansion occurred during the 19th century and Bishop Auckland became an important market town and administrative centre for the region.

Auckland Castle, at one time the principal country residence of the Prince Bishops, is now the official residence of the Bishop of Durham. The castle began as a small 12th century manor house and over the years successive bishops have added to it; looking at it today, it appears largely 17th or 18th century. But the fabric is still basically medieval, although parts of it were destroyed during the Civil War, when it was the headquarters of Sir Arthur Hazlerigg, Governor of the North. Bishop Cosin set about making it windproof and watertight after the Restoration, turning the Great Hall into a magnificent private chapel in 1665. Dedicated to St Peter, it is reputed to be the largest private chapel in Europe. Tel: 01388 601627.

A market has been held in Bishop Auckland for centuries. Opposite the present market place is the imposing Franco-Flemish Bishop Auckland Town Hall, built in the early 1860s.

While the villages immediately surrounding Bishop Auckland are mainly industrial, there are still some attractions worth seeing. At South Church is the cathedralesque St Andrew's Church, 157 feet long and said to be the largest parish church in the county. On display in a working men's club at West Auckland can be seen the most unlikely of trophies - the World Cup, no less. In 1910 the village's football team went to Italy to represent England in the first ever 'World Cup'. The team beat Juventus 2-0 in the final. The team successfully defended the title the following year, earning the right to retain the trophy for all time. The trophy on show is actually a replica, the original having been stolen.

12 TIME FOR YOU TEA ROOMS

Bishop Auckland

Outstanding tea rooms located within the Four Clocks Centre, offering freshly prepared treats and a wide selection of hot and cold drinks.

See entry on page 87

AROUND BISHOP AUCKLAND

BINCHESTER

1 mile N of Bishop Auckland off the A689

Binchester Roman Fort, known to the Romans as Vinovia, was built in around AD 80. It was one of a chain of forts built along Dere Street, and has the best preserved Roman military bathhouse in Britain, complete with a pillared hypocaust heating system. In addition to acting as a military centre controlling the local area, the fort also provided a stopping-off place for troops and supplies heading towards Hadrian's Wall. A portion of Dere Street has been preserved here.

ESCOMB

2 miles NW of Bishop Auckland off the A688

In the small village of Escomb is one of the true hidden gems of County Durham - the 7th century **Church of St John the Evangelist**, built using stone from nearby Binchester Roman Fort. This is one of only three complete Saxon churches in Britain, and is typically Saxon in layout, with its long, high nave and tiny chancel arch. In the south wall of the nave is a curious sundial surrounded by serpents and surmounted by what may be a mythical beast. This church is one of Northern Europe's finest examples of early Christian architecture.

WITTON-LE-WEAR

4 miles NW of Bishop Auckland off the A68

Overlooking the River Wear are the hillside terraces of the village of Witton-le-Wear, noted for its handsome green, its open views, attractive cottages and a pele tower attached to fragments of a medieval manor house in the High Street. **Low Barns Nature Reserve** is a 40-hectare reserve with a nature trail, bird hides, observatory, woodland, ponds, meadow, lakes and river. The Nature Reserve and Visitor Centre are in the care of the Durham Wildlife Trust.

CROOK

5 miles NW of Bishop Auckland on the A689

Crook is a small, spacious, town with a wide square, which, in summer, is full of flowers.

13 THE COLLIERY INN

Crook

A fine old free house renowned for the quality and variety of its food.

See entry on page 88

14 DOWFOLD HOUSE

Crook

An award-winning bed & breakfast offering superior guest bedrooms and quality breakfasts.

See entry on page 90

At one time it was a centre of coal mining, and the quaintly named Billy Row to the north of the town centre is a typical coalfield hamlet of miners' cottages.

SHILDON

2 miles SE of Bishop Auckland on the B6282

Timothy Hackworth served from 1825 as the resident engineer on the Stockton to Darlington Railway. In 1840 he resigned and left in order to develop the Soho Engine Works at Shildon, and make his own locomotives. The first trains to run in Russia and Nova Scotia were built here. Today the Engine Works, plus his house, form Locomotion: The National Railway Museum. The displays, including 60 vehicles and a workshop, give a fascinating insight into the early days of rail and steam power in England. Among the main attractions is a restored 1979 full-size replica of the Sans Pareil locomotive, built by Hackworth in 1829 for the Rainhill Trials on the Liverpool to Manchester railways. Open seven days a week all year.

It was at Shildon, in September 1825, that *Locomotion No 1* was attached to 12 coal wagons, 21 wagons with seats and a passenger coach named *Experiment*. With George Stephenson on the footplate, and a signalman riding ahead, the train carried nearly 600 passengers at 12 mph on the historic run from Darlington to Stockton (see also under Darlington).

HARTLEPOOL

There are really two Hartlepools - the old town on the headland, and the newer part

15 COTTONS CAFÉ AND RESTAURANT

Crook

This fully licensed establishment has a fantastic reputation for its home cooked food and friendly atmosphere.

See entry on page 89

Hartlepool Marina

with the marina and town centre, formerly known as West Hartlepool. A proud maritime town, the old part of Hartlepool dates back centuries. In the Middle Ages it was the only port within County Durham that was allowed to trade outside the Palatinate, thus confirming its importance. After the Norman Conquest, the Bruce family, whose most notable member was Robert the Bruce, King of Scotland, acquired the town. In 1201 King John bestowed the market charter on Hartlepool and ordered that the walls be built to defend it against the marauding Scots. Today parts of the wall remain and continue to stand guard over the Headland. There is a particularly fine gatehouse, called the Sandwellgate, with solid turrets on either side. Go through the pointed archway, and you find yourself on the beach.

Built by the Bruces as a burial place, the ornate 13th century St Hilda's Church stands on the site of a monastery founded by St Aidan in AD 647. The church is dedicated to St Hilda - its most famous abbess, celebrated for her teachings and her mentoring of a poor cowherd Caedmon, now regarded as the creator of religious verse. Hilda subsequently went on to found the great monastery at Whitby, where the Synod of Whitby was held in AD 664. The church houses a collection of religious artefacts, Saxon wall carvings and a tomb, made of Frosterley marble, believed to be that of Robert the Bruce. Parts of the cemetery were excavated in the 19th century, and some of the finds are on display in Durham and Newcastle.

Hartlepool's harbour gradually went into decline, and by the early 18th century the place was no more than a fishing village. In 1835 work started on opening up the harbour once more, and rail links were established with the coalfields. But it faced stiff competition. In 1847 work started on the West Harbour and Coal Dock, and by 1860 it was thriving with timber and shipyards. Other docks were opened and Ralph Ward Jackson, a local entrepreneur, instigated the building of a new town with streets of terraced houses to house the workers. A park with many sporting and leisure facilities named in his honour is linked by a walkway to Burn Valley Gardens, the town's central green belt.

On December 16, 1914 Hartlepool was the first town in Britain to suffer from enemy

16 THE CAUSEWAY

Hartlepool

Entertainment, real ales, and home cooked food comprise to make this public house a real social hub.

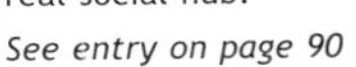

See entry on page 90

17 HARTLEPOOL HISTORIC QUAY

Hartlepool

Open every day all year round and voted one of the top six Heritage & History attractions in the UK, Hartlepool Historic Quay and Museum is a fun day out for all the family.

See entry on page 90

18 NIP IN CAFÉ

Hartlepool

With a Romanian/ English menu, this popular café has enjoyed great success since it opened in March 2010.

See entry on page 91

action during the First World War when it was shelled from German warships lying off the coast.

Nowadays the town is a thriving shopping centre, with some interesting tourist attractions, including **Hartlepool's Maritime Experience**. The multi-award-winning Heritage and History attraction (Tel: 01429 860077) tells the story of life at sea in the time of Nelson, Napoleon and the Battle of Trafalgar. Grouped round the small dock are various businesses and shops, such as a printer, gunsmith, naval tailor, swordsmith and instrument maker. Visitors can also go aboard HMS *Trincomalee*, a British warship originally launched in 1817. Hartlepool's lifeboat station has an all-weather Trent Class boat and a B Class Atlantic 75. The station can be visited between 9 and 5 (9-12 weekends). Crew training takes place on Thursday evenings and Sunday mornings.

Next door is the **Museum of Hartlepool**, with exhibits depicting life in the town through the ages. It features a new display of bronze Age man, axes, toys, Anglo-Saxon jewellery, Georgian silver, tales of sea monsters and the legend of the Hartlepool monkey. Washed ashore on a piece of wreckage during the Napoleonic Wars, local fishermen, unable to understand the monkey's gibberings, presumed it to be a French spy and hanged it from a gibbet on Fish Sands. (One of the nicknames of Hartlepool FC is the Monkeyhangers!) Visitors to the museum can have coffee aboard the PSS *Wingfield Castle*, an old paddle steamer. Hartlepool Art Gallery is housed within a beautifully restored Victorian church (bult by E B Lamb in 1854) on Church Square. It contains a collection of contemporary art and photography and a 100-foot viewing tower commands great views of the town. The Tourist Information centre is located in this building.

Summerhill Visitor Centre is a 100-acre country park on the western edge of Hartlepool that has been transformed for conservation and outdoor sports.

AROUND HARTLEPOOL

SEAL SANDS

3 miles S of Hartlepool off the A689

Standing in the shadows of Hartlepool Nuclear Power Station is **Seal Sands** and the Teesmouth Field Centre. Local organisations have come together to protect and enhance the marshes, tidal flats and dunes here on the north shore of the Tees estuary. The area is protected as a Nature Reserve and popular with people who come to view its large Common and Grey seal population and thousands of migratory birds. Visits by appointment only - Tel: 01429 264912.

BILLINGHAM

5 miles SW of Hartlepool, off the A19

Modern Billingham grew up as a result of the great chemical plants that surrounded the River Tees. Although the town looks modern, it is in fact an ancient place, possibly founded by Bishop Ecgred of Lindisfarne in the 9th century. **St Cuthbert's Church** has a 10th century Saxon tower, and Saxon walls survive in the nave. The chancel was rebuilt and widened in 1939 to provide for the town's growing population due to the influx of workers to the chemical plants. **Billingham Beck Valley Country Park** is a country park with wetlands, wildflower meadows and a 10-acre ecology park with a visitor centre.

Billingham Beck Country Park

ELWICK

4 miles W of Hartlepool off the A19

Elwick is a small, pretty village with patches of village green running up each side of a main street lined with neat, unassuming cottages. St Peter's Church has a nave dating from the 13th century. The chancel was rebuilt in the 17th century using materials from the previous chancel, and its tower was added on in 1813. On either side of the chancel arch are two small Saxon carvings - possibly fragments of grave markers.

TRIMDON

9 miles W of Hartlepool on the B1278

There are three villages with the word Trimdon in their name - Trimdon Grange, Trimdon Colliery and Trimdon itself. It's a quiet village with a wide main street and the unpretentious medieval St Mary Magdalene's Church.

At **Trimdon Colliery**, two miles to the northeast, a great underground explosion in 1882 claimed the lives of 74 miners.

HART

2 miles NW of Hartlepool on the A179

In this quiet village stands the mother church of Hartlepool - St Mary Magdalene's Church with its varied examples of architecture. The nave is Saxon, the tower and font are Norman and the chancel is early 19th century.

On the outer wall of the White Hart Inn is a figurehead, said to have been a relic from the Rising Sun, which was shipwrecked off Hartlepool in 1861.

PETERLEE

6 miles NW of Hartlepool off the A19

Peterlee is a new town, established in 1948 to re-house the mining families from the colliery villages around Easington and Shotton. The town has a modern shopping centre, a tourist information office and a market. Close by is the village of Easington, whose fine old St Mary's Church sits on a low hill. The church tower is Norman, and the interior contains some examples of Cosin-style woodwork.

On the south side of Peterlee, **Castle Eden Dene National Nature Reserve** is one of the largest woodlands in the North East that has not been planted or extensively altered by man.

DARLINGTON

Darlington is an important regional centre serving the southern part of County Durham, Teesdale, the Tees valley and much of North Yorkshire. It was founded in Saxon times, and has a bustling town centre with one of the largest market places in England. On its west side are the Old Town Hall and indoor market, with an imposing Clock Tower designed by Alfred Waterhouse in 1864.

Darlington

There are many fine buildings in Darlington, most notably **St Cuthbert's Church** on the east side of the market place, with its distinctive tall spire. It is almost cathedral-like in its proportions, and was built by Bishop Pudsey between 1183 and 1230 as a collegiate church. Its slender lancet windows and steep roof enhance its beauty, which has earned it the name 'The Lady of the North'.The church was restored by George

Locomotion, Darlington Railway Museum

Gilbert Scott in the 1860s.

Perhaps Darlington's greatest claim to fame lies in the role it played, with neighbouring Stockton, in the creation of the world's first commercially successful public railway, which opened in 1825. It was the Darlington Quaker and banker Edward Pease who became the main driving force behind the scheme to link the Durham coalfields with the port of Stockton.

The original Darlington Station, built in 1842, was located at North Road Station. Today it serves as **Head of Steam - Darlington Railway Museum** - a museum of national importance which houses relics of the pioneering Stockton and Darlington Railway. These include a replica of Stephenson's Locomotion No 1, a Stockton and Darlington first-class carriage built in 1846, a World War 11 newsstand, the Derwent, (the earliest surviving Darlington-built locomotive) and even Victorian loos. The present Darlington Station, Bank Top, was constructed at a later date as part of the East Coast line linking England with Scotland. So much early railway history is to be seen hereabouts that British Rail have named their local Bishop Auckland-Darlington-Middlesbrough line the Heritage Line.

Continuing with Darlington's railway theme, there's an unusual engine to be seen in Morton Park - **Train** is a life-size brick sculpture, designed by sculptor David Mach and unveiled by Lord Palumbo of Walbrook in 1997. During the summer months you can see a floral replica of George Stephenson's Locomotion No 1 in the town centre, at the foot of Post House Wynd.

AROUND DARLINGTON

PIERCEBRIDGE

4½ miles W of Darlington on the A67

Driving past the picturesque village green of Piercebridge, most motorists will be unaware that they are passing through the centre of a once important **Roman Fort**. Piercebridge was one of a chain of forts on Dere Street, which linked the northern Roman headquarters at York with the north. Other forts in the chain were located at Catterick to the south and Binchester, just outside Bishop Auckland, to the north. The remains of the fort, which are still visible today, can be dated from coin evidence to around AD 270. The site is always open and admission is free. Finds from this site are housed in the Bowes Museum at Barnard Castle.

GAINFORD

7 miles W of Darlington on the A67

Gainford village sits just north of the Tees. At its core is a jostling collection of quaint 18th and 19th century cottages and houses grouped around a village green. At the south west corner of the green is St Mary's Church - a large church, built mostly in the 12th

19 THE CARLBURY ARMS

Piercebridge

Lovers of fine food, well-kept real ales and unbeatable hospitality need look no further as this fine establishment has it all.

See entry on page 91

20 THE BRIDGEWATER ARMS

Winston

This delightful village pub has a glowing reputation for fine food, well-kept ales and unbeatable hospitality.

See entry on page 92

century from stone that is believed to have come from Piercebridge Roman fort, three miles to the east. Certainly a Roman altar was found built into the tower during the restoration of 1864-65, and it can be seen in the museum of Durham Cathedral.

Gainford Hall is a large Jacobean mansion built by the Reverend John Cradock in the early 1600s. Though not open to the public, it can be viewed from the road. It's hard to believe that in the 19th century the now quiet village of Gainford was a spa, visited by people from all over the North of England. Some way away along the banks of the Tees to the west, a basin can be seen where the sulphurous waters were collected.

Raby Castle

STAINDROP

9 miles W of Darlington on the A688

Set in a magnificent 200-acre deer park on the outskirts of the village, **Raby Castle** is one of the country's finest medieval castles - a romantic, fairy-tale building, which was once the home of the powerful Nevill family. Built in the 14th century, it houses a fine art collection and sumptuous interiors. In the 16th century over 700 barons assembled in the great Baron's Hall to plot the overthrow of Elizabeth 1 - an action which was to cost the Nevill family dearly, for it resulted in the castle and all the Nevill estates being seized by the Crown. In 1626 the castle was leased to Sir Henry Vane, James 1's Secretary of State, and has remained with the Vane family ever since. The castle was besieged during the Civil War, but luckily survived and remains an impressive example of defensive and domestic architecture. Much of the interior is now Georgian and Victorian, although the Great Kitchen remains virtually unaltered since its construction over 600 years ago. The Castle, the beautiful walled garden and the coach house are all open to the public. Tel: 01833 660202

Staindrop itself is a delightful, very typical, Durham village with a long village green lined with Georgian houses. St Mary's Church, with its Saxon core, houses tombs of the Nevill and Vane families.

21 THE BLACK SWAN

Staindrop

A superb village pub serving locally brewed ale and traditional hearty food.

See entry on page 93

HEIGHINGTON

5 miles N of Darlington off the A6072

Heighington is an attractive village with neat cottages and a large green. St Michael's Church is predominantly Norman, and has a pre-Reformation oak pulpit with prayers inscribed on it for its donors, Alexander and Agnes Fletcher. About three miles west of the village, near Bolam, is the shaft of a 9th century cross known as the Leggs Cross.

SEDGEFIELD

9 miles NE of Darlington on the A689

Sedgefield, well known for its National Hunt racecourse, is a small town whose market charter was issued in 1315. The grand 15th century tower of St Edmund's Church dominates the village green and the cluster of Georgian and early Victorian houses. It is

Hardwick Hall, Sedgefield

famous for its intricately carved Cosin woodwork, which was on a par with the woodwork lost when Brancepeth church was destroyed by fire in 1998. The Laudian Bishop Cosin's son-in-law, Denis Granville, was rector here in the late 17th century, and it was at this time that the woodwork was installed. A wheelchair-friendly Heritage Trail takes a 1.75-mile tour of the town's major sights.

Hardwick Hall Country Park lies to the west of the town, beyond the A 177. Developed as a pleasure garden between 1748 and 1792 the gardens were all laid out and the ornamental buildings were designed by the architect James Paine. The hall is now a luxury hotel, but the park with its network of woodland walks and Gothic folly is open to the public.

MIDDLETON ST GEORGE

3 miles E of Darlington off the A67

Middleton St George is a pleasant village on the banks of the River Tees to the east of Darlington, close to Teesside International Airport - once an airfield from which British and Canadian bombers flew during World War II. St George's Church dates from the 13th century with 18th and 19th century additions, and stands away from the village among fields. Curiously, the stonework has been heavily patched with brick at some point. It is thought to have been built on the site of an old Saxon church and the Victorian pews are rather incongruous - rather more like old-fashioned waiting room seats than pews.

Near Middleton St George, the village of **Middleton One Row** is aptly named - it consists of a single row of Georgian cottages. The cottages were inevitably altered over the years as the arrival of the railway inspired development throughout the region.

See entry on page 93

STOCKTON-ON-TEES

9 miles E of Darlington on the A166

Stockton-on-Tees found fame with the opening of the Stockton to Darlington railway in 1825, constructed so that coal from the mines of South Durham could have access to the Tees, where it would be shipped south to London. The opening of the railways encouraged the growth of industry, and the subsequent discovery of ironstone in the Cleveland Hills in the 1850s was to transform the fortunes of the town, providing considerable wealth for many of its citizens.

In the centre of Stockton's High Street are the Old Town Hall and market cross dating from the mid 18th century, and in Theatre Yard off the High Street is the **Green Dragon Museum**, set in a former sweet factory warehouse. This lively museum features displays of local history and an excellent photographic gallery.

Stockton's redbrick parish church was completed in 1713 and is one of only a handful of Anglican churches in England without a dedication. Its official title is The Parish Church of Stockton-on-Tees, though for many years it has been informally called St Thomas's. This unofficial dedication came from a chapel of ease that stood on the site when Stockton was a part of the parish of Norton.

Captain James Cook is said to have served the early part of his apprenticeship in Stockton. A full-size replica of his ship, *HM Bark Endeavour* is moored at Castlegate Quay

Preston Hall, Stockton-on-Tees

on Stockton's riverside. Alongside is the *Teesside Princess*, a river cruiser that takes visitors on a pleasure trip as far inland as Yar

Preston Hall Museum, set in 110 acres of parkland to the south of the town on the banks of the Tees, is housed in the former home of the local shipbuilder Robert Ropner. Exhibits describe how life was lived in the area at the time the Hall was built in 1825. There is a re-created period street, a fully furnished drawing room of the 1820s and a collection of arms and armoury in the cellar. The museum's most famous exhibit is *The Diceplayers*, painted by Georges de la Tour in the 17th century. As we went to press in spring 2011, the museum was under restoration.

Stockton may no longer be a busy port, but in recent years there has been a lot of development along the banks of the Tees. The spectacular **Tees Barrage**, built to stop the flow of chemical waste being carried upstream, has transformed an 11-mile stretch of the river.

YARM

9 miles E of Darlington on the A67

Set within a loop of the River Tees, Yarm was a prosperous river port as far back as the 14th century. Its broad main street, one of the widest in England, is lined with some fine Georgian houses and coaching inns, but the bustling river traffic has gone. Standing in the centre of this elegant street is the Town Hall of 1710 with marks on its walls recording the levels of past river floods, but the town's most impressive structure is the railway viaduct with its 40 arches soaring above the rooftops and extending for almost half a mile. It was at a meeting in Yarm's George & Dragon Hotel in 1820 that plans were drawn up for the Stockton & Darlington Railway, the first of all passenger-carrying railways.

LOW DINSDALE

4 miles SE of Darlington off the A67

A visit on foot or by car to Low Dinsdale is well worth while, as the 12th century red sandstone St John the Baptist Church surrounded by copper beeches is worthy of a postcard. Opposite stands a 16th century manor house built on the site of a moated Norman manor owned by the Siward family. They later changed their name to Surtees, and became well known throughout the north.

MIDDLESBROUGH

Dominating the skyline of this busy town is the **Transporter Bridge**, opened in 1911 and the only working bridge of its kind in England. The bridge can carry nine cars or 200 people on each crossing. Captain Cook was born in Middlesbrough in 1728, and in the **Captain Cook Birthplace Museum** in Stewart Park, Marton, visitors can chart his life story and experience life below decks in the 18th century through original objects and hands-on displays. Tel: 01642 311211. The Museum stands next to the site of the cottage where he was born (the cottage no longer exists). Also well worth a visit when in Middlesbrough is the **Dorman Museum**, with themed displays of natural history, social history and world cultures spread over 8 themed galleries and 2 exhibition spaces.

mima, Middlesbrough Institute of Modern Art, is a new gallery in the heart of Middlesbrough. mima showcases an internationally significant programme of fine art and applied art from the 19th century to the present day. Tel: 01642 726720

On the southeastern edge of Middlesbrough is the National Trust's **Ormesby Hall**, a beautiful 18th century mansion with a magnificent stable block attributed to Carr of York and a superb model railway layout and exhibition. Tel: 01642 324188. Signed off the A19 at Acklam on the southern edge of Middlesbrough, **Nature's World** is a pioneering eco-experience featuring organic demonstration and ornamental gardens, wildlife areas, ponds and hydroponicum (indoor tropical garden). The centre is powered by geothermal, solar and wind power. Tel: 01642 594895.

AROUND MIDDLESBROUGH

KIRKLEATHAM

5 miles E of Middlesbrough on the A174

Two good reasons for a visit here. **Kirkleatham Museum** is an early 18th century house (built as a Free School)with exhibitions on art, coast and country, and the region's ironstone mining and iron and steel heritage, with activities for children and family groups. Tel: 01642 479500. **Kirkleatham Owl Centre** has one of the country's most important collections of owls, also falcons, buzzards, vultures, kites and caracaras. Call 01642 480512 for opening times.

GUISBOROUGH

8 miles E of Middlesbrough on the A171

The stark ruins of **Guisborough Priory** stand on an elevated site overlooked by the Cleveland Hills. Founded by the great landowner Robert de Bruis II in 1119, the monastery became one of the most powerful in Yorkshire. Much extended in 1200, and rebuilt after a fire destroyed the whole site, the estate was sold in 1540 to a Thomas Chaloner, who cannibalised much of the fabric to grace ornamental gardens at his grand mansion nearby. Nothing remains of that mansion, and of the Priory itself the great arch at the east end is the most striking survival. The grounds are a popular venue for picnics.

Guisborough Priory

REDCAR

This popular town and resort on the coast is home to the oldest lifeboat in the world, on display at the **RNLI Zetland Lifeboat Museum**. It was built in 1802 by H Greathead and stands among exhibitions on fishing history, models, photographs, paintings and cards in a handsome listed building in King Street. Tel: 01642 494311.

Redcar's Lifeboat Station can be visited on Sunday mornings, or by appointment. Tel: 01642 484491.

Saltburn Pier and Tramway

AROUND REDCAR

SALTBURN-BY-THE-SEA

5 miles SE of Redcar on the A174

This charming seaside town (complete with a pier) at the northern end of the 36-mile Heritage Coast is largely the work of the Victorians, and in particular the entrepreneur Henry Pearse. It stands on a cliff high above a long, sandy beach, and to transport visitors from the town to the promenade and beach the ingenious water-balanced **Inclined Tramway** was built. It is still in use, the oldest such tramway to have survived in Britain. A miniature (15" gauge) railway, first established in 1947 and run entirely by volunteers, runs from the seafront to the **Valley Gardens** and the **Woodland Centre**, set between the formal pleasure gardens and the wild natural woodland beyond. The pre-Victorian Saltburn was a notorious haunt of smugglers, and those days are brought to life with costumed characters, sounds and smells in the **Saltburn Smugglers Heritage Centre**, set in old fishermen's cottages next to the Ship Inn in Old Saltburn. Tel: 01287 625252.

At Skinningrove, a few miles east of Saltburn, is the **Cleveland Ironstone Mining Museum**, where visitors can discover the special skills and customs of the miners who helped make Cleveland the most important ironstone mining district in Victorian and Edwardian England. Tel: 01287 642877.

23 THE CLARENDON HOTEL

Redcar

Close to the beach, golf club and racecourse, this family run hotel offers fantastic en-suite accommodation and a good selection of food.

See entry on page 94

24 RAPPS CAFÉ & THE KINGS GRILL

Saltburn by the Sea

This delightful café and fine dining restaurant stand side by side and both attract plenty of diners through their doors.

See entry on page 95

LOCATION MAP

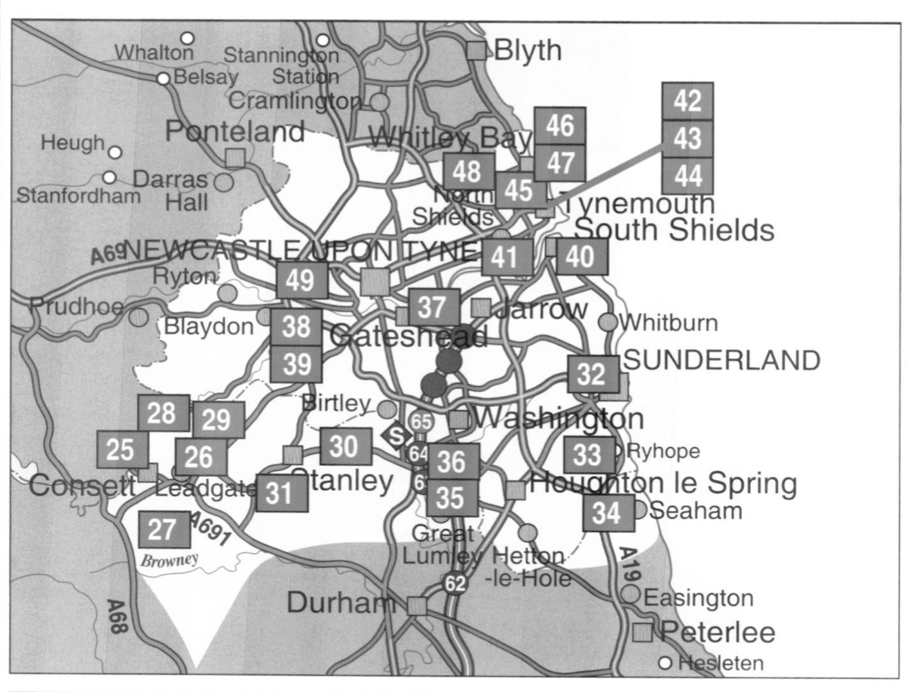

Accommodation

27	The Old Mill, Knitsley	pg 23, 97
28	The Manor House Inn, Shotley Bridge	pg 23, 96
30	Beamish Mary Inn, Beamish, Stanley	pg 24, 99
44	Martineau Guest House, Tynemouth	pg 35, 108

Food & Drink

25	The Scotch Arms, Blackhill, Consett	pg 22, 96
26	The Jolly Drovers, Leadgate, Consett	pg 22, 96
27	The Old Mill, Knitsley	pg 23, 97
28	The Manor House Inn, Shotley Bridge	pg 23, 96
29	The Miners Arms, Medomsley	pg 23, 98
30	Beamish Mary Inn, Beamish, Stanley	pg 24, 99
31	Mr Crusty's Café, South Moor, Stanley	pg 24, 100
33	The Albion, Ryhope, Sunderland	pg 26, 101
34	Featherbed Rock Cafe, Seaham	pg 27, 102
35	The Floaters Mill, Woodstone Village, Houghton-le-Spring	pg 27, 103
36	The Dun Cow, Bournmoor, Houghton-le-Spring	pg 27, 102
38	LG Coffee Bar, Whickham, Newcastle-upon-Tyne	pg 30, 104
39	Poachers Pocket, Whickham, Newcastle-upon-Tyne	pg 30, 105
41	The Spread Eagle, Preston Village, North Shields	pg 35, 106
42	Country House Tea Rooms, Tynemouth	pg 35, 107
43	Gingersnaps Victorian Tea Rooms, Tynemouth	pg 35, 108
45	Queens Head, Cullercoats, North Shields	pg 36, 108
46	The Cornerstone, Whitley Bay	pg 36, 109
47	Barnacle Cafe Bistro, Whitley Bay	pg 36, 110
48	Brown Sugar Lounge, Monkseaton	pg 36, 110
49	The Boathouse, Newburn	pg 37, 111

Places of Interest

32	Sunderland Museum and Winter Gardens, Sunderland	pg 25, 101
37	Gateshead Millenium Bridge, Gateshead	pg 28, 104
40	South Shields Museum and Art Gallery, South Shields	pg 31, 105

NORTH COUNTY DURHAM WITH TYNE AND WEAR

The area south of the Tyne is largely industrial in character, encompassing the large towns and cities of Gateshead, Sunderland and South Shields in Tyne & Wear and, further out in County Durham, the smaller communities of Chester-le-Street and Consett. There is plenty for the visitor to see, particularly in Gateshead and Sunderland, which, like so many large British conurbations, are re-discovering themselves and their heritage. The coastline is a dramatic landscape of beaches, limestone cliffs and headlands. Awarded Heritage Coast status in 2001, a scenic attraction is the Durham Coastal Footpath - an 11-mile clifftop route from Seaham to Crimdon.

Gateshead lies immediately south of Newcastle, on the banks of the River Tyne, and in recent years both have benefited from a tremendous amount of regeneration work. In Gateshead this has revolutionised the riverside area, with such attractions as the Gateshead Millennium Bridge and Baltic Arts Centre.

To the east, South Shields is an area associated with a famous writer. The town is now well established as Catherine Cookson Country, with a Catherine Cookson Trail and a Catherine Cookson Exhibition in the local museum. The origins of Christianity can be explored in Jarrow, where the Venerable Bede lived and worked as a monk. Sunderland, to the south, is one of England's newest cities, and has the first minster to be created in England since the Reformation. Sunderland is undergoing a reformation of its own. Once an industrial centre the city is thriving again, boosted by the opening in 2002 of a link with Tyneside's Metro system. Attractions include the Sunderland Museum, with its splendid Winter Gardens, and the National Glass Centre.

The area inland from the north bank of the Tyne was an important focus of the Industrial Revolution and the region is steeped in tradition and hard work. Local people - often referred to as Geordies - were employed in the coal mines, engineering works and shipyards. They didn't travel far to spend their leisure time or holidays, heading for the likes of Whitley Bay or Tynemouth, eight miles east of Newcastle city centre on the North Sea coast, but a lifetime away from their harsh living and working conditions. Today, much of that industry has now gone but the pride and passion remains, as 21st century life, leisure and industry have injected a new vibrancy in the air.

Dominating the region is Newcastle-upon-Tyne, which with Gateshead is one of Britain's most exciting conurbations. An ambitious regeneration programme has transformed the city; stroll down Grey Street one of the most elegant streets in Europe; enjoy the view of the Tyne bridge from the Quayside; visit one of several superb museums and be sure to sample the legendary nightlife. There is a real buzz in the air. Away from Newcastle there are areas of rural calm and beauty waiting to be explored. To the west, and actually in Northumberland, stand the romantic ruins of Prudhoe Castle. One of the North East's greatest sons - George Stephenson - was born in Wylam, a village to the west of Newcastle in Northumberland. One room of the small stone cottage where he was born in 1781 is open to the public, but his story is told in greater detail in the Stephenson Railway Museum in North Shields. Legacies of the past can be explored at Segedunum Roman fort, Wallsend - so called because this was where Hadrian's Wall ended; it is now the beginning (or end) of the new Hadrian's Wall National Trail.

Terris Novalis, Consett

CONSETT

Steel-making first started in this area of County Durham at Shotley Bridge, when craftsmen from Germany set up their furnaces in the 17th century and began making swords and cutlery. When the railway came here to serve the local iron works and surrounding collieries in the 19th century, Shotley Bridge began to develop something of a reputation as a spa town, and its popularity as such is evident from the many fine houses to be seen here, such as Dial House.

Steel-making on a grand scale began in Consett in 1840, when the Derwent Iron Company built two blast furnaces. By 1890 over 7,500 people were employed in the industry, and over 1 million tonnes of steel were being produced. In the late 1960s, 6,000 people were still employed in the steelworks, though this wasn't to last. The demand for steel dropped, and in 1980 the works closed forever.

Terris Novalis by Tony Cragg is two mammoth engineering tools, a theodolite and an engineer's level which are 20 times the scale of the original instruments. Made of stainless steel, the instruments sit on giant animal feet supports. The sculptures are located on what was once the site of the largest steelworks in Europe and they are widely viewed locally as a fitting monument and landmark to the steel industry which was once synonymous with Consett.

Land reclamation schemes have smartened up the area where the steelworks once stood, and its attendant spoil heaps have made way for green hillocks dotted with young trees. The countryside outside the town has some interesting places to visit.

A redundant railway line north of the town is linked to **The Derwent Walk Country Park**. The park covers 425 acres of woodland and riverside meadow, and the Derwent Walk itself is the track bed of the old Derwent Valley Railway between Consett and Swalwell. The main walk is 11 miles long, and suitable also for cycles, horses and wheelchairs. It gives access to a number of paths which include nature trails, the South Tyne Cycleway and the Heritage Way. Swalwell Visitor Centre, situated at the northern end of the Derwent Walk, is the starting point for a history trail and has a large pond and butterfly garden. There is

See entry on page 96

See entry on page 96

another visitor's centre at Thornley Woodlands.

To the south of the town is **Hownsgill Viaduct**, constructed in 1857 to take the track of the Stanhope and Tyne Railway. Visitors can now walk across it, and there are some spectacular views.

AROUND CONSETT

EBCHESTER

3 miles N of Consett on the A694

Ebchester is the site of a Roman fort called **Vindomora**, and some scant remains can be seen in the churchyard of St Ebba's Church. It was one of a string of forts on Dere Street, the Roman road which linked York with the north. Inside the church are a number of inscribed Roman stones, including an altar to the god Jupiter, 'the greatest and the best'.

Inside Ebchester's church is the tomb of R S Surtees, creator of Jorrocks, probably the leading character in fox-hunting fiction. Surtees, born in Durham in 1805, inherited his father's Hamsterley estate in 1838, giving him the time and resources to spend his days hunting and shooting. He became High Sheriff of Durham in 1856 and died in Brighton in 1864.

27 THE OLD MILL - KNITSLEY

Knitsley

Outstanding accommodation, food and real ale can be found at this impressive property that is set within 100 acres of beautiful countryside.

See entry on page 97

28 THE MANOR HOUSE INN

Shotley Bridge

Expect a warm welcome, real ales, excellent food, log fires in winter and comfortable accommodation.

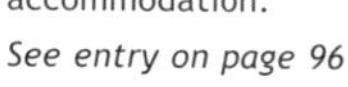

See entry on page 96

29 THE MINERS ARMS

Medomsley

Dating back to the early 19th century, this pub is well-known in the area for the delicious traditional pub fayre it serves.

See entry on page 98

CHESTER-LE-STREET

Chester-le-Street is a busy market town built around the confluence of Cong Burn and the River Wear. There was a Roman fort here at one time, and the street on which the town once stood was a Roman road, later replaced by the Great North Road.

The medieval **St Mary's and St Cuthbert's Church** is built on the site of a cathedral established in AD 883 by the monks of Lindisfarne carrying the body of St Cuthbert. His coffin rested here for 113 years until the monks took it to its final resting place at Durham. There are no fewer than 14 effigies (not all of them genuine) of members of the Lumley family within the church, though they don't mark the sites of their graves. Next to the church is the **Ankers House Museum**, situated in the medieval anchorage. Between 1383 and 1547, various anchorites, or Christian hermits, lived here. These holy people were what might be called extreme hermits, living walled up, with a squint to

Lumley Castle

Tanfield Railway, Beamish

see the altar, an opening for food and a grave ready outside when the time came.

Lumley Castle, to the east across the River Wear, was built in 1389 by Sir Ralph Lumley, whose descendant, Sir Richard Lumley, became the 1st Earl of Scarborough in the 1690's. In the early 18th century it was refashioned by the architect Vanbrugh for the 2nd Earl, and turned into a magnificent stately home. But gradually the castle fell out of favour with the Lumley family and they chose to stay in their estates in Yorkshire instead. For a while it was owned by Durham University before being turned into the luxurious hotel that it is today.

Waldridge Fell Country Park, two miles south-west of Chester-le-Street and close to Waldridge village, is County Durham's last surviving area of lowland heathland. A car park and signed footpaths give access to over 300 acres of open countryside, rich in natural history.

AROUND CHESTER-LE-STREET

BEAMISH

4 miles NW of Chester-le-Street on the A693

The award-winning **Beamish, The North of England Open Air Museum** is situated in 300 acres of beautiful County Durham countryside and vividly illustrates life in the North of England from the early 1800s to 1913.. This is one of the North East's leading tourist attractions. Buildings from throughout the region have been brought to Beamish, rebuilt and furnished as they once were. Costumed staff welcome visitors and demonstrate the past way of life. The museum has acquired the Victorian steam locomotive Dunrobin, built in 1895 for the duke of Sutherland to pull his private train at Dunrobin Castle. Tel: 0191 370 4000.

Two miles to the northwest is **Causey Arch**, reputed to be the world's first single-arch railway bridge and in its day the longest single span bridge in England. It was designed by Ralph Wood, a local stonemason, and financed by a group of local coal owners to carry the **Tanfield Railway** - opened in 1725 - between Sunniside and Causey. In those days the wagons were pulled by horses, though steam power eventually took over. The first bridge fell down and the unfortunate designer Wood was so frightened that the second attempt would also fail that he threw himself off the bridge to his death. Steam-hauled trains now run along three miles of line between Sunniside and East Tanfield, and at Old Marley Hill are collections of locomotives and carriages and a steam-driven vintage workshop. Tel: 0191 388 7545. There's a car park and picnic area close by, and rights of

30 BEAMISH MARY INN

Beamish

Many people are very fond of this historic inn, which supports local micro breweries by serving a fantastic selection of eight real ales.

See entry on page 99

31 MR CRUSTY'S CAFÉ

South Moor, nr Stanley

Hearty daytime eating in a cheerful café with friendly family owners.

See entry on page 100

way link them to Beamish. The restored railway started its 40th anniversary celebrations with a weekend-long freight festival in February 2010.

SUNDERLAND

Sunderland's history is told in an exhibition in **Sunderland Museum** on Burdon Road (Tel: 0191 553 2323). Displays take the visitor back in time to discover the region's proud heritage in textile traditions and coal. Other exhibits include a large collection of Sunderland Pottery and a display of paintings by LS Lowry, who spent much of the last 15 years of his life in the region, finding inspiration for his work in the industrial cities and their coastline. The original **Winter Gardens**, badly damaged in the Second World war, have been re-created - a green oasis in a glass rotunda, with over 1,500 flowers and plants from all over the world. The Museum and the Winter Gardens are contained within Mowbray Park, which has been fully restored with themed walkways, poetry inscriptions, historical monuments, a lake and a bowling green. Visitors can bet 'nose-to-beak' with endangered species at Close Encounters. The award winning **Northern Gallery for Contemporary Art** is on the top floor of the City Library and on Ryhope Road, south of the city centre, is the university-owned Reg Vardy Art Gallery, which supports exhibitions, projects and events that explore contemporary art practice..

The **Exchange Building**, the oldest public building in the city, is a venue for the whole community to enjoy. Exhibitions, meetings and functions take place there, plus there is a restaurant and café. The famous Empire Theatre - a Sunderland institution - attracts all the top productions.

On the north side of the Wear, in the suburb of Monkwearmouth, is **St Peter's Church**, one of the most important sites of early Christianity in the country. This tiny Saxon church was founded in AD 674 by Benedict Biscop, a Northumbrian nobleman and thane of King Oswy, who had travelled to Rome and was inspired to found a monastery on his return. This was to become a great centre of culture and learning, rivalled only by Jarrow. The Venerable Bede, England's first great historian, lived and worked at St Peter's Church for a time and described the monastery's foundation in his Ecclesiastical History of England. The west tower and the wall of this most fascinating church have survived from Saxon times and the area around the church, where shipyards once stood, has been landscaped.

Close to St Peter's Church, in Liberty Way, Monkwearmouth, is the **National Glass Centre** (Tel: 0191 515 5555). Glass was first made in Sunderland in the 7th century at St Peter's Church, so it's fitting that the centre was built here. Visitors can see how glass was made all those years ago, and watch modern glass blowing. There is a Glass Gallery,

32 SUNDERLAND MUSEUM AND WINTER GARDENS

Sunderland

Sunderland Museum & Winter Gardens combines a museum, art gallery, exhibition space and Winter Gardens to create a stunning visitor attraction.

See entry on page 101

Light Transformer, National Glass Centre

devoted to all forms of glass art, and in the Kaleidoscope Gallery there are several interactive exhibits showing glass's many amazing properties. Walking on the roof is not for the faint hearted, as it's made of clear glass panels 30 feet above the riverside. However, some panels are opaque, so people who don't have a head for heights can still walk there and enjoy the view. A stunning restaurant overlooks the River Wear.

Art of another kind is to be found in the St Peter's Riverside Sculpture Trail. It was established in 1990, and comprises various works of outdoor sculpture - in metal, wood, glass and stone - placed along the banks of the Wear - mostly on the Monkwearmouth side.

Roker is one of Sunderland's suburbs, located to the north of the great breakwaters that form the city's harbour. The northern breakwater, known as Roker Pier, is 825 metres long and was opened in 1903. Roker Park, once the home of Sunderland Football Club, has been carefully restored to its former Victorian splendour, and from Roker and Seaburn through to Sunderland there is a six-mile-long seaside promenade. Crowds of people gather here in July to witness front line jet fighters and vintage planes in action during the Sunderland International Air Show. Tel: 0191 553 2000. On Old Washington Road, the **North East Aircraft Museum** houses a collection of aircraft in various stages of restoration and aero engines. The **Stadium of Light** is now the magnificent home of Sunderland FC - tours are available daily except on matchdays. Tel: 0191 551 5055. On Newcastle Road, **Fulwell Windmill** is the only working windmill in the North East. Built in 1808, it has been restored to full working order and has a visitor centre. Tel: 0191 516 9790

St Andrew's Church in Talbot Road, Roker, has been described as 'The Cathedral of the Arts and Crafts Movement'. Built by E S Prior in the early 20th century, it is crammed with treasures by the leading craftsmen of the period - silver lectern, pulpit and altar furniture by Ernest Gimson, a font by Randall Wells, stained glass in the east window by H

Fulwell Windmill

A Payne, a painted chancel ceiling by Macdonald Gill, stone tablets engraved by Eric Gill, a Burne-Jones tapestry and carpets from the William Morris workshops.

Sunderland's Lifeboat Station is the oldest in the country, and it was from here that the first experimental motor lifeboat in the RNLI fleet operated. The Station can be visited on Sunday mornings and Tuesday evenings.

AROUND SUNDERLAND

SEAHAM

4 miles S of Sunderland on the B1287

Seaham was developed by the Marquises of Londonderry. In 1821 the family bought what

33 THE ALBION

Ryhope

A much loved village pub offering home-made food, a warm welcome and a well stocked bar.

See entry on page 101

was then the old village of Seaham, in order to build a harbour from which to transport coal from the family's collieries to London and the Continent. The present town grew up around the harbour, and although most of the collieries have now closed, Seaham is still very much a working town.

There is a fine sandy beach in Seaham and a sculpture trail running between the harbour and Seaham Hall celebrating the town's heritage.

Penshaw Monument

A major feature of the coast is the **Durham Coastal Footpath**, an 11-mile route that runs from Seaham northwards to Crimdon. It passes through dramatic clifftop scenery and deep ravines carved into the Magnesian limestone rock.

PENSHAW

4 miles W of Sunderland off the A183

This mining village is famous for the **Penshaw Monument** - a fanciful Doric temple modelled on the Temple of Theseus, and built in 1844 in memory of John George Lambton, 1st Earl of Durham and Governor of Canada. A waymarked circular walk of just over three miles links Penshaw Monument with the River Wear.

All Saints Church dates from 1745, and has one unusual feature: inside it there is a monument to the Eliot family carved on a piece of stone from the Pyramid of Cheops in Egypt.

To the west is Lambton Castle, scene of an old tale about The Lambton Worm. Legend has it that many years ago, the heir to the Lambton estate was fishing in the Wear one Sunday morning when he should have been at worship. Instead of a fish, he caught a huge worm, which he promptly threw into a well, where it grew to an enormous size. The worm became so big that it could coil itself around hillsides, and began to terrorise the neighbourhood. Meanwhile the heir, away in the Holy Land fighting in the Crusades, knew nothing of this. On his return he met a witch who told him the secret of how the worm could be killed, on the premise that having done so he must then kill the first living

34 FEATHERBED ROCK CAFÉ

Seaham

Overlooking Seaham's famous historic harbour this café draws in plenty of passers-by with the aroma of home cooking.

See entry on page 102

35 THE FLOATERS MILL

Woodstone Village, nr Houghton-le-Spring

With the very friendly staff and fantastic atmospherse, The Floaters Mill the perfect place to go for a quiet drink with friends and family.

See entry on page 103

36 THE DUN COW

Bournmoor, nr Houghton-le-Spring

Local produce is the main focus of the superb menu offered to diners at this superb public house.

See entry on page 102

thing he met on returning to his village. If he failed to do so the family would be cursed and no Lambton would die peacefully in his or her bed for nine generations. His father, hearing of this, released an old dog close by. Unfortunately, having successfully slain the worm, the young heir didn't see the old dog but his father first, he refused to kill him and the witch's prophesy about the next nine generations came true.

WASHINGTON

6 miles W of Sunderland on the A1231

Present-day Washington is a new town with modern districts scattered over a wide area surrounding the town centre. Built to attract industry into an area whose mining industry was in decline, the town has achieved its aim. Within the old village of Washington to the east of the town centre, is an attraction well worth visiting - **Washington Old Hall**, the ancestral home of the Washington family, ancestors of George Washington, the first American president.

The Hall was originally a manor house built in the 12th century for the de Wessington family, whose descendants through a female line finally left the house in 1613, when it was acquired by the Bishop of Durham.

The present Washington Old hall, in local sandstone, was rebuilt on the medieval foundations in about 1623. In 1936 it was to be demolished, but a hastily formed preservation committee managed to save it, thanks to money from across the Atlantic. In 1955 it was officially reopened by the American Ambassador, and two years later it was acquired by the National Trust. The interiors re-create a typical manor house of the 17th century, and there are some items on display which are connected to George Washington himself, though the man never visited or stayed there. A peaceful stroll can also be enjoyed in the formal Jacobean garden. Tel: 0191 416 6879

Washington is also the home to the **Washington Wetland Centre** - a conservation area and bird watchers' paradise covering some 45 hectares of wetland, woodland,

Washington Wildfowl and Wetland Centre

ponds and lakes sloping down to the River Wear. There are over 1,000 birds representing 85 different species, including grey herons, mallard, widgeon, nene (the state bird of Hawaii), heron, Chilean flamingos, redshank and lapwing. Other attractions include wildflower meadows, dragonflies, the Close Encounter feeding area, a Discovery Centre, Waterside Café, picnic areas, gift shop and Splash Zone play area. Excellent disabled access and free wheelchair hire. Tel: 0191 416 5454

GATESHEAD

For generations Gateshead lived very much in the shadow of neighbouring Newcastle, but no longer. Today the city is at the heart of an impressive regeneration programme that has

37 GATESHEAD MILLENIUM BRIDGE

Gateshead

See one of the world's most stunning riverside landmarks - the Gateshead Millenium Bridge.

See entry on page 104

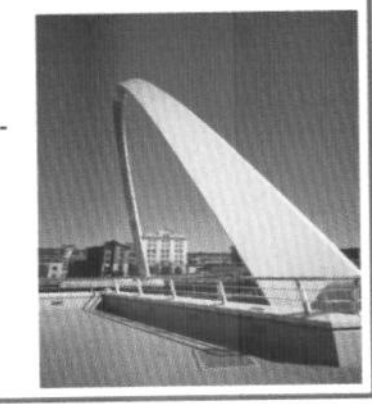

revitalised the area. In a bid hosted jointly with Newcastle, the city was shortlisted for Capital of Culture 2008, narrowly missing out to Liverpool in the final stage.

Visitors arriving in the city from the South are greeted by one of North East England's most important modern icons - **The Angel of the North**. Commissioned by Gateshead Council and created by renowned sculptor Antony Gormley, this vast and most impressive statue, made from 200 tonnes of steel, is 65 feet high and has a wingspan of 175 feet. Erected in February 1998, the statue has attracted worldwide attention.

Nowhere is the city's transformation more evident than on the Gateshead Quays, a major new arts, leisure and cultural venue on the banks of the River Tyne. One of the most spectacular attractions in Gateshead is the £21 million **Gateshead Millennium Bridge**, erected across the Tyne in 2001 and designed to take both cyclists and pedestrians. A tilting mechanism enables the bridge to pivot at both ends, forming a gateway arch, underneath which ships can pass. This operation, which has been likened to a giant blinking eye, is an engineering world first for which the bridge has received many accolades. The bridge is particularly impressive at night when it is lit by a high tech, multi-colour light display.

The **Baltic Centre for Contemporary Art** is a major international centre for Contemporary art, housed in a converted 1950s grain warehouse on the south bank of the Tyne. It is one of the largest temporary art spaces in Europe: five galleries display an ever changing programme of work from resident artists. There is also a viewing platform with spectacular views of the Tyne Bridge. Admission is free. Next to the Baltic is the open air performance square, Baltic Square, a venue for street artists and musical events.

Further along the Quayside, in a spectacular Norman Foster building, is **The Sage Gateshead** music centre. The venue boasts a 1650-seat performance hall, 450-seat secondary hall and a school of music, as well as being home to the Northern Sinfonia orchestra. It caters for all tastes - jazz, classical, folk and rock. Linking the Baltic with the Sage Gateshead is a leisure complex with an 18 screen cinema, bowling alley, nightclubs, fitness suites and restaurants.

The **Gateshead Quay Visitor Centre** is housed in the former St Mary's parish church, a grade I listed church with Norman origins. It includes a display on Gateshead's history and future development plans and a tourist information centre.

Saltwell Park is an elegant Victorian park dating back to the 13th century that has impressive floral displays. Gateshead has achieved some notable successes in Britain in Bloom competitions, and in June Gateshead Central Nursery hosts a major flower show.

Shipley Art Gallery houses a nationally renowned collection of contemporary craft, as well as William C Irving's painting of the Blaydon Races. The races were originally horse races, which took place from 1862 to 1916. they are now

Angel of the North, Gateshead

a 6-mile running race from Newcastle to Blaydon. In November 2009 a charity version of Geordie Ridley's anthemic song was recorded by the stars of Auf Wiedeersehen pet in aid of the Sir Bobby Robson Foundation.

AROUND GATESHEAD

GIBSIDE CHAPEL

6 miles SW of Gateshead on the A694

The large mansion at Gibside Estate was owned by the Bowes family, and partially demolished in 1958. Now the place is chiefly visited for the **Palladian Gibside Chapel**, owned by the National Trust. Building work began in the 18th century but it wasn't until 1812 that the chapel was finally consecrated.

A stately building, looking more like a small mansion than a church, Gibside was built for Sir George Bowes, whose mausoleum lies beneath it. For viewing times call 01207 541820. The Georgian Gardens, designed by Capability Brown, have miles of walks through the wooded slopes and riverside of the Derwent Valley. At nearby Rowlands Gill is the **Derwent Walk Country Park** with woodlands, riverside meadows, the Derwent Walk and the Northern Kites project.

38 L G COFFEE BAR

Whickham

All dishes, cakes and scones etc are homemade on the premises and the smell inside will make your mouth water.

See entry on page 104

39 POACHERS POCKET

Whickham

Offering locally sourced food, real ales and live entertainment the Poachers Pocket has it all.

See entry on page 105

SPRINGWELL

3 miles S of Gateshead on the B1288

Springwell is home to the **Bowes Railway**, once a private rail system pulling coal-filled wagons from pit to port. The original wagonways would have been made of wood, with horses pulling the wagons. The line finally closed in 1974, and today the site is a Scheduled Industrial Monument, the only one of its type in the country. The railway is home to a magnificent collection of around 80 colliery wagons, many of them actual Bowes Railway stock, including some former Stockton & Darlington wagons bought secondhand from the North Eastern Railway.

Many of the buildings of the original **Springwell Colliery** have been retained, as well as the hauliers' houses at Blackham's Hill, where there are demonstrations of the only preserved working inclines in the country, designed and built by George Stephenson. The railway organises special events and open days, and a passenger service operates between the museum centre at Springwell and Wrekenton, with an intermediate stop at Blackham's Hill. Tel: 0191 416 1847

JARROW

4 miles E of Gateshead on the A184/A194

Mixed memories surround the town of Jarrow. Once a thriving centre for the Tyneside shipbuilding industry, it gained fame during the famous Jarrow Hunger March when hundreds of unemployed men from the area walked to London to draw attention to their plight. A bas-relief at the Metro Station commemorates the event, which took place in 1936, as does a sculpture outside Morrison's Supermarket.

At Church Bank, **Bede's World** (Tel: 0191 489 2106) is a museum and outdoor interpretation centre where visitors can discover the exciting early medieval world of the Venerable Bede. It encompasses both a monastery and a church founded in the 7th century and dedicated to St Paul. The

Sundial, Bede's World

original dedication stone can still be seen within its chancel, together with fragments of Anglo-Saxon stained glass - shown to be the oldest ecclesiastical stained glass in Europe, if not the world. A modern glass by Piper depicts the Jarrow double cross in a deep blue background. It was unveiled by the princess of Wales in 1985. It was at Jarrow monastery that Bede wrote his *Ecclesiastical History of England*. He was undoubtedly Britain's first genuine historian, employing methods of checking and double checking his information that are still in use today. Jarrow Hall, a Georgian building incorporated into the museum, contains a re-created Anglo-Saxon farm.

MARSDEN

9 miles E of Gateshead on the A183

The coast between South Shields and Roker is magnificent, with rocky cliffs projecting into the sea at Lizard Point and the impressive Marsden Bay. Marsden Rock was once a famous County Durham landmark - a rock formation shaped like the Arc de Triomphe that stood in the bay. In 1996, however, it finally succumbed to the forces of nature and collapsed, leaving two tall stumps. The smaller stump proved so unstable that in 1997 it was demolished. The Rock has a famous bird colony of kittiwakes and cormorants. The caves, which were once home to smugglers, have been transformed into a bar and restaurant.

Souter Lighthouse at Lizard Point was built in 1871, and was the first reliable electric lighthouse in the world. It's a perfect example of Victorian technology, and features an engine room, foghorns and lighthouse keeper's living quarters. Owned by the National Trust, and open to the public. Tel: 0191 529 3161. **The Leas**, in the care of the Trust, is a 2½-mile stretch of spectacular coastline running from Trow Rocks to Lizard Point; it includes Marsden Bay, Marsden Rock and many grottoes and sea stacks.

SOUTH SHIELDS

8 miles E of Gateshead on the A184/A194

South Shields stretches out along the southern shore of the Tyne estuary. Though close to Newcastle and Gateshead, the North Sea coastline here is remarkably unspoiled, and can be walked along for many miles. No less a personage than King George V declared that the beach at South Shields was the finest he had seen. This is a stretch of fine firm sand, behind which a small but pleasant resort thrives.

However, it is the older part of South Shields that has given the town a new claim to fame, thanks to the work of one of the world's most popular novelists - Dame Catherine Cookson, who died in 1998. She was born Katie McMullen in 1906, in a house in Leam Lane amid poverty and squalor, the illegitimate child of a woman called Kate Fawcett. The house is gone now, but a plaque

40 SOUTH SHIELDS MUSEUM & ART GALLERY

South Shields

South Shields Museum & Art Gallery explores the story of South Tyneside through sensational displays, hands-on exhibits and stunning art.

See entry on page 105

has been erected marking the spot.

Catherine Cookson wrote a series of best-selling novels which captured the world of her own childhood, and that of her parents and grandparents, with vivid clarity. It was a world that was shaped in the 19th century around the narrow streets and coal mines - a world of class warfare and conflict, passion and tragedy, violence and reconciliation.

Tyne Bridges

A **Catherine Cookson Trail** has been laid out in the town, showing places associated with her and her books, and a leaflet is available to guide you round. The South Shields Museum, which recently underwent a major redevelopment, includes an enhanced Catherine Cookson's gallery and an Arts Adventure Centre.

Much of the old harbour at South Shields has been restored, particularly around the Mill Dam which is home to the Customs House offering a cinema, theatre, art galleries and an excellent Italian restaurant. Fine Georgian buildings and warehouses still survive in this area along the riverside. In Baring Street the remains of a Roman fort can be seen; the West Gate of Arbeia has been faithfully reconstructed to match what experts believe is its original appearance.

NEWCASTLE-UPON-TYNE

Newcastle, the region's capital, is rapidly becoming one of Britain's most exciting cities, and contains many magnificent public buildings and churches. Situated above the River Tyne, it is linked to its neighbour Gateshead as one visitor destination.

The **Tyne Bridge** has long been the icon by which Newcastle is internationally known. Opened in 1928, it bears an uncanny resemblance to the Sydney Harbour Bridge, which isn't surprising as both were designed by the same civil engineering company. The bridge is the start point of the world's biggest half marathon: on Sunday, October 5th, 2008, some 50,000 will cross the bridge before running, jogging or walking their way to the seaside finish at South Shields.

Newcastle has enjoyed a varied and colourful history and in its time has acted as a Roman frontier station, a medieval fortress town, an ecclesiastical centre, a great port, a mining, engineering and shipbuilding centre and a focal point of the Industrial Revolution that was to change the face of the world.

The **Quayside** is the first view of Newcastle for visitors from the south, whether travelling by road or rail. The area is the symbolic and historic heart of this elegant city and boasts some 17th-century merchants' houses mingling with Georgian architecture, and the beautiful Guildhall contains a state of the art visitor information centre. It has been a focal point for activity since the first bridge was built across the river in Roman times and has been revitalised in recent years with some sensitive and imaginative restoration of the river front area. There are now a number of lively cafés and wine bars along with a regular Sunday market.

To the west of the Quayside is Central Station, designed by local architect John Dobson and officially opened by Queen Victoria in 1850.

Grainger Town, the historic centre, contains many fine examples of classical Victorian architecture.

Grey's Monument, an 18th century landmark dedicated to the former Prime

Minister Earl Grey, stands at the head of Grey Street, about which John Betjeman wrote that "not even Regent Street in London, can compare with that subtle descending curve". With over 40% of its buildings officially listed, Grey Street was awarded the title of Britain's favourite street by listeners to the Radio 4 Today programme.

The **Castle Keep** at Castle Garth was built by Henry II in the 12th century on the site of the 'new castle', built in 1080 by Robert, eldest son of William 1, on the site of the Roman fortifications of Pons Aelius. This earlier wooden castle, from which the city takes its name, is thought to have been the start of Hadrian's Wall before it was extended east. It was built after uprisings against the new Norman overlords that followed the killing of Bishop Walcher in Gateshead at a meeting to discuss local grievances.

Henry's impressive new structure was built entirely of stone, and reached 100 feet in height. Although the battlements and turrets were added in the 19th century, much of it is Norman. The only other remaining castle building is Black Gate, dating back to 1247. If at first glance the structure looks a little unusual, it is because of the house built on top of it in the 17th century. The castle was in use during the Civil War, when it was taken by the Scottish army after the Royalist defeat at the Battle of Newburn, five miles west of Newcastle, in 1640.

Grey's Monument, Newcastle-Upon-Tyne

Many of the other medieval buildings were demolished in the mid-19th century to make way for the railway, and the Castle and Black Gate were fortunate to survive.

At one time, Newcastle was surrounded by stout walls that were 20 to 30 feet high in places and seven feet thick. Parts of these survive and include a number of small towers, which were built at regular intervals. Begun in 1265, the walls were eventually completed in the mid-14th century. They were described as having a "strength and magnificence" which "far passeth all the walls of the cities of England and most of the cities of Europe". The best remaining sections are the West Walls behind Stowell Street, and the area between Forth Street and Hanover Street, south of Central Station, which leads to spectacular views of the River Tyne from the gardens perched on the cliff side.

One unusual feature of the walls was that they passed right through the grounds of a 13th century Dominican monastery, known as Blackfriars, causing the prior to protest loudly. To keep the peace, a door was cut through to allow the monks access to their orchards and gardens. Blackfriars was later converted and turned into almshouses for the destitute. Earmarked for demolition in the 1960s, the building was eventually saved. The church is long gone, but the remaining buildings have been renovated and opened as a craft centre and restaurant grouped around a small square. It's another of the area's hidden places, and well worth a visit.

Newcastle has two cathedrals - the Anglican **St Nicholas's Cathedral** on St Nicholas Street, and the Roman Catholic **St Mary's Cathedral** on Clayton West Street. St Nicholas, dating from the 14th and 15th centuries, was formerly the city's parish church, and it still has the feel of an intimate parish church about it. Built in 1844, St Mary's was one of A W H Pugin's major works; the spire he originally designed was never built, and the present one dates from 1872.

This is a metropolitan city of great vibrancy and activity, and there's plenty to do, with a rich variety of entertainment on offer. There is a choice of theatres, cinemas, concert venues and an opera house. The **Laing Art Gallery** on New Bridge Street has a permanent collection of 18th and 19th century paintings and changing displays of contemporary artwork.

The city boasts a wide range of museums and art galleries: The **Discovery Museum**, Blandford Square, depicting Newcastle's social and industrial past; the **Great North Museum: Hancock**-incorporates collections from the city's Museum of Antiquities, Shepton Museum and the Hatton Gallery ; the **Life Science Centre**, Times Square - genetic science brought to life; the **Hatton Gallery**, Newcastle University Art Dept - a permanent collection of West African sculpture; the **Museum of Antiquities**, King's Road; the **Shefton Museum of Green Art & Archaeology**, Newcastle University - Greek Art and Archaeology; the **Side Gallery**, The Side - documentary photography exhibitions; and the **Newburn Hall Motor Museum**, Townfield Gardens - a private collection of vintage vehicles.

Down near the quayside is a unique group of half-timbered houses known as **Bessie Surtees House**, owned by English Heritage. The rooms are richly decorated with elaborate plaster ceilings, and there is some beautiful 17th century wall panelling.

To the west of the city, on the south bank of the Tyne, is **Blaydon**, famous for its races, which inspired one of Newcastle's anthems, *The Blaydon Races*. But horse racing hasn't been held here since 1916, and the racecourse is no more. Gosforth Park, to the north of the city, is where horse racing now takes place (Tel: 0191 222 7849 for details of race days). See under Gateshead. Near Blaydon is the Path Head Water Mill, a restored 18th century mill.

Newcastle is a true Northern capital - a proud city that doesn't look to the South for inspiration and guidance. There is an unmistakable air of confidence in the future. Along with neighbouring Gateshead, Newcastle staged a bid to become European City of Culture 2008. Narrowly missing out to Liverpool in the final stages, the city has none the less been designated as a Centre of Cultural Excellence with a wide range of events planned for the coming years.

The Metro Rapid Transport System, Britain's largest after London, links Newcastle with Gateshead, South Shields, Sunderland and the northern coastal areas of Tynemouth and Whitley Bay.

NORTH AND EAST OF NEWCASTLE-UPON-TYNE

WALLSEND

3 miles E of Newcastle on the A193

In Wallsend the mighty shipyards tower over **Segedunum Roman Fort, Baths and Museum** on Buddle Street. The fort, on the banks of the River Tyne, was the last outpost on Hadrian's Wall. Segedunum (it means 'strong fort') stood at the eastern end of the Hadrian's Wall. Originally the wall only went as far as Newcastle, but it was decided to extend it to deter sea attacks. There are only scant remains of the structure in the district nowadays.

Segedunum is a reconstruction of what the Roman fort would have looked like. Over 600 Roman soldiers could have been garrisoned here at any one time, and the area must have been a bustling place. Now visitors can explore the reconstructed fort, get a stunning view from a 114-feet viewing tower, and watch archaeologists uncovering yet more foundations of the original wall. The reconstructed bath house is the only one of its kind in Britain.

NORTH SHIELDS

5 miles E of Newcastle on the A193

Standing at the mouth of the River Tyne the town is named after the shielings (fishermens' huts) on the riverbank. The **Fish Quay**, dating back to 1225, grew up when fishermen were called upon to supply Tynemouth Priory. While the boats are smaller in number than in its heyday the port is still a hive of activity, the best time to see fishing boats come into port and experience the hustle and bustle of the landing of catches is between 6 and 7pm. Fabulous fresh fish can be bought from the numerous fishmongers. Many of the buildings on the Fish Quay are linked to the fishing industry. The 'High' and 'Low' lights are prominent landmarks on the upper and lower banks of the Fish Quay that were designed to guide vessels entering the Tyne.

Well worth a visit in North Shields is the **Stephenson Railway Museum** in Middle Engine Lane. George Stephenson began his career as a humble engine-man at Willington Ballast Hill before moving to Killingworth, where he eventually became an engine-wright. The museum remembers the man and his achievements as well as covering steam, diesel and electric trains and explaining how trains work. Tel: 0191 200 7146. See also under Shildon and Darlington.

TYNEMOUTH, WHITLEY BAY AND CULLERCOATS

8 miles E of Newcastle on the A193

These three towns form a linked resort. Nestling at the mouth of the River Tyne, Tynemouth boasts a proud maritime heritage. In 1864 the first Volunteer Life Brigade was created here (still in operation today), and visitors can learn more about this vital service in the small museum attached to the lifeboat station. Overlooking the river is the notable **Collingwood Monument**, the grand statue of Admiral Lord Collingwood, Nelson's second-in-command at Trafalgar, who went on to win the battle after Nelson's death. The four guns below the statue are from his ship, the *Royal Sovereign*. Tynemouth Priory was built over the remains of a 7th century monastery, which was the burial place of St Oswin, King of Deira (the part of Northumbria south of the Tees), who was murdered in AD 651. The priory was as much a fortress as a monastery, which explains the existence of the adjoining 13th century castle ruins. Tynemouth station is the venue for a popular antique market held every weekend. The Palace building on Grand Parade at Tynemouth is home to the **Toy Museum**, where over 8,000 toys are on display. It also has a toy hospital. Tel: 0191 259 1776. Tynemouth's Lifeboat Station can be visited between 9 and 4 on weekdays or by appointment (Tel: 0191 257 0913). The lifeboat *Spirit of Northumberland* is named in memory of the first lifeboat stationed at north Shields more than 200 years ago.

Long Sands is an award winning and

gloriously sandy beach that stretches from Tynemouth to Cullercoats, a small town renowned for its history of salt production. In the 1700s around 2180 tons of salt were gathered here each year, abandoned caves were once the hiding place of smugglers who made their fortune illegally transporting it to Scotland. Much quieter than the neighbouring resorts of Tynemouth and North Shields, Cullercoats was a favourite retreat of the famous American artist Winslow Homer, who painted some of his finest works here.

The seaside resort of Whitley Bay has a unique atmosphere at weekends and bank holidays when young people from all over the country come to sample its legendary nightlife. The town has some excellent safe beaches and in July hosts the Whitley Bay International Jazz Festival.

On a small island, easily reached on foot from Whitley bay at low tide, is **St Mary's Lighthouse**. The reward for climbing the 137 steps to the top is magnificent views of the Northumberland coast. Completed in 1898, the Lighthouse remained in operation until 1984, when it was superseded by modern navigational techniques. North Tyneside council now runs the Lighthouse and former keeper's cottages as a visitor centre and nature reserve.

SEATON SLUICE

8 miles NE of Newcastle on the A193

Inland from Seaton Sluice is **Seaton Delaval Hall**. This superb Vanburgh mansion, the ancestral home of the Delavals, was built in the Palladian style in 1718 for Admiral George Delaval. Gutted by fire in 1822, it was never restored. Tel: 0191 237 1493. In the grounds of the house stands the Norman St Mary's Chapel.

BLYTH

12 miles NE of Newcastle on the A193

Blyth is a small industrial town at the mouth of the River Blyth. Much of the town's industrial heritage is linked to the Northumberland coalfields, their rapid decline in recent years is a loss from which the area is only slowly recovering. The oldest part of the town is set around an 18th century lighthouse called the High Light. Blyth claims its own piece of railway history with one of the country's earliest wagonways, the **Plessey Wagonway**, dating from the 17th century and built to carry coal from the pits to the riverside. As well as coal mining and shipbuilding, the town was once a centre of salt production, and in 1605 it is recorded that there were eight salt pans in Blyth.

45 QUEENS HEAD

Cullercoats

A much loved village pub offering a varied menu, real ales and fine views of the seafront.

See entry on page 108

46 THE CORNERSTONE

Whitley Bay

A family run cafe offering a tasty array of homemade treats, hot and cold drinks and a warm welcome.

See entry on page 109

47 BARNACLE CAFE/BISTRO

Whitley Bay

A beach cafe by day and a bistro by night. The Barnacle offers fantastic food, friendly staff, a great atmosphere and spectacular sea views.

See entry on page 110

48 BROWN SUGAR LOUNGE

Monkseaton

A fantastic cafe bistro, offering a relaxed atmosphere and good honest food all reasonable prices.

See entry on page 110

Blyth's industrial landscape and coastline was the inspiration for several paintings by L S Lowry. The building that is now the headquarters of the Royal Northumberland Yacht Club was a submarine base during the Second World War.

NORTH AND WEST OF NEWCASTLE-UPON-TYNE

WYLAM

5 miles W of Newcastle off the A69

Wylam is the birthplace of George Stephenson, railway pioneer, and one room in the little stone cottage on the north bank of the Tyne where he was born in 1781, the second son of Robert, the fireman of a colliery engine.

PRUDHOE

9 miles W of Newcastle on the A695

The romantic ruins of **Prudhoe Castle** are in the care of English Heritage. King William the Lion of Scotland unsuccessfully attacked the castle in 1173 and 1174, and the threat of further attacks led Henry II to agree to the building of a new stone castle. Completed in the 12th century, it was one of the finest in Northumberland, and was later provided with a moat and drawbridge, a new gatehouse and a chapel. There is an impressive oriel window above the altar of the chapel. A Georgian manor house in the courtyard houses an exhibition, which tells the history of the castle. Tel: 01661 833459

Prudhoe Castle

49 THE BOATHOUSE

Newburn

This pub boasts a beautiful riverside location and attracts plenty of hungry walkers through its doors.

See entry on page 111

MICKLEY

10 miles W of Newcastle on the A695

A signpost at Mickley Square points visitors to **Cherryburn**. The house is noted as the birthplace of Thomas Bewick, the well-known illustrator and wood engraver, famous for his portrayal of birds, animals and country life. Now owned by the National Trust, the house contains an exhibition of his woodcuts and hosts regular demonstrations of the printing techniques used in his time. Tel: 01661 843276

PONTELAND

7 miles NW of Newcastle on the A696

Though this small town has largely become a dormitory town for Newcastle-upon-Tyne, resulting in a lot of recent development, it still retains a character of its own. **St Mary's Church**, much altered but essentially 12th century, stands opposite the attractive Blackbird Inn, housed in a 13th and 14th century fortified house. Within the gardens of the Old Vicarage is a 16th century vicar's pele.

A few miles north of Ponteland are **Kirkley Hall Gardens**, which are open to the public from 10 to 3 except weekends out of season. Tel: 01670 841200. There are 35,000 different species of labelled plants here, and it is home to the national collections of beech, dwarf willow and ivy. Other attractions include a Victorian walled garden, sunken and woodland garden, greenhouse plants and herbaceous and ornamental borders.

LOCATION MAP

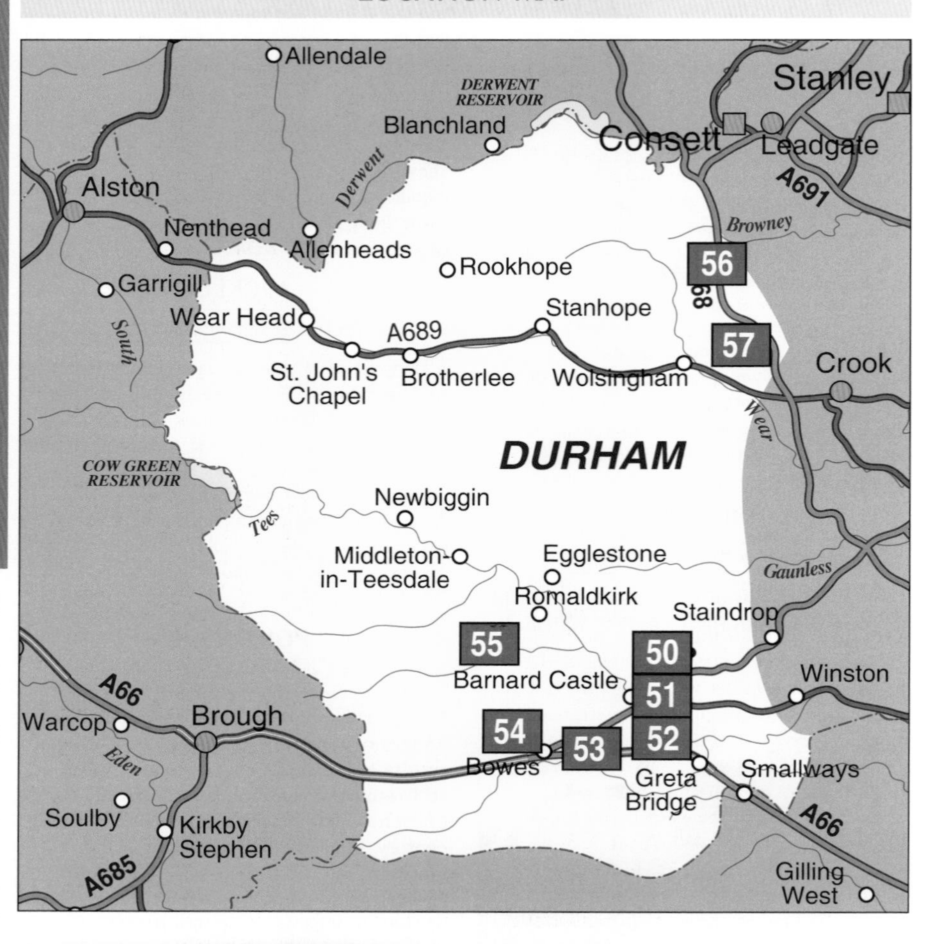

Accommodation

- 53 The George & Dragon, Boldron, Barnard Castle *pg 41, 114*
- 54 The Ancient Unicorn, Bowes, Barnard Castle *pg 41, 115*
- 55 Clove Lodge, Baldersdale, Barnard Castle *pg 42, 116*
- 57 Helme Park Hall Hotel, Fir Tree Village, Bishop Auckland *pg 45, 118*

Food & Drink

- 51 Cafe Nest, Barnard Castle *pg 40, 112*
- 53 The George & Dragon, Boldron, Barnard Castle *pg 41, 114*
- 54 The Ancient Unicorn, Bowes, Barnard Castle *pg 41, 115*
- 56 The Pantry, Tow Law, Bishop Auckland *pg 45, 117*
- 57 Helme Park Hall Hotel, Fir Tree Village, Bishop Auckland *pg 45, 118*

Places of Interest

- 50 Barnard Castle, Barnard Castle *pg 40, 111*
- 52 Bowes Museum, Barnard Castle *pg 40, 113*

WEARDALE, TEESDALE AND THE PENNINES

To the west, County Durham sweeps up to the Northern Pennines - a hauntingly beautiful area of moorland, high fells and deep, green dales. Officially designated as an Area of Outstanding Natural Beauty in 1988, the North Pennines covers almost 2,000 square kilometres. It is one of the most remote and unspoiled places in the country and has been called 'England's last wilderness'.

The great northern rivers of the Wear, the Tees, the Tyne and the Derwent have their sources here. Tumbling mountain streams have cut deep into the rock, creating the impressive waterfalls of Low Force, High Force, and Cauldron Snout. These are magical places, and show just how water has shaped the Durham Dales. The area is rich in wildlife. Hen harriers, merlins and other rare species breed here, and in spring and summer the plaintive call of the curlew can be heard.

This is ideal country for walking and cycling, though in the winter months it can be wild and inhospitable. There are numerous rights-of-way to be explored, including the C2C (Coast to Coast) cycle path. The Pennine Way cuts through County Durham in the south, close to the towns of Barnard Castle and Middleton-in-Teesdale, continuing westward through Upper Teesdale until it enters Cumbria. Further north it enters Northumberland to the west of Haltwhistle and then the Northumberland National Park.

Man has left his mark here too, for this is working countryside. The lower reaches have been farmed for centuries, and the high fells are home to many flocks of sheep. At one time there were woollen mills in Barnard Castle, providing a ready market for local sheep farmers. Lead mining was a thriving industry, with mines located at Killhope, Ireshopeburn and St John's Chapel. Middleton-in-Teesdale was once the headquarters of the London Lead Company, a great Quaker business venture.

There are two great County Durham dales - Teesdale to the south and Weardale to the north. Of the two, Teesdale is the softer, particularly in its lower reaches, which share an affinity with the Yorkshire Dales. This isn't surprising, for at one time part of the River Tees formed the boundary between County Durham and Yorkshire. The lower Dale is dotted with charming villages that nestle along the bank of the River Tees, as it winds its way between the historic towns of Barnard Castle and Middleton-in-Teesdale. Small farmsteads, whitewashed in the local tradition, are surrounded by dry stone wall enclosures. Travelling up the dale the vista opens out into miles of open moorland, home to a multitude of wildlife and unique flora. Beyond Middleton-in-Teesdale the B6277 winds up and over some bleak but beautiful scenery until it arrives at Alston in Cumbria, England's highest market town.

The A689, which winds its way through Weardale further north, follows an alternative route to Alston, passing through a dale that was once the hunting ground of Durham's Prince Bishops. Life, at one time, must have been harsh here and the houses and villages seem grittier somehow than those of neighbouring Teesdale. The scars on the landscape expose the regions past as one of the most heavily industrialised upland landscapes in England. Farming developed hand in hand with mining, as the miners supported their variable income with produce from their smallholdings. Methodism was very strong within the communities and many former Methodist chapels can still be seen in the area. There is however plenty to see here, such as the lead mining museum at Killhope, the curious fossilised tree stump at Stanhope, and the village of Blanchland, a few miles to the north in Derwentdale.

BARNARD CASTLE

This historic market town is a natural centre for exploring Teesdale and the Northern Pennines. Set beside the River Tees, 'Barney' is recognised nationally as one of the 51 most historically and architecturally important towns in Great Britain. The town derives its name from **Barnard Castle**, founded in the 12th century by Bernard, son of Guy de Baliol, one of the knights who fought alongside William I. The castle played an important role in the defeat of the Northern Earls who rose against Elizabeth I in 1569. Besieged by rebel forces for 11 days, the castle was ultimately forced to surrender, but not before its resistance had provided time for Queen Elizabeth's army, under the Earl of Sussex, to speed to York and force the rebels to flee. Many were executed and those leading families who had supported the plans to overthrow Elizabeth I lost their lands.

The castle ruins, with the imposing round keep overlooking the River Tees, have a gaunt beauty. Riverside walks wind through the woods that once formed part of the castle's hunting grounds. County Bridge, a narrow arched bridge built in 1569, traverses the fast flowing River Tees close to the Castle. It formerly spanned the boundaries of two counties and the lands of two bishops, and illicit weddings were regularly conducted in the middle of the bridge, where neither bishop could object.

The town has an especially rich architectural heritage, with handsome houses, cottages, shops and inns dating from the 17th to the 19th centuries. The octagonal **Market Cross** is a most impressive building, which dates back to 1747 and has served numerous purposes such as courthouse, town hall and jail. Underneath the veranda (a later addition) a lively butter market took place. You can still see the bullet holes in the weather-vane, resulting from a wager by two local men in 1804, shooting from outside the Turk's Head, 100 yards away, to determine who was the best shot. The building was fully restored in 1999. The Bank was once the town's main commercial street; Blagraves house is the oldest inhabited building and it is here that Oliver Cromwell is reputed to have stayed in 1648. At the bottom of The Bank glimpses of the town's industrial roots can still be found in Thorngate and Bridgegate. Weavers' cottages have been converted into modern dwellings and grassy slopes cover the remains of riverside woollen mills.

A walk along Newgate will bring visitors to the **Bowes Museum**, one of County Durham's great surprises and surely one of the most spectacular buildings in England. This magnificent French-style château was the inspiration of John Bowes, son of the Earl of Strathmore, and Joséphine, his French actress wife. The designer of the Bowes building was a Frenchman, Jules Pellechet, who apparently took his inspiration from the grand Town Hall in Le Havre. The couple's love of the arts and a desire that people

50 BARNARD CASTLE

Barnard Castle

Set on a high rock above the River Tees, imposing Barnard Castle was the stronghold of the Balliol family.

See entry on page 111

51 CAFÉ NEST

Barnard Castle

This place houses a superb Cafe & Gallery that offers a relaxed and informal atmosphere and is the ideal meeting place for work or pleasure.

See entry on page 112

52 BOWES MUSEUM

Barnard Castle

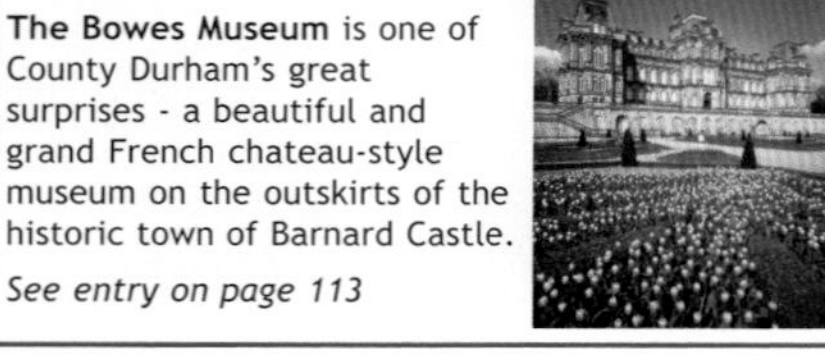

The Bowes Museum is one of County Durham's great surprises - a beautiful and grand French chateau-style museum on the outskirts of the historic town of Barnard Castle.

See entry on page 113

Bowes Museum

from all walks of life should be able to partake in such riches resulted in this superb legacy. Sadly both died before their dream could be realised, but the museum was completed and opened to the public in 1892. Today the museum, open daily at 10am, houses one of England's finest art collections including paintings by Canaletto, Goya and Turner, as well as fine textiles, ceramics, glass, clocks and watches and antique furniture. . The most famous and best loved exhibit is undoubtedly the Silver Swan, a 230-year-old, beautifully crafted life-size mechanical bird that appears to pick up and swallow a fish to the backdrop of a tinkly music box. Set in 23 acres of parkland, the museum boasts a splendid parterre garden; a Tree Trail in the grounds highlights unusual trees from around the world. The museum is open daily from 10 to 5.

AROUND BARNARD CASTLE

GRETA BRIDGE

4 miles SE of Barnard Castle on the A66

Lovers of romantic landscape should make their way south of Barnard Castle to Greta Bridge on the A66 - the graceful old bridge immortalised in paintings by great English water-colourists such as Cotman and Turner. Footpaths run by the riverside, through the edge of Rokeby Park. Close by are the ruins of medieval **Mortham Tower**, subject of Sir Walter Scott's narrative poem of colourful chivalry and courtly love, *Rokeby*. The elegant Palladian house, where Scott stayed to write his poem, is open to the public during the summer months. Charles Dickens travelled up the Great North Road from London with his illustrator Hablot K Browne to gather material for his third novel Nicholas Nickleby, and they spent their first night in Greta Bridge (see also under Bowes).

EGGLESTONE ABBEY

2 miles S of Barnard Castle, near the A66

South East of Barnard Castle the road leads over an old pack horse bridge to Egglestone Abbey. It is made up of the ruins of a Premonstratensian abbey of which most of the nave and chancel, built in the 13th and 14th century, survives. Close by is the Meeting of the Waters where the river Greta joins the River Tees, creating splendid views.

BOWES

4 miles W of Barnard Castle off the A66

The ruined Norman castle of Bowes was built on the site of a Roman fort, guarding the approach to Stainmore Pass. In 1838 Charles Dickens visited the village to collect material for *Nicholas Nickleby*, and noticed a boys'

53 THE GEORGE AND DRAGON INN

Boldron

With a recent new lease of life this picturesque inn offers freshly prepared home cooked food, real ale and two en-suite guest bedrooms.

See entry on page 114

54 THE ANCIENT UNICORN

Bowes

Standing in an Area of Outstanding Natural Beauty this pub-lover's pub has plenty of character and is an ideal resting spot for visitors to the area.

See entry on page 115

academy run by William Shaw in the main street. The school became the model for Dotheboys Hall and Shaw was immortalised as Wackford Squeers. Shaw is buried in the churchyard of St Giles' Church along with George Taylor, Dickens's inspiration for Smike. "I think," Dickens later said, "his ghost put Smike into my head upon the spot."

Eggleston Hall Gardens

ROMALDKIRK

4 miles NW of Barnard Castle on the B6277

Between Middleton and Barnard Castle, the B6277 follows the south bank of the River Tees passing through pretty unspoiled villages such as Cotherstone and Romaldkirk. The church at Romaldkirk, known as the **Cathedral of the Dales**, is dedicated to the little-known St Romald or Rumwald, son of a Northumbrian king who could miraculously speak at birth. Beautiful stone houses are set around spacious greens and there are delightful walks close to the river.

EGGLESTON

6 miles NW of Barnard Castle on the B6281

Within the grounds of Eggleston Hall are **Eggleston Hall Gardens**, which are open to the public all year. There are four acres of garden here within the high wall that once enclosed the kitchen garden. The ornamental gardens are laid out informally, with many rare herbaceous plants and shrubs to be seen. Vegetables are cultivated using the traditional organic methods. The Gardens are open all year, 10 to 5 daily.

55 CLOVE LODGE

Baldersdale

Offering B&B and self-catering options in a wonderfully rural location, this place is popular with walkers and cyclists.

See entry on page 116

MIDDLETON-IN-TEESDALE

10 miles NW of Barnard Castle on the B6277

Middleton-in-Teesdale, the capital of Upper Teesdale, is a small town in a dramatically beautiful setting with the River Tees running below, while all around is a great backcloth of green hills, within the North Pennines Area of Outstanding Natural Beauty. The town's links with the lead-mining industry can be seen in the Market Square, where there is a handsome cast-iron fountain which was purchased and placed there in 1877 by the employees of the Quaker-owned London Lead Mining Company. The expense was covered from subscriptions raised for the retirement of the company's local superintendent, Robert Bainbridge. At the west end of Hude is Middleton House, the company's former headquarters.

Although the lead-mining industry disappeared at the beginning of the 19th century, Middleton still retains the strong feeling of being a busy working town. The surrounding hills still bear the scars, with the remains of old workings, spoil-heaps and deep, and often dangerous, shafts. The town's agricultural links remain strong, with streets bearing names such as Market Place,

Horsemarket and Seed Hill.

Like Barnard Castle, Middleton is increasing in popularity as a centre from which to explore Teesdale and the Northern Pennines. Middleton is the centre for some magnificent walks in Upper Teesdale. The most famous of these is The Pennine Way, which passes through the town on its 250-mile route from Derbyshire to Kirk Yetholm in Scotland. Turning west along Teesdale the track passes through flower-rich meadows, traditional, whitewashed farmsteads and spectacular, riverside scenery, including the thrilling waterfalls at Low Force, High Force and Cauldron Snout.

From its modest rise at the top of the North Pennines to the top of the Whin Sill rock at Forest in Teesdale, the River Tees steadily grows and gathers pace. Then it suddenly and spectacularly drops 70 feet. The majestic **High Force** is England's largest waterfall in terms of water flow, with this dramatic drop over Great Whin Sill at the end of a wooded gorge. After heavy rainfall its rumble can be heard over a mile away. **Low Force** isn't so much a waterfall as a series of cascades, and whilst less spectacular than its upstream neighbour, it is equally beautiful.

Low Force

Further up the Dale from High Force is Cow Green Reservoir and below it Cauldron Snout, which cascades down dolerite steps. A nature trail leads from Cow Green car park to Cauldron Snout and Moor House Nature Reserve, home to some rare Alpine plants, including the Blue Gentian.

About three miles northwest of Middleton-in-Teesdale, near the village of Newbiggin, is the **Bowlees Visitor Centre**, where information on the natural history and geology and the people of the area is displayed. The picnic area has four small waterfalls and a footpath to Gibson's Cave and Summerhill Force.

HAMSTERLEY FOREST

9 miles N of Barnard Castle off the A68

Hamsterley Forest is one of the Forestry Commission's most attractive Forest Parks. This huge area encompassing over 5,500 acres of mature woodland is managed for timber production, and has 1,100 acres available for recreation. A wide range of activities are on offer for visitors including informal or guided walks, orienteering, horse-riding and cycling (bikes can be hired). There is a visitors centre with displays on forestry, wildlife and timber usage, and large, grassy areas make splendid picnic spots.

Surprisingly enough, the Forest is largely artificial and relatively recent in origin, having been planted only 40 to 50 years ago. Much of it covers areas once worked by the lead-mining industry. This is a good area to discover a range of wild flowers and, in the damper places, fungi. Red squirrels can still be seen in the forest, along with roe deer, badgers, adders and up to 40 species of birds including heron, woodcock, sparrow hawk, woodpeckers, fieldfare and goldfinch.

STANHOPE

Stanhope, the capital of Upper Weardale, is a small town of great character and individuality, which marks the boundary between the softer scenery of lower Weardale and the wilder scenery to the west.

The stone cross in the market place is the only reminder of a weekly market held in the town by virtue of a 1421 charter. The market continued until Victorian times, but today the town continues to serve the surrounding villages as an important local centre for shops and supplies.

Enjoying an attractive rural setting in the centre of the Dale, with a choice of local walks, Stanhope, in its quiet way, is becoming a small tourist centre with pleasant shops and cafés. Stanhope enjoyed its greatest period of prosperity in the 18th and 19th centuries when the lead and iron-stone industries were at their height, as reflected in the town's buildings and architecture.

The most dominant building in the Market Square is **Stanhope Castle**, a rambling structure complete with mock-Gothic crenellated towers, galleries and battlements. The building is, in fact, an elaborate folly built by the MP for Gateshead, Cuthbert Rippon in 1798 on the site of a medieval manor house. In 1875 it was enlarged to contain a private collection of mineral displays and stuffed birds for the entertainment of Victorian grouse-shooting parties. In the gardens is the **Durham Dales Centre**, which contains the Tourist Information Centre, a tea room and a sculptured children's animal trail. The Dales Garden was first developed as an exhibit at the Gateshead National Gardens Festival in 1990 and has been re-created here using typical Dales cottage garden plants.

Stanhope Old Hall

St Thomas's Church, by the Market Square, has a tower whose base is Norman, and some medieval glass in the west window. In the churchyard is a remarkable fossil tree stump which was discovered in 1962 in a local quarry.

The **Weardale Railway** runs for five miles between Stanhope and Wolsingham in the North Pennines Area of Outstanding Natural Beauty. Subject to availability, the trains are steam-hauled.

Stanhope Old Hall, above Stanhope Burn Bridge, is generally accepted to be one of the most impressive buildings in Weardale. This huge, fortified manor house was designed to repel Scottish raiders. The privately owned hall itself is part medieval, part Elizabethan and part Jacobean. The outbuildings included a cornmill, a brew house and cattle yards.

One of the most important Bronze Age archaeological finds ever made in Britain was at Heathery Burn, a side valley off Stanhope Burn. In 1850, quarrymen cut through the floor of a cave to find a huge hoard of bronze and gold ornaments, amber necklaces, pottery, spearheads, animal bones and parts of chariots. The treasures are now kept in London's British Museum.

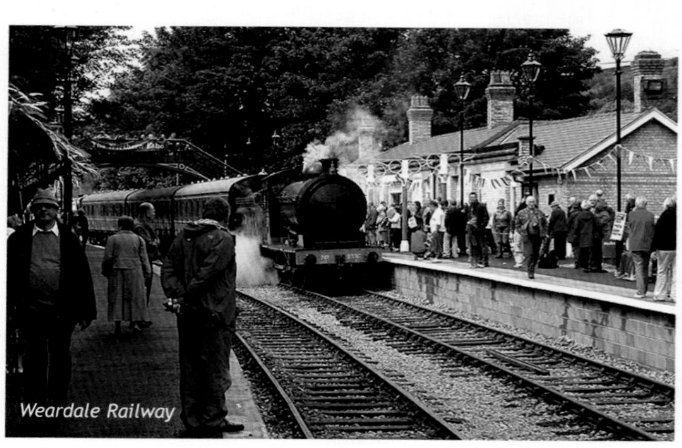

Weardale Railway

AROUND STANHOPE

FROSTERLEY

3 miles E of Stanhope on the A689

The village is famous for Frosterley marble, a black, heavily fossilised limestone that in former times was used extensively for rich decorative work and ornamentation on great public and private buildings throughout the north. The Chapel of the Nine Altars in Durham Cathedral makes extensive use of Frosterley Stone, sometimes called Durham Marble.

WOLSINGHAM

5 miles E of Stanhope on the A689

Wolsingham is one of the oldest market towns in County Durham and has its origins in Saxon times. The town has strong links with the iron and steel industries; Charles Attwood who was one of the great pioneers in the manufacture of steel founded the town steelworks, which once cast a variety of anchors and propellers for ships.

Tunstall Reservoir

Tunstall Reservoir, north of Wolsingham, and reached by a narrow lane, lies in a valley of ancient oak woods alongside Waskerley Beck. The reservoir was built in the mid 19th century, originally to provide lime-free water for the locomotives of the Stockton and Darlington Railway to prevent their boilers from scaling like a domestic kettle. It now forms part of a delightful area to stroll, picnic or go fishing.

56 THE PANTRY

Tow Law

Delicious home cooked food ensures this light and modern tea room is always bustling with eager diners.

See entry on page 117

57 HELME PARK HALL HOTEL

Fir Tree Village, nr Bishop Auckland

Quality accommodation with easy access to both country and town, this charming property is a popular venue that caters for all occasions.

See entry on page 118

BLANCHLAND

7 miles N of Stanhope on the B6306

A small, serene estate village on the Northumberland and Durham border. This is another of the area's hidden places, and one well worth seeking out. The name Blanchland (white land) comes from the white habits worn by the canons of the Premonstratensian Order who founded Blanchland Abbey in 1665. The abbey was dissolved by Henry VIII in 1537. In 1702, Lord Crewe, the Bishop of Durham bought the Blanchland estate. On his death in 1721 the estates were left to the Lord Crewe Trustees who were responsible for building the picturesque village of Blanchland which you see today, using stone from the ruined Abbey buildings. Small cottages snuggle round a village square opposite the popular Lord Crewe Arms, housed in part of the priory next to the ancient abbey church of St Mary the Virgin.

Pow Hill Country Park

POW HILL COUNTRY PARK

7 miles N of Stanhope on the B6306

Set in moorland overlooking the Derwent Reservoir, Pow Hill lies on the south shore and has great views of the lake. Conserved for its special wildlife interest, this valley bog habitat is home to goldcrests, coal tits, roe deer and red squirrels. The western end of the lake is protected as a nature reserve. In winter large flocks of migrant waders and wildfowl gather here. The Park is open for visits throughout the year.

ROOKHOPE

3 miles NW of Stanhope off the A689

Rookhope (pronounced Rook-up), in lonely Rookhope Dale, is on the C2C cycle route, and has a history lost in antiquity, dating back to Roman times.

Another old fashioned Dale village, Rookhope is set in a hidden North Pennine valley. The remains of lead and iron mine activity now blend into quiet rural beauty. At one point the road climbs past Rookhope Chimney, part of a lead-smelting mill where poisonous and metallic-rich fumes were refined in long flues.

ALLENHEADS

9 miles NW of Stanhope on the B6295

Allenheads also has lead-mining connections, with its scatter of stone miners' cottages and an irregular village square with pub and chapel in a lovely setting. The village is a centre for fine, upland rambles through the surrounding hills, which still retain many signs of the former industrial activity. From Allenheads the main road climbs over Burtree Fell into Weardale, with wild moorland roads branching across to Rookhope to the east and Nenthead to the west.

WESTGATE AND EASTGATE

4 miles W of Stanhope on the A689

The area between the lovely stone built villages of Westgate and Eastgate was once the Bishop of Durham's deer park, kept to provide him with an abundant supply of venison. The villages are so called because they were the east and west 'gates' to the park. The foundations of the Bishop's castle can still be seen at Westgate along with an old mill and water wheel. In 1327 the troops of Edward III camped at Eastgate en route to Scotland to face the Scottish army.

ST JOHN'S CHAPEL

7 miles W of Stanhope on the A689

St John's Chapel is named after its parish church, dedicated to St John the Baptist. Like many of the surrounding villages, it was once a lead mining centre and is still the home of an annual Pennine sheep auction in September that attracts farmers from all over the North Pennines. This is the only village in Durham to boast a town hall, a small building dating from 1868 overlooking the village green.

The road from St John's Chapel to Langdon Beck in Teesdale rises to 2,056 feet as it passes over Harthope Fell, making it the highest classified road in England.

Killhope Lead Mining Museum, nr Cowshill

COWSHILL

8 miles W of Stanhope on the A689

In a hollow between Cowshill and Nenthead lies Killhope Mine. The Pennines have been worked for their mineral riches, lead in particular, since Roman times but until the 18th century the industry remained relatively primitive and small scale.

Mechanisation in the late 18th and early 19th century allowed the mining industry to grow until it was second only to coal as a major extractive industry in the region. Now the country's best-preserved lead-mining site, Killhope Mine is the focal point of what is now the **North of England Lead Mining Museum**, dominated by the massive 34-feet water wheel. It used moorland streams, feeding a small reservoir, to provide power for the lead ore crushing mills, where the lead ore from the hillside mines was washed and crushed ready for smelting into pigs of lead. Much of the machinery in the Museum has been carefully restored by Durham County Council over recent years, together with part of the smelting mill, workshops, a smithy, tools and miners' sleeping quarters. The Museum stands on the site of the former Park Level Mine alongside Killhope Burn, off the A689 between Stanhope and Alston. Open for visits April to October.

IRESHOPEBURN

8 miles W of Stanhope on the A689

At Ireshopeburn, between Cowshill and St John's Chapel, is the delightful little **Weardale Museum & High House Chapel** situated in the former minister's house next to an 18th century Methodist chapel. The exhibits include a carefully re-created room in a typical Weardale lead-miners' cottage kitchen, with period furnishings and costumes, local history and mineral displays, and a room dedicated to John Wesley, who visited the area on several occasions. The museum is open during summer months only. This delightful small folk museum was formed in 1985 by a group of senior volunteers. The building is now the oldest Methodist chapel in the world in continuous weekly use since 1760.

River Wear, Ireshopeburn

LOCATION MAP

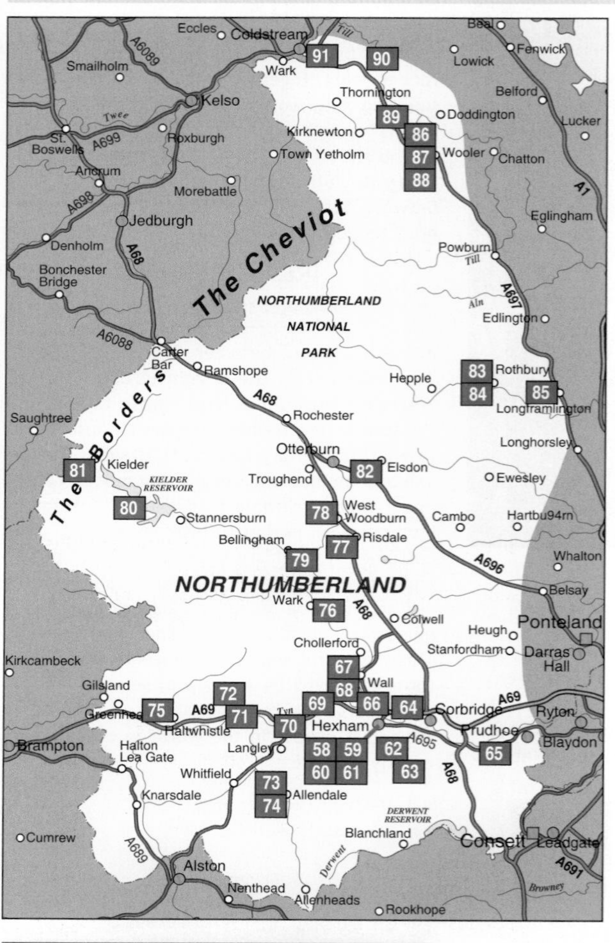

Accommodation

62	Loughbrow House, Hexham	pg 52, 121
63	Travellers Rest, Slaley, Hexham	pg 52, 122
66	The Sun Inn, Acomb	pg 53, 123
67	The Hadrian Hotel, Wall, Hexham	pg 54, 125
69	Red Lion, Newbrough	pg 54, 126
70	Anchor Hotel, Haydon Bridge	pg 54, 127
71	Bowes Hotel, Bardon Mill	pg 55, 128
74	Allendale Tea Rooms and Bed & Breakfast, Allendale	pg 56, 129
75	The Manor House Inn, Haltwhistle	pg 56, 130
76	The Black Bull, Wark	pg 57, 130
77	The Gun Inn, Ridsdale	pg 57, 131
78	The Bay Horse Inn, West Woodburn	pg 58, 132
79	The Cheviot Hotel, Bellingham	pg 58, 133
83	Newcastle House Hotel, Rothbury	pg 59, 136
85	Embleton Hall, Morpeth	pg 61, 138
86	The Anchor Inn, Wooler	pg 61, 139
88	The Black Bull Hotel, Wooler	pg 62, 141
89	The Red Lion Inn, Milfield	pg 62, 142
90	The Black Bull, Etal Village, Cornhill-on-Tweed	pg 63, 143
91	The Collingwood Arms Hotel, Cornhill-on-Tweed	pg 63, 143

HADRIAN'S WALL AND THE NORTHUMBERLAND NATIONAL PARK

Hadrian's Wall, Walltown Crags

West Northumberland, where the North Pennines blend into the Cheviots, is an exhilarating mixture of bleak grandeur, beauty and history. Stretching north towards the Scottish border are the 398 square miles of the Northumbrian National Park and the Kielder Forest Park, while to the south is Hadrian's Wall, that monumental feat of Roman civil engineering built on the orders of Emperor Hadrian in AD 122. A 73-mile-long World heritage Site, the wall marked the northern limit of the Roman Empire. Almost 2,000 years later it is still one of the world's most famous landmarks, stretching across mile after mile of glorious countryside.

Towards the east of the area, the hills slope down towards a stretch of fertile land with little towns like Rothbury and Wooler, which in themselves deserve exploration. But

Food & Drink

Places of Interest

Northumberland National Park

up on the high ground a person could walk for miles without meeting another soul. The highest point, at 2,650 feet, is the Cheviot itself, a few miles from the Scottish border.

This is the land of the Border Reivers, or mosstroopers, bands of marauding men from both sides of the Border who rustled, pillaged and fought among themselves, incurring the wrath of both the English and Scottish kings. A testament to their activities is the fact they gave the word blackmail to the English language. The 'mail' part of blackmail is an old Scottish word for a tax payment, and blackmail was a payment made by Border farmers to the Reivers as protection money. The Pennine Way passes over the moorland here, dipping occasionally into surprisingly green and wooded valleys. There are also less strenuous walks, circular routes and cycle tracks laid out, with maps and leaflets available from the park visitor centres, at Rothbury, the quaintly-named Once Brewed, and Ingram. Here you can also learn about the history of the area as well as things to see.

Three main valleys penetrate the park from the east - Harthope Valley, Breamish Valley and Coquetdale. Harthope Valley is accessed from Wooler, along the Harthope Burn. Part of it is called Happy Valley, and is a popular beauty spot. There are a number of circular walks from the valley floor up into the hills and back again.

Breamish Valley is the most popular of the valleys, and it's here that the Ingram Visitors Centre, open in the summer months only, is located. Again, there are trails and walkways laid out.

Coquetdale is the gentlest of the three, and is popular with anglers. It winds up past Harbottle towards Alwinton and Barrowburn, but in so doing passes through the Otterburn Training Area, where up to 30,000 soldiers a year come to practise their artillery skills. This has actually preserved the upper part of Coquetdale from modern development, and farming here has changed little over the years. The valley is rich in wildlife, and heron, sandpiper and grey wagtail are common. The exposed crags support rock-rose and thyme, and there are patches of ancient woodland.

The Kielder Forest covers 200 square miles, and is situated to the west of the National Park. It contains Europe's largest man-made lake, Kielder Water, opened by the Queen in 1982.

In the south of the National Park is by far the greater part of Hadrian's Wall, the best known Roman monument in Britain, and the best known Roman frontier in Europe.

HEXHAM

The picturesque market town of Hexham sits in the heart of Tynedale, and is its capital and administrative centre. It's rich in history and character and an ideal base from which to explore the Tyne Valley and Hadrian's Wall.

Hexham Abbey, one of the most important churches in the north of England, was at one time known as 'the largest and most magnificent church this side of the Alps'. It was founded by St Wilfrid in AD 674 after Queen Etheldreda of Northumbria

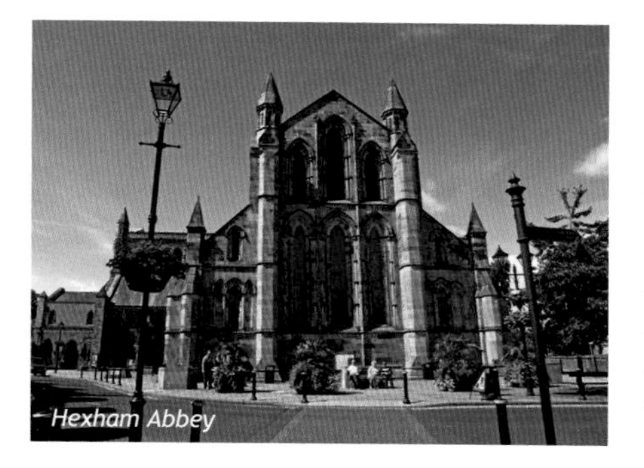
Hexham Abbey

granted him some land. The crypt of this early church remains almost intact, and access to it is via a stairway from the nave. The crypt was built using Roman stones, and on some of them you can still see inscriptions and carvings. Frith Stool, also known as St Wilfrid's chair, is a 1,300-year-old stone chair that is believed to have been used as a coronation throne for the ancient kings of Northumbria.

In 1130 a group of Augustinian canons set up an abbey on the site. The present church dates from the 13th century and contains some wonderful late-medieval architecture, which later restoration has not diminished. It has a rich heritage of carved stonework, and the early 16th century rood screen has been described as the best in any monastic church in Britain.

The Abbey was ransacked many times by the Scots armies, who at one time poured over the border into England. However, this was a two-way traffic, and the English did likewise to the abbeys at Melrose and Kelso.

The Abbey overlooks the Market Place, where a lively and colourful market is held each Tuesday. Nearby is the early 14th century Moot Hall, built of Roman stone. In olden days it served as the courtroom of the Archbishop of York, who held the grand title of Lord of the Liberty and Regality of Hexham. Today the hall houses the **Border History Library**, which contains material on Border life, in particular the music and poetry of the region.

Nearby, the Manor Office was England's first purpose-built prison and was built by the Archbishop in 1332 as a gaol for his courthouse. The **Border History Museum** is located within the gaol and tells, in a vivid way, the story of the border struggles between Scotland and England. For centuries the borderlands were virtually without rule of law, ravaged by bands of men known as

58 KNIGHTS CAFE

Hexham

This popular cafe has been welcoming hungry passersby for the past 34 years and is well known for its tasty breakfasts.

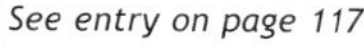

See entry on page 117

59 THE GARDEN COFFEE HOUSE (FORMERLY PHAT KATZ)

Hexham

Homemade lunches, cakes and locally produced ice cream are extremely popular at this wonderful child-friendly coffee house.

See entry on page 119

60 UPPER TEAS CAFE

Felton

Delicious homemade cakes and lunches are available Monday - Saturday at this popular cafe that offers a pleasant and friendly service.

See entry on page 119

Reivers - cattle rustlers and thieves who took advantage of the disputed border lands. Powerful wardens, or Lords of the Marches, themselves warlords of pitiless ferocity, were given almost complete authority by the king to control the Reivers and anyone else who crossed their path. However, for all their power and ferocity they were singularly unsuccessful in controlling the bloodshed. This was the period of the great border ballads, violent and colourful tales of love, death, heroism and betrayal, which have found an enduring place in literature.

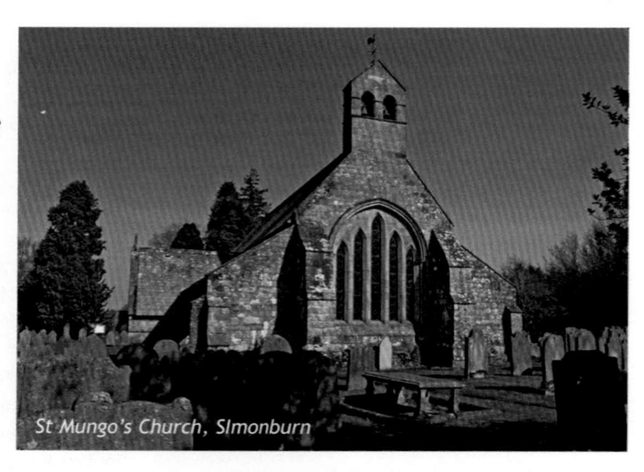

St Mungo's Church, Simonburn

The award-winning **Queens Hall Arts Centre** with theatre, café, library and exhibitions presents a full and varied programme throughout the year. Tel: 01434 652477.

The town of Hexham has retained much of its character, with winding lanes and passageways, attractive 18th and 19th century houses, handsome terraces and some delightful shops and a market. There are some fine gardens around the abbey, and several attractive areas of open space. Tyne Green Country Park features attractive walks along the riverside and a picnic and barbecue site.

Hexham National Hunt Racecourse at Acomb is one of the most picturesque courses in the country. Call 01434 606881 for details of meetings. At Simonburn, just north of Hadrian's Wall, **St Mungo's Church** is the Mother Church of the North Tyne Valley.

61 IN THE CHARE

Hexham

The aroma of home cooking attracts plenty of passersby to this wonderful cafe, which offers the very best in hospitality and homemade food.

See entry on page 120

62 LOUGHBROW HOUSE

Hexham

This impressive guest house standing 600ft above the River Tyne provides the ideal base for visitors wanting to explore Northumberland.

See entry on page 121

AROUND HEXHAM

SLALEY

4 miles SE of Hexham, off the B6306

Slaley is a quiet village consisting of one long street with some picturesque houses dating from the 17th, 18th and 19th centuries. One of the finest houses - Church View - stands opposite the 19th century St Mary's Church. Two miles southwest, Slayley Hall has some interesting gardens.

63 TRAVELLERS REST

Hexham

Offering quality accommodation and fine food in an isolated scenic location this place has a fantastic reputation as a B&B and as a place to dine out.

See entry on page 122

CORBRIDGE

3 miles E of Hexham on the A69

The lively market town of Corbridge was, for a time, the capital of the ancient Kingdom of Northumbria. The original Roman town, **Corstorpitum**, lay half a mile to the northwest, and was an important military headquarters. Visitors to the site can see the substantial remains of this strategic river crossing, which include a fine example of military granaries and two fortified medieval towers, which are evidence of more troubled times. The museum houses finds from the excavation of the site, the most famous of which is the Lion of Corbridge - a stone fountainhead. The 14th century Vicar's Pele was, as the name implies, formerly the home of the vicar, and the other, Low Hall, dating from the 13th century, was converted into a private house in 1675.

The finest building in Corbridge is undoubtedly **St Andrew's Church**. It still retains many Saxon features, and the base of the tower was once the west porch of the Saxon nave. Within the tower wall is a complete Roman arch, no doubt removed from Corstorpitum at some time.

Corbridge is also the site of the **Northumberland County Show**, the region's biggest single rural attraction, held each year on the late May Bank Holiday Monday.

AYDON

4 miles E of Hexham off the B6321

Aydon Castle is a superb example of a fortified manor house, such protection being necessary in this region in times past to keep the Reivers at bay. Built by Robert de Reymes in the late 13th century, it remains remarkably intact, and is often described as one of the best preserved fortified manor houses in Britain, thanks to its early owners and now to English Heritage.

CHOLLERFORD

5 miles N of Hexham on the B6318

The Roman fort of **Chesters**, or Cilurnum, to give it its Roman name, is situated in the parkland created by Nathaniel Clayton around the mansion he had built in 1771. The fort covers nearly six acres and was large enough to accommodate a full cavalry regiment. The **Museum** houses a remarkable collection of Roman antiquities. Remains of the Roman fort include a well preserved bath house and barracks. Near the bath house can be seen the foundations of a Roman bridge that carried a road across the Tyne.

Five minutes' walk from the Roman Fort is **Chesters Walled Garden**, laid out as a unique, organically run herb and herbaceous garden, with the original box hedges and cruciform layout giving it a timeless quality enhanced by the informal planting. The gardens house the national collections of thyme and marjoram, and other attractions include the Roman Garden and the giant Tibetan rhubarb. Many of the garden's 900 herbs are sold in the adjoining nursery. Open

64 THE RAT INN

Anick, nr Hexham

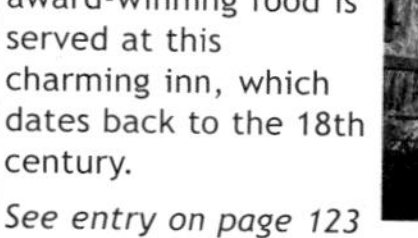

Locally-sourced, award-winning food is served at this charming inn, which dates back to the 18th century.

See entry on page 123

65 THE BLUEBELL INN

Stocksfield

With plenty of charm and character and a spectacular hidden beer garden, this pub serves home cooked food and real ales.

See entry on page 124

66 THE SUN INN

Acomb

Fine home cooking attracts a loyal clientele at this popular pub which has a cosy bar and games room.

See entry on page 123

Chesters Walled Garden, Chollerford

daily Easter to the end of October, otherwise by appointment. Tel: 01434 681483.

CHOLLERTON

5 miles N of Hexham on the A6079

Chollerton, six miles north of Hexham, enjoys an exceptionally fine setting. Nearby is the site of the Battle of Heavenfield, where King (later St) Oswald defeated the army of Cadwalla, a Welsh king.

BARRASFORD

7 miles N of Hexham off the A6079

Barrasford sits on the North Tyne across from **Haughton Castle**, of which there are fine views. The castle is one of the finest great houses in Northumberland, and dates originally from the 13th century. Over the succeeding years, additions and alterations have been made, with the west wing being designed by Anthony Salvin and built in 1876. The castle isn't open to the public.

HAYDON BRIDGE

6 miles W of Hexham on the A69

Two bridges cross the Tyne here - a modern concrete one dating from 1970, and an older one dating from 1776. North of the village is Haydon Old Church, close to where the

67 THE HADRIAN HOTEL

Wall, nr Chollerford

This country hotel offers comfortable accommodation and delicious wholesome food in the unspoilt territory of Hadrian's Wall.

See entry on page 125

68 HADRIAN'S WALL

Wall, nr Chollerford

Welcome to the unspoilt beauty of Hadrian's Wall Country, where the rugged countryside hides a wealth of activities and attractions.

See entry on page 125

69 RED LION

Newbrough

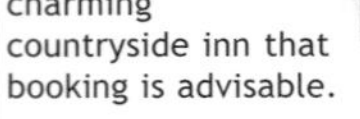

The freshly made food with a twist is so popular at this charming countryside inn that booking is advisable.

See entry on page 126

70 ANCHOR HOTEL

Haydon Bridge

Quality food, real ale and comfortable accommodation can all be found at this hotel, which boasts a superb location next to the South River Tyne.

See entry on page 127

medieval village of Haydon lay. It dates partly from the 12th century.

LANGLEY

6 miles W of Hexham on the B6295

Langley Castle, now a hotel and restaurant, was built in around 1350. In 1450, Henry 1V had it destroyed, but it was restored in the 1890s by a local historian, Cadwallader Bates. In the 17th and early 18th centuries the Castle was owned by the Earls of Derwentwater, and in 1716 the third earl, James, was beheaded in London for his part in the 1715 Jacobite rebellion. His brother Charles was later beheaded for his part in the 1745 uprising. A memorial to them sits beside the A686 not far from the castle. Guided tours of the Castle and grounds are available by prior arrangement - Tel: 01434 688888.

Garden Station at Langley is an attractive, restored Victorian railway station in a woodland garden. A tranquil place with gardening and art courses, unusual plants and refreshments. Tel: 01434 684391.

BARDON MILL

10 miles W of Hexham on the A69

Bardon Mill, a former mining village, stands on the north bank of the South Tyne. An important drovers' road crossed the river here and cattle were fitted with iron shoes at Bardon Mill to help them on their way to southern markets. The village is a convenient starting point for walks along **Hadrian's Wall** and the Roman forts of **Vindolanda** and **Housesteads** are nearby. At Vindolanda (the Vindolanda Trust Tel: 01434 344277) excavations continue to reveal fascinating insights into Roman life. The open-air **Roman Army Museum** features a reconstructed temple, shop and house (Tel: 01697 747485). Perched high on a ridge, with splendid views of the surrounding countryside, the remains of Housesteads Fort cover over five acres and is one of the finest sections of Hadrians Wall. Nearby, **Once Brewed** is the main Visitor Centre for Hadrians Wall and the Northumberland National Park.

Between Bardon Mill and Haydon Bridge lies the confluence of the South Tyne and the River Allen, which, like the Tyne, comes from two main tributaries - the East Allen and West Allen. The valleys of the East and West Allen really are hidden jewels. The 22,667 acres of Allen Banks, as the lower part of the valley near the Tyne is known, is a deep, wooded, limestone valley, rich in natural beauty, now owned by the National Trust.

ALLENDALE

10 miles SW of Hexham on the B6295

Allendale Town lies on the River East Allen, set against a backdrop of heather clad moorland, and was once an important centre of the north Pennine lead-mining industry. It retains attractive houses from prosperous times and a surprisingly large number of existing or former inns around the Market Square. A sundial in the churchyard in Allendale records the fact that the village

71 BOWES HOTEL

Bardon Mill

Superb accommodation and delicious food can all be found under one roof at this establishment, which stands at the heart of Hadrian Wall country.

See entry on page 128

72 VINDOLANDA

Bardon Mill

Vindolanda, once a Roman frontier military and civilain site displays rare and fascinating objects from the

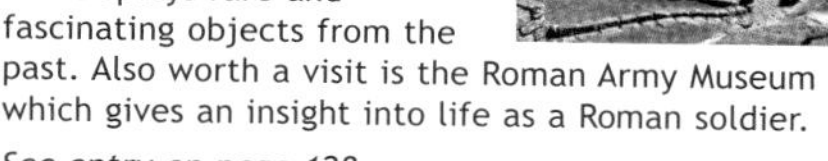

past. Also worth a visit is the Roman Army Museum which gives an insight into life as a Roman soldier.

See entry on page 128

73 THE GOLDEN LION

Allendale

Home cooked food, real ale and live

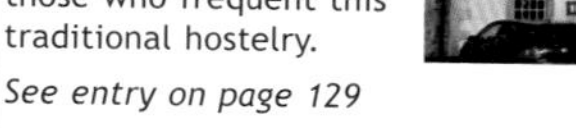

entertainment are regularly enjoyed by those who frequent this traditional hostelry.

See entry on page 129

lies exactly at the mid point between Beachy Head in Sussex and Cape Wrath in Scotland, making it the very centre of Britain.

HALTWHISTLE

15 miles W of Hexham on the A69

The origins of the name Haltwhistle are unknown but two suggestions are the watch (wessel) on the high (alt) mound, or the high (haut) fork of two streams (twysell). It is difficult to imagine that this pleasant little town with its grey terraces was once a mining area, but evidence of the local industries remain. An old pele tower is incorporated into the Centre of Britain Hotel in the town centre. Holy Cross Church, behind the Market Place, dates back to the 13th century and is said to be on the site of an earlier church founded by William the Lion, King of Scotland in 1178, when this area formed part of Scotland. The town lies close to the best-preserved stretch of Hadrian's Wall, which here follows the dramatic line of the Whin Sill ridge and provides breathtaking views across five counties.

Three miles northwest of Haltwhistle, off the B6318, is **Walltown Quarry**, a recreation site built on the site of an old quarry. Today part of the Northumberland National Park, it contains laid-out trails and it is possible to spot oystercatchers, curlews, sandpipers and lapwings.

***Walltown Quarry**, Haltwhistle*

74 ALLENDALE TEA ROOMS AND BED & BREAKFAST

Allendale

The aroma of home cooking attracts plenty of locals and visitors through the doors of this recently transformed establishment.

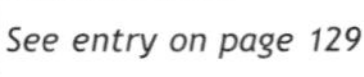

See entry on page 129

75 THE MANOR HOUSE INN

Haltwhistle

This place offers a fantastic base from which to explore Northumberland, and serves tasty home cooked food daily.

See entry on page 130

OTTERBURN

The village of Otterburn stands close to the centre of the National Park, in the broad valley of the River Rede. It makes an ideal base for exploring the surrounding countryside, an exhilarating area of open moorland and rounded hills. It was close to here, on a site marked by the 18th century Percy Cross, that the **Battle of Otterburn** took place in 1388 between the English and the Scots. By all accounts it was a ferocious encounter, even by the standards of the day, and one commentator said that it "was one of the sorest and best fought, without cowards or faint hearts".

Under the command of Earl Douglas, a gathering of Scottish troops at Jedburgh in 1388 had resolved to enter England in a two-pronged attack - one towards Carlisle and one down into Redesdale. In charge of the Redesdale contingent was the Earl of Douglas, who got as far as Durham before being forced back to the border by Henry

Percy, better known as Hotspur, and his brother Ralph.

In August the English caught up with the Scottish army at Otterburn, and went straight into attack. The battle continued for many hours, gradually descending into a series of hand to hand fights between individual soldiers. Gradually the Scots got the upper hand, and captured both Percys. But it was a hollow victory, as the Earl of Douglas was killed. A second force under the Bishop of Durham hurried north when it heard the news, but it wisely decided not to engage in battle. A series of markers known as Golden Pots are said to mark the journey of Douglas's body when it was taken back to Melrose. Otterburn Mill dates from the 18th century, though a mill is thought to have stood on the site from at least the 15th century. Production of woollens ceased in 1976, but the mill can be visited and on display are Europe's only original working tenterhooks, where newly woven cloth was stretched and dried.

There are some interesting walks around Otterburn, and some well preserved remains of Iron Age forts can be seen on both Fawdon Hill and Camp Hill.

North of the village are the remains of **Bremenium** Roman fort. It was first built by Julius Agricola in the 1st century, though what the visitor sees now is mainly 3rd century. In its day the fort could hold up to 1,000 men, and was one of the defences along the Roman road now known as Dere Street. Close by is the **Brigantium Archaeological Reconstruction Centre**, where you can see a stone circle of 4000 BC, Iron Age defences, a drystone walled round house, cup and ring carvings and a section of Roman road.

AROUND OTTERBURN

BELLINGHAM AND WARK

7 miles SW of Otterburn on the B6320

The North Tyne is fed by the Kielder Water, which on its way down to join the South Tyne above Hexham passes by the interesting villages of Bellingham and Wark.

Bellingham (pronounced Bellin-jam) is a small market town in a moorland setting, with a broad main street, market place and the austere little **St Cuthbert's Church**, reflecting the constant troubles of the area in medieval times. To prevent marauding Scots from burning it down, a massive stone roof was added in the early 17th century.

In the churchyard an oddly shaped tombstone, somewhat reminiscent of a peddler's pack, is associated with a foiled robbery attempt that took place in 1723. A peddler arrived at Lee Hall, a mansion once situated between Bellingham and Wark, and asked if he could be put up for the night. As her master was away at the time the maid refused, but said that he could leave his heavy pack at the Hall and collect it the next day.

Imagine her consternation when some time later the pack began to move. Hearing her screams for help, a servant rushed to the scene and fired his gun at the moving bundle. When blood poured out and the body of an armed man was discovered inside, the servants realised that this had been a clever attempt to burgle the Hall. They sounded a horn, which they found inside the pack next to the body, and when

76 THE BLACK BULL

Wark

Comfortable accommodation, traditional pub grub and well-kept ales can all be found at this picturesque village inn.

See entry on page 130

77 THE GUN INN

Ridsdale

This isolated village inn offers tourists and locals the very best in hospitality, home-cooked food and facilities.

See entry on page 131

the robber's accomplices came running in response to the prearranged signal, they were speedily dealt with.

Wark, to the south of Bellingham, is an attractive estate village, once part of the lordship of Wark. The Scottish kings are said to have held court here in the 12th century. **Chipchase Castle**, is a combination of 14th century tower, Jacobean mansion and Georgian interior.

Kielder Water

On the slopes overlooking the North Tyne are a large number of unusually named prehistoric settlements, such as Male Knock Camp, Good Wife Camp, Nigh Folds Camp, Carryhouse Camp and Shieldence Camp.

KIELDER

16 miles W of Otterburn off the B6320

Kielder village was built in the 1950s to house workers employed in the man-made **Kielder Forest**, which covers 200 square miles to the west of the **Northumberland National Park**.

Here at Kielder Forest you'll find one of the few areas in Britain that is home to more red squirrels than grey, thanks to careful forest planning that ensures a constant supply of conifer preferred by red squirrels. Otters, too, are resident in Kielder, and the area abounds with deer and rare birds and plants.

There's some excellent walking to be had, with several marked trails and routes to suit all abilities, from a leisurely stroll to an energetic climb, with maps and leaflets to guide you round. There are also cycle routes, including the 17 mile Kielder Water Cycle Route, and bicycles can be hired from the local visitors centre.

78 THE BAY HORSE INN

West Woodburn

This immaculate inn is a delightful place to pause for a drink, relax over a leisurely meal or enjoy a break in a picturesque setting.

See entry on page 132

79 THE CHEVIOT HOTEL

Bellingham

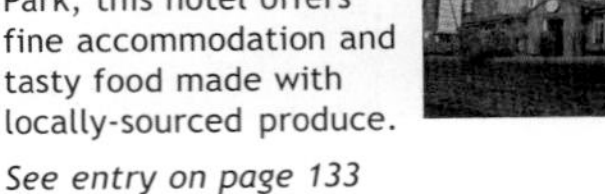

At the heart of the Northumberland National Park, this hotel offers fine accommodation and tasty food made with locally-sourced produce.

See entry on page 133

80 KIELDER WATER BIRDS OF PREY CENTRE

Kielder

The centre contains one of the largest and most fascinating collections of Birds of prey in the north of England.

See entry on page 134

81 THE ANGLERS ARMS

Kielder

Genuine hospitality, outstanding food and great real ales combine to provide a great overall experience at this popular pub and restaurant situated in a tranquil location on the edge of Kielder Water.

See entry on page 135

Within the forest is **Kielder Water**, opened by the Queen in 1982; it is the largest man-made lake in Northern Europe with over 27 miles of shoreline. The visitor can take a pleasure cruise aboard the Osprey, an 80-seat passenger cruiser that stops at several points of interest along the lake.

Located at sites around the lake and within the forest is an art and sculpture trail of works inspired by the surroundings. **Leaplish Waterside Park** has a range of activities and attractions for all ages, including the **Kielder Water Birds of Prey Centre**, one of the largest and most fascinating collections of birds of prey in the North of England. Tel: 01434 250500

To the northwest is **Kielder Castle**, at one time a hunting lodge for the Duke of Northumberland, and later offices for the Forestry Commission. It is now a fascinating visitor centre with exhibits describing the development of the forest and the birdlife that is found in Kielder.

ELSDON

3 miles E of Otterburn on the B6341

The village of Elsdon is of great historical importance. Built around a wide green, with **St Cuthbert's Church** in the middle, it was the medieval capital of Redesdale - the most lawless place in Northumberland, and scene of some of the worst border fighting. In later years it became an important stopping point on the drovers' road.

In the late 19th century, when the church was being restored, over 1,000 skulls were uncovered. They are thought to be those of soldiers killed at the Battle of Otterburn.

Elsdon Tower, which in 1415 was referred to as the 'vicar's pele', dates from the 14th century, though it was largely rebuilt at a later date. It is one of the most important pele towers of the region and is now a private residence.

ROTHBURY

12 miles E of Otterburn on the B6341

The attractive town of Rothbury is a natural focal point from which to explore the valley of the River Coquet. It is an excellent starting point for some delightful walks, either along the valley or through the nearby woodland. The most famous perhaps being the trail to the Rothbury Terraces, a series of parallel tracks along the hillside above the town.

Simonside, a hill offering a fine viewpoint, is steeped in history and the subject of several legends. Flint arrowheads have been recovered there, as well as bronze swords, shards of pottery, axe heads and ornaments. Burial cairns abound, as do carved stones and ancient paths. The Northumberland National Park has prepared a leaflet, which guides you on a walk up and onto the hill.

To the north of Simonside is Lordenshaws, with a well defined hill fort, Bronze Age burial mounds, rock carvings and cairns.

From the 18th century the village of Rothbury developed into a natural marketplace for Upper Coquetdale, to which cattle and sheep were brought for sale, and the drovers were provided with numerous alehouses. Since the mid 19th century Rothbury has been a holiday resort for walkers and fishermen, and the railway, which opened in 1870, contributed further to its growth.

The former Saxon parish church of

See entry on page 136

See entry on page 136

Cragisde House, Rothbury

Rothbury, which was almost entirely rebuilt in 1850, is worth visiting to see the font, which stands on part of the 9th century Rothbury cross.

Just outside Rothbury is the house and estate of **Cragside**, once the home of Sir William Armstrong, arms manufacturer and industrialist. He bought 14,000 acres in the valley of the Debden Burn, and employed architect Norman Shaw to extend the existing house and make it suitable to entertain royalty and other wealthy guests. Work began in 1864, and what finally emerged in 1884 was a mock-Tudor Victorian mansion. A pioneer of the turbine, Armstrong designed various pieces of apparatus for the house, and devised his own hydroelectric systems, with man-made lakes, streams and miles of underground piping, making Cragside the first house in the world to be lit by hydroelectricity and a wonder of its age. Cragside is now owned by the National Trust, and has been sympathetically restored to show how upper middle class Victorians were beginning to combine comfort, opulence and all the latest technology in their homes.

With one of Europe's largest rock gardens, 40 miles of walks and 7 million tress and shrubs, including England's tallest Douglas fir, Cragside is a garden of superlatives and great drama. The 1,000 acres include 8,000 heathers and a vast woodland garden famous for its rhododendron and azalea displays. In 2009 the newly restored Iron Bridge was open for the first time in 30 years.The adventure play area and labyrinth make Cragside a great place for a family visit. Tel: 01669 620333.

WELDON BRIDGE

15 miles E of Otterburn on the A697

Weldon Bridge is an exceptionally elegant bridge across the River Coquet, dating from 1744. Although it no longer carries the main road, it remains an impressive feature.

Nearby is **Brinkburn Priory**, standing in secluded woodland on the banks of the river. It was established in about 1135 by William de Bertram, 1st Baron Mitford, and is thought to have been built by the same masons who constructed nearby Longframlington church. It is in a beautiful setting surrounded by ancient trees and rhododendrons, and was once painted by Turner as a romantic ruin. Its church was restored in 1859 by Thomas Austin on behalf of the Cadogan family, and has many fine architectural features. It is also the setting for famous annual summer concerts.

LONGFRAMLINGTON

15 miles E of Otterburn on the A697

Longframlington derives its name from its

principal family, the de Framlingtons, who are recorded as the 12th-century benefactors of Brinkburn Priory. The route of the Devil's Causeway, a Roman road between Hadrian's Wall and the Scottish border, can easily be traced west of the village, along what is now a farm lane past Framlington Villa.

There are few shops here but the village retains the traditional craftsmanship of a Northumbrian pipe maker. The workshop, where you can see the production of these unique and beautiful musical instruments, is open to the public.

HEPPLE

8 miles NE of Otterburn on the B6341

Hepple has a reminder of the difficulty of life near the borders in the form of **Hepple Tower**, a 14th century pele tower built so strongly that attempts to demolish it and use the stone for a new farmhouse had to be abandoned. The chances are that the tower was erected by Sir Robert Ogle - he was known to own at least six similar buildings! West of the village, on the moors, are some fine examples of fortified houses and farms.

WOOPERTON

20 miles NE of Otterburn off the A697

Wooperton is close to the site of the **Battle of Hedgeley Moor**, which took place in 1464. In truth this was more of a skirmish, in which the Yorkist Lord Montague defeated the Lancastrian Sir Ralph Percy, who was killed. The site of the Battle of Hedgeley Moor is marked by a carved stone called the Percy Cross and can be reached along a short footpath leading from the A697.

85 EMBLETON HALL

Longframlington

As one of the most renowned hotels in Northumberland you can expect luxury accommodation and top of the range cuisine here.

See entry on page 138

WOOLER

Wooler is a small town standing on the northern edge of the Cheviots, midway between Newcastle and Edinburgh, and is an excellent centre for exploring both the Cheviots and the border country. In the 18th and early 19th centuries it became an important halt on the main north-south coaching route and now holds regular markets of sheep and cattle.

There are superb walking opportunities in the area surrounding Wooler, for example, the Iron Age hill fort immediately west of the town, Earle Whin and Wooler Common, or via Harthope onto The Cheviot itself. Alternatively, the visitor can take a vehicle into the Harthope Valley with a choice of walks, easy or strenuous, up and through the magnificent hillsides of this part of the Northumberland National Park.

The visitor can also climb **Humbleton Hill**, on top of which are the remains of a hill fort, built about 300 BC. The Battle of Humbleton Hill was fought here in 1402 between the English and the Scots, who had been on a raiding mission as far south as Newcastle. Due to the firepower of Welsh bowmen in the English army, the Scottish army assembled within the fort was easily

86 THE ANCHOR INN

Wooler

This place is always busting with locals and visitors after a traditional pub meal or real ales. For overnight guests it is in an ideal location for exploring the Border country.

See entry on page 139

87 BREEZE

Wooler

This wonderful place offers fine homemade food, beverages and an array of arts, crafts and gifts at the heart of walking country.

See entry on page 140

Humbleton Hill

defeated. Human and horse bones have been uncovered while Humbleton Hill's northern slopes were being ploughed, and an area is still known to this day as Red Riggs from the blood, which stained the ground during and after the battle.

AROUND WOOLER

KIRKNEWTON

6 miles W of Wooler on the B6351

Kirknewton is a typical border village made up of cottages, a school and village church. **St Gregory's Church** dates mainly from the 19th century, though there are medieval fragments such as an unusual sculpture, which shows the Magi wearing kilts - a fascinating example of medieval artists presenting the Christian story in ways their audience could understand.

Josephine Butler, the great Victorian social reformer and fighter for women's rights, who retired to Northumberland and died here in 1906, is buried in the churchyard. Her father had been a wealthy landowner, and a cousin of British Prime Minister Earl Grey of Howick Hall, near Craster.

Half a mile east of Kirknewton, in what are now fields by the River Glen, lay the royal township of Gefrin or Ad-Gefrin, better known as Yeavering. Discovered in 1948 thanks to aerial photography, this was where, in the 7th century, King Edwin of Northumbria built a huge wooden palace that included a royal hall over 100 feet long, storehouses, stables, chapels and living quarters. A stone, and a board explaining the layout, now mark the place where this long-vanished royal establishment once stood.

BRANXTON

8 miles NW of Wooler off the A697

The site of the decisive **Battle of Flodden Field** can be found near Branxton, marked by a cross in a cornfield reached by a short path. Following the terms of a Scottish alliance with the French King James IV of Scotland led his 30,000 troops into England after Henry VIII had invaded France. An

Flodden Battlefield Memorial, Branxton

English army of some 20,000 men under the Earl of Surrey marched north in response and in the ensuing battle the Scots were routed, with the loss of up to 10,000 men, and the king killed. The tragedy is commemorated in the lament *The Flowers of the Forest*, played by pipers at the Remembrance Sunday ceremony.

FORD AND ETAL

4 miles E of Cornhill-on-Tweed on the B6353 (Ford) or B6354 (Etal)

The twin estate villages of Ford and Etal were built in the late-19th century. Ford is a 'model' village with many beautiful stone buildings and well-tended gardens. Dating originally from the 14th century but heavily restored in the 19th, **Ford Castle** was the home of Louisa Ann, Marchioness of Waterford. In 1860 she built the village school and spent the years from 1862 to 1883 decorating it with life-size murals depicting biblical scenes, often including local people in the scenes and thus creating a pictorial gallery of life and work in the area at that time. Now known as **Lady Waterford Hall**, it is open daily in the summer for visits. Etal is an attractive village within which are the ruins of the 14th century castle destroyed by King James IV of Scotland. The **Church of the Blessed Virgin Mary** was built in 1858 by Lady Augusta Fitzclarence in memory of her husband and daughter.

CORNHILL-ON-TWEED

10 miles NW of Wooler at junction of A697 and A698

An unusual attraction, on the banks of the River Till near Cornhill, is **Heatherslaw Cornmill**, a 19th century cornmill restored to working order, producing stoneground wholemeal flour with wheat grown in the surrounding fields. It's open daily in summer. Tel: 01890 820488 for visiting and milling times.

90 THE BLACK BULL

Etal Village

This charming pub is well-regarded for its locally produced meals, genuine hospitality and community spirit.

See entry on page 143

91 THE COLLINGWOOD ARMS HOTEL

Cornhill-on-Tweed

Fine home cooking attracts a loyal clientele at this popular three star hotel, promoting local produce with Rod Rooms and Kennels.

See entry on page 143

LOCATION MAP

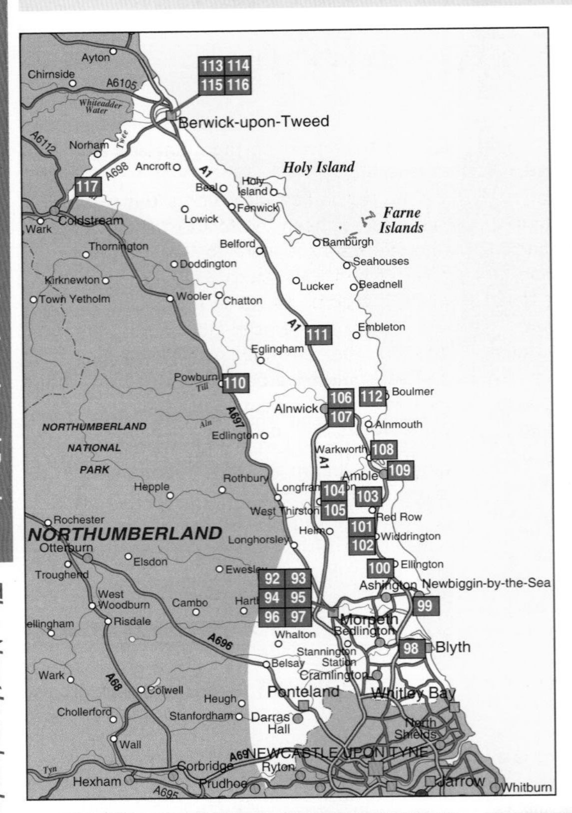

Accommodation

95	Lansdown House, Morpeth	pg 66, 145
99	The New Ship Inn, Newbiggin-by-the-Sea	pg 69, 147
100	The Plough Inn, Ellington	pg 69, 148
103	The Trap Inn , North Broomhill, Morpeth	pg 69, 151
104	The Northumberland Arms Hotel, West Thirston, Morpeth	pg 70, 150
105	Stags Head, Felton	pg 70, 152
108	Hermitage Inn, Warkworth	pg 72, 154
109	The Schooner, Amble	pg 73, 155
110	Crawley Farmhouse & Crawley Tower Cottage , Powburn, Alnwick	pg 73, 155
111	Coach House, Brownieside, Alnwick	pg 74, 156
116	The Cat Inn , Berwick-upon-Tweed	pg 77, 159
117	The Old School House, Tillmouth, Cornhill-on-Tweed	pg 80, 159

Food & Drink

92	Old Red Bull Inn, Morpeth	pg 66, 144
93	Sour Grapes Wine Bar, Morpeth	pg 66, 144
94	Pepperpot Cafe-Bistro, Morpeth	pg 66, 145
96	The Joiners Arms, Morpeth	pg 67, 146
97	Beetroot Grill & Cafe, Morpeth	pg 67, 146
98	Windmill Inn, Blyth	pg 68, 148
99	The New Ship Inn, Newbiggin-by-the-Sea	pg 69, 147
100	The Plough Inn, Ellington	pg 69, 148
101	Widdrington Inn, Widdrington Village, Morpeth	pg 69, 150
102	The Country Barn Farm & Coffee Shop, Widdrington Village, Morpeth	pg 69, 149

THE NORTHUMBERLAND COASTAL AREA

Stretching from the edge of the Cheviots to the East Coast, and from the River Blyth in the south to Berwick-upon-Tweed in the north, this is an area of quiet villages and small market towns, majestic castles, and what many people consider to be the finest coastline in England. Designated as the North Northumberland Heritage Coast, the area boasts a wealth of historical attractions such as Bamburgh Castle, Lindisfarne and the Farne Islands. Bamburgh was the birthplace, in 1814, of Grace Darling, who became an internationally feted heroine when with her father she rescued survivors of a paddle steamer wrecked in a violent storm.

For all its beauty, it's a quiet coastline, and you can walk for miles along the dunes and beaches without meeting another soul. No deck chairs or noisy ice cream vans here - just a quietness broken occasionally by the screeching of gulls. Coquet Island is a renowned bird sanctuary where the visitor can see puffins, roseate terns, razorbills, cormorants and eiders.

Lindisfarne, a small island lying between Bamburgh and Berwick, is perhaps the most evocative place of all on the coast. It was to here that St Aidan and a small community of Irish monks came from Iona in AD 635 to found a monastery from which missionaries set out to convert northern England to Christianity.

The region has withstood a tempestuous past and has been the focus of fierce fighting, nowhere more so than the Border town of Berwick, whose strategic location made it a prime target in the endless skirmishes between the English and the Scots. All along the coastline can be seen superb castles; some have been converted into grand mansions for the great families of the area, while others are now no more than ruins.

Inland from the coast the land is heavily farmed, and there is a pleasant landscape of fields, woodland, country lanes and farms. The villages, with their ancient parish churches and village greens, are especially fine. The village green was essential in olden times, as the Scots constantly harried this area, and the villagers needed somewhere to guard their cattle after bringing them in from the surrounding land.

The area to the southeast, around Ashington, was once coal mining country, though the scars are gradually being swept away. The industry is remembered in a museum of mining at Woodhorn. Even here however, an earlier history is evident, as the former Woodhorn church is one of the most interesting in Northumberland.

Food & Drink

Places of Interest

MORPETH

The county town of Morpeth seems far removed, both in spirit and appearance, from the mining areas further down the Wansbeck valley. An attractive market town, Morpeth was once a stopping point on the A1 from Newcastle and Edinburgh, before the days of bypasses, and some fine inns were established to serve the former travellers.

The Norman's built a castle here that stood in what is now **Carlisle Park**. It was destroyed by William Rufus in 1095. A second castle was built close by, but was demolished by King John in 1215. It was subsequently rebuilt, but was mostly destroyed yet again by Montrose in 1644. Known as **Morpeth Castle**, it is now a restored gatehouse, managed by the Landmark Trust and is open once a year.

The third - which isn't really a castle but has the appearance of one - was built by John Dobson in 1828 as the county gaol and courthouse. Still standing, it is now private apartments and self catering accommodation.

Morpeth Castle

The **Clock Tower** in the middle of Oldgate has been heightened several times. It probably dates from the early 17th century, though medieval stone was used in its construction. In its time it has served as a gaol and a place from where the nightly curfew was sounded. Its bells were a gift from a Major Main, who was elected MP for the town in 1707. He had intended them for Berwick, but they didn't elect him, so, as a local saying goes, "the bells of Berwick still

92 OLD RED BULL INN

Morpeth

Family-owned inn that is well-regarded for its well-kept ales, friendly atmosphere and tasty toasted sandwiches.

See entry on page 144

93 SOUR GRAPES WINE BAR

Morpeth

The mouth-watering food and fine selection of beverages makes this establishment an extremely popular place to dine out as well as a fantastic place to socialise.

See entry on page 144

94 PEPPERPOT CAFE-BISTRO

Morpeth

A destination venue for lovers of fine food and hospitality since it opened at the end of 2010.

See entry on page 145

95 LANSDOWN HOUSE

Morpeth

Situated in a fantastic location this superb B&B has four en-suite fresh, modern guest rooms.

See entry on page 145

Morpeth Clock Tower

ring at Morpeth". The Clock Tower is one of only a handful of such buildings in England. The Town Hall was built to designs by Vanbrugh, and a handsome bridge over the Wansbeck was designed by Telford.

Morpeth's St Mary's Church, lying to the south of the river, dates from the 14th century. It has some of the finest stained glass in Northumberland. In the churchyard is the grave of Suffragette Emily Davison, who was killed under the hooves of Anmer, the king's horse, during the 1913 Derby meeting. Her funeral attracted thousands of people to Morpeth. Her epitaph is 'Deeds Not Words', with the Biblical quotation 'Greater love hath no man than this, that a man lay down his life for his friends'. About a mile west of the town are the scant remains of Newminster Abbey, a Cistercian foundation dating from the 12th century. It was founded by monks from Fountains Abbey in Yorkshire.

Not to be missed is the 13th century **Morpeth Chantry** on Bridge Street, one of only five bridge chantries still in existence. Originally the Chapel of All Saints, it has been in its time a cholera hospital, a mineral water factory and a school where the famous Tudor botanist William Turner was educated. Nowadays it houses the **Chantry Bagpipe Museum**, a unique museum specialising in the history and development of Northumbrian small pipes and their music; open Monday to Saturday and summer Sundays and Bank Holidays. The town's tourist information centre is also located here, as are a craft centre, a picture framers and a mountain sports shop.

There are two attractions for animal-lovers in the area: the Sanctuary Wildlife Care Centre at Crowden Hill Farm, Ulgham, with 100 or so rescued animals (Tel: 01670 791778), and the Whitehouse Farm Centre with hundreds of animals to feed, hold or stroke (Tel: 01670 789988). Until 1997 this was a poultry farm, and the owners now raise a few sheep and cattle, as well as looking after many other creatures, from birds of prey to meerkats.

96 THE JOINERS ARMS

Morpeth

A superb free house that serves up to seven real ales all day every day. It also has an impressive display of stuffed animals above the bar.

See entry on page 146

97 BEETROOT GRILL AND CAFE

Morpeth

Offering fine food and drink this place is fast becoming one of the area's must visit dining establishments.

See entry on page 146

AROUND MORPETH

CAMBO

11 miles W of Morpeth off the B6342

The renowned landscape gardener Lancelot 'Capability' Brown was born here in 1716. **Wallington Hall**, lying deep in the heart of the Northumbrian countryside, is a National

Trust property dating from 1688. The two great families associated with the place - the Blacketts and the Trevelyans - have each made their own mark on what must be one of the most elegant houses in Northumberland. In the Great Hall is a famous collection of paintings about Northumbrian history, and one of the rooms has an unusual collection of dolls' houses. The 18th century landscaped grounds (influenced by local man Lancelot 'Capability' Brown, who went to school in the estate village) include lawns, shrubberies, lakes and woodland, ornamental buildings, sculptures and water features.

BELSAY

7 miles SW of Morpeth on the A696

Belsay Hall was built for Sir Charles Monck on an estate that already had a castle and a Jacobean mansion. Set in 30 acres of landscaped gardens, Belsay Hall is Greek in style and contains the architecturally splendid Great Hall. Two miles west is the Bolam Lake Country Park, with a 25 acre lake, trails and picnic areas

BEDLINGTON

5 miles SE of Morpeth off the A189

Bedlington, formerly known as the county town of Bedlingtonshire, was a district of the County Palatinate of Durham until 1844, when it was incorporated into Northumberland. The town became the centre of a prosperous mining and iron-founding community and has two important links with railway history. The rolled-iron rails for the Stockton and Darlington Railway were manufactured here, and it is also the birthplace of the great locomotive engineer, Sir Daniel Gooch. One of the greatest engineers of his day, Sir Daniel was the locomotive superintendent on the Great Western Railway, and the man who first linked up North America and Europe via a telegraph line.

There is an attractive country park near Bedlington at Humford Mill, with an information centre and nature trails. At Plessey Woods, south west of the town, another country park extends along the wooded banks of the River Blyth, around Plessey Mill, with trails and a visitor centre.

ASHINGTON

5 miles E of Morpeth on the A197

Ashington is a sprawling town around the River Wansbeck, built to serve the mining industry. The two-mile-long **Wansbeck Riverside Park**, which has been developed along the embankment, offers sailing and angling facilities, plus a four mile walk along the mouth of the River Wansbeck. The famous footballing brothers Bobby and Jackie Charlton were born in Ashington in the 1930s, and the cricketer Stephen Harmison is also a son of the town. In the stunning modern Cutter building and original colliery structures **Woodhorn Colliery Museum**, in the QEII Country Park, tells the story of coal mining and miners. Woodhorn is

Wansbeck Riverside Park, Ashington

98 WINDMILL INN

Blyth

Popular pub with locals and tourists alike serving great beer with live entertainment at the weekends including karaoke on Friday nights and live music every Saturday.

See entry on page 148

also home to Northumberland's archival treasures, with all kinds of records dating back 800 years. Tel: 01670 528080.

WOODHORN

6 miles E of Morpeth on the A197

At Woodhorn, close to Ashington, there is the fascinating late-Anglo-Saxon St Mary's Church, said to be the oldest church building in Northumberland. The outside was heavily restored in 1843, though inside it is almost wholly pre-Norman. There is a 13th century effigy of Agnes de Velence, wife of Hugh de Baliol, brother of the Scottish king, John Baliol.

NEWBIGGIN BY THE SEA

7 miles E of Morpeth on the A197

Newbiggin by the Sea is a fishing village and small resort enjoying an attractive stretch of coastline with rocky inlets and sandy beaches, now much improved after the ravages of the coal industry. St Bartholomew's Church has a particularly interesting 13th century interior. The village has the oldest operational lifeboat house in Britain, built in 1851. During its 160 years the lifeboat station has had 12 different lifeboats, the current craft being an Atlantic 75 inshore boat.

99 THE NEW SHIP INN

Newbiggin-By-The-Sea

With accommodation all year round and home cooked food this is the ideal public house to call at if you are visiting the north east coast of the UK.

See entry on page 147

100 THE PLOUGH INN

Ellington

A destination hot spot for lovers of good food, real ale and fine hospitality. Four guest rooms are available all year round.

See entry on page 148

DRURIDGE BAY

12 miles NE of Morpeth off the A1068

Druridge Bay Country Park includes Ladyburn Lake, where there is sailing and windsurfing, plus walking trails, a visitor centre and picnic area. The whole area was once a huge opencast coalmine before it was landscaped and opened as a park in 1989. Nearby are the ruins of medieval Chibburn Preceptory - a small medieval house and chapel that belonged to the Knights Hospitaller.

LONGHORSLEY

6 miles N of Morpeth off the A697

Longhorsley is noted for being the home of Thomas Bell, inventor of self-raising flour. He called it Bell's Royal, but the name was later changed to Bero.

Born at Blackheath in London in 1872,

101 WIDDRINGTON INN

Widdrington Village

Lovers of fine food regard this establishment very highly. Locals and visitors come here to drink, eat and socialise.

See entry on page 150

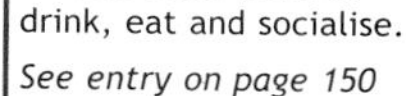

102 THE COUNTRY BARN FARM & COFFEE SHOP

Widdrington Village

Overlooking Druridge Bay this splendid establishment offers tempting homemade treats made with quality local produce.

See entry on page 149

103 THE TRAP INN

North Broomhill

A warm family welcome is assured at this charming family run Inn serving home cooked food and real ales alongside great entertainment and bed and breakfast accommodation.

See entry on page 151

Emily Davison spent a lot of time in the village. A plaque on the wall of the post office, her former home, commemorates her death under the hooves of the King's horse at Epsom in 1913. Her suffragette activities are remembered by the local Women's Institute each year when flowers are placed on her grave in the family grave in Morpeth (qv).

ALNWICK

Alnwick (pronounced Annick) is one of Northumberland's most impressive towns. It still retains the feel and appearance of a great medieval military and commercial centre, being an important market town since the granting of its charter in 1291. The town is dominated by the huge fortress of **Alnwick Castle**, set in beautiful parklands designed and landscaped in the 18th century by Capability Brown and Thomas Call. Alnwick Castle began, like most of Northumberland's castles, as a Norman motte and bailey. In the 12th century this was replaced by a stone castle, which was greatly added to over the centuries. In 1309, the castle came into the possession of Henry de Percy, who strengthened the fortifications. Henry's great grandson was made an earl, and the castle was then passed down 11 generations of Earls. When the male Percy line died out, it passed through the female line to Sir Hugh Smithson, who took the Percy name and was created Duke of Northumberland. When the Duke inherited the castle in 1750 it was falling into disrepair and he commissioned the renowned Robert Adam to restore the castle into a residence fit for a Duke. The superb ceilings and fireplaces can still be seen today. Further sweeping changes were made in the 1850s and 1860s, when the 4th Duke commissioned the Victorian architect Anthony Salvin to transform the castle into a great country house with all modern comforts while recapturing its former medieval glory. Visitors can admire the Italian Renaissance-style State Rooms and treasures that include paintings by Titian, Tintoretto, Canaletto and Van Dyck, collections of Meissen china and exquisite furniture.

There is also an impressive archaeological museum and extensive archive collections, as well as the Fusiliers of Northumberland Museum housed in The Abbot's Tower.

The castle is the home of the Percys to this day, and is a favourite location for making films, including Robin Hood Prince of Thieves and the Harry Potter films, where it doubles as Hogwart's School.

The present Duke and Duchess of

104 THE NORTHUMBERLAND ARMS HOTEL

West Thirston

Dating back to the 18th century this charming hotel offers five quality guest rooms and serves meals created using the finest local produce.

See entry on page 150

105 STAGS HEAD

Felton

Specialising in English and Indian cuisine, this recently renovated pub also has three quality bunk rooms to offer visitors.

See entry on page 152

106 ALNWICK CASTLE

Alnwick

Owned by the Percy family since 1309, Alnwick is one of the finest castles in the British Isles.

See entry on page 152

107 ALNWICK CASTLE GARDEN

Alwick

A garden which is a place of contemplation, a place of fun, a place of inspiration and education.

See entry on page 153

Alnwick Gardens

Northumberland are responsible for one of the most exciting contemporary gardens to be developed in recent years. The Duchess's vision was to create a beautiful public space open to everyone for contemplation, fun, inspiration and relaxation - and she has realized it on a grand scale. The impressive **Alnwick Garden**, officially opened by its patron HRH the Duke of Wales in 2002, boasts a superb Grand Cascade - one of the finest water features in Europe, and other gardens include the Rose Garden, the Serpent garden, the Labyrinth, the ornamental Garden, the Poison Garden with ivy-covered tunnels, one of the world's largest treehouses and a new pavilion and visitor centre. There are 3 miles of box hedges, every inch of which are hand-clipped twice a year. Tel: 01665 511350

Hulne Park, landscaped by the great Northumbrian born 'Capability Brown', encompasses the ruins of Hulne Priory, the earliest Carmelite Foundation in England dating from 1242.

Alnwick town itself is worthy of a leisurely exploration among the evocatively named ancient narrow streets of Pottergate, Fenkle Street, Green Batt, Bondgate Without and Bondgate Within. A road leads through the narrow arch of Hotspur Tower, the one surviving part of the town's fortifications, built by the second Duke of Northumberland in the 15th century. All that's left of the once mighty Alnwick Abbey is its 15th century gatehouse, situated just beyond Canongate Bridge.

St Michael's Church in Alnwick overlooks the River Aln, and dates from the 15th century. It was unusual in a place as lawless as Northumberland at that time to build a church as large and as splendid as St Michael's.

The popular and colourful Alnwick Fair, dating from the 13th century, takes place each June. Each year on Shrove Tuesday Alnwick is host to an annual tradition that begins with the Duke of Northumberland throwing a ball over the castle wall into the town and ends when the ball is retrieved from the river.

AROUND ALNWICK

ALNMOUTH

3 miles E of Alnwick off the A1068

Alnmouth is a small seaside resort at the mouth of the River Aln, with fine sandy beaches and two golf courses. The village dates back to the 8th century and was the main sea port for the town of Alnwick in the Middle Ages. John Paul Jones, the Scot who founded the American navy, bombarded the port during the American War of Independence.

The village of Alnmouth is the starting point for many excellent walks along superb stretches of coastline both southwards, past extensive dunes to Warkworth, and north to the former fishing village of Boulmer.

WARKWORTH

6 miles SE of Alnwick on the A1068

At the southern end of Alnmouth Bay, on the River Coquet, lies **Warkworth Castle**. The site has been fortified since the Iron Age, though the first stone castle was probably built by one 'Roger, son of Richard', who had

Warkworth Castle

been granted the castle by Henry II in the 12th century.

What can be seen now is mainly late 12th and 13th century, including the great Carrickfergus Tower and the West Postern Towers, built by Roger's son, Robert. The castle came into the ownership of the Percys in 1332 and the family lived here up until the 16th century. The family crest can be seen on the Lion Tower.

The most famous of all the Percy's, Harry (known as Hotspur) was brought up here.

In 1399 the family created history for the role they played in placing Henry Bolingbroke on the throne as Henry IV. The castle is now in the care of English Heritage and is a delightful sight in spring when the grass mound on which it stands is covered with thousands of daffodils. Tel: 01665 711423

An unusual and interesting walk is signposted to The Hermitage, along the riverside footpath below the castle, where a ferry takes you across the river to visit the tiny chapel hewn out of solid rock. It dates from medieval times and was in use until late in the 16th century.

Warkworth is an interesting and beautiful village in its own right. An imposing fortified gatehouse on the 14th century bridge, now only used by pedestrians, would enable an invading army to be kept at bay north of the Coquet. **St Lawrence's Church** is almost entirely Norman, though its spire - an unusual feature on medieval churches in Northumberland - dates from the 14th century.

108 HERMITAGE INN

Warkworth

This former coaching inn has all year round accommodation and is well known in the area for the delicious meals served from its a la carte menu.

See entry on page 154

AMBLE

7 miles SE of Alnwick on the A1068

Amble is a small port situated at the mouth of the River Coquet, once important for the export of coal, but now enjoying new prosperity as a marina and sea-fishing centre, with a carefully restored harbour. It is a lively place, particularly when the daily catches of fish are being unloaded. Amble's Lifeboat Station can be visited daily between 10 and 4. The RNLI's last Waveney Class boat left service from here.

A mile offshore lies **Coquet Island**. It was here that St Cuthbert landed in AD 684. The island's square-towered lighthouse was built in 1841 on the ruins of a 15th century monastery known as Cocwadae. Parts of the monastic building have survived, including a Benedictine cell dating from the 14th century.

Coquet Island had a reputation in former times for causing shipwrecks, but is now a celebrated bird sanctuary, noted for colonies of terns, puffins and eider ducks, with as many as 35,000 nesting birds in the summer. Managed by the Royal Society for the Protection of Birds, the island can be visited by boat trips departing from Amble quayside throughout the summer. Landing is not permitted, but visitors can see live images of the birds at the Notrhumberland Seabird centre on Amble's quayside.

EDLINGHAM

5 miles SW of Alnwick on the B6341

Edlingham mustn't be confused with the villages of Eglingham and Ellingham, both a few miles to the north. Here at Edlingham the moorland road crosses Corby's Crags, affording visitors one of the finest views in Northumberland. The panorama encompasses the Cheviot Hills in the north, whilst to the south a rolling landscape of heather moors and crags stretches as far as Hadrian's Wall. On a clear day it's possible to catch a glimpse of the high peaks of the North Pennines.

Edlingham Castle was built in the 12th century, but abandoned in 1650 when parts of it collapsed. The ruins were originally thought to be of a simple Northumbrian tower house, but excavations in the late 1970s and early 1980s showed it as having been much more substantial than that.

EGLINGHAM

6 miles NW of Alnwick on the B6346

St Maurice's Church dates from about 1200, and was built on a site granted to the monks of Lindisfarne in AD 738 by King Ceowulf of Northumbria. In 1596 it was attacked by the Scots, and part of the chancel had to be rebuilt in the early 17th century.

A few bumps in a field not far away indicate where the village once stood, and a mile to the southwest is a small hill fort with the quaint name of The Ringses.

CHILLINGHAM

11 miles NW of Alnwick off the B6348

Chillingham is a pleasant estate village best known for the herd of wild, horned white cattle that roam parkland close to Chillingham Castle. Descendants of the cattle that once roamed Britain's forests, they are the only herd of wild white cattle in the country. Chillingham village was built by the Earls of Tankerville and contains many Tudor style houses.

Chillingham Castle is beautifully sited within a 365-acre park. Begun in 1245, the castle belonged for many years to the Grey family who fought many battles with the Scots and the Percy's of Alnwick. Sadly the

Chillingham Castle

109 THE SCHOONER

Amble

Close to the fishing town's bustling harbour, this delightful B&B and pub offers comfortable accommodation and home cooked food.

See entry on page 155

110 CRAWLEY FARMHOUSE & CRAWLEY TOWER COTTAGE

Powburn

Spacious and comfortable farmhouse Bed and Breakfast accommodation in a perfect location for exploring the surrounding area with additional self catering holiday cottage nearby.

See entry on page 155

castle fell into ruin in the 1930s, but was bought in the 1980s by Sir Humphrey Wakefield, a descendant of the Grey family, and has been splendidly restored. Attractions include the impressive Grand Hall, a jousting course, dungeon and torture chamber. The castle and surrounding gardens are open to the public in the summer (not Saturdays except Easter Saturday). Tel: 01668 215359. Two signposted walks have been laid out through Chillingham Woods, giving superb views over the surrounding countryside. Just outside Chillingham is the National Trust's hill fort Ros Castle, once a vital beacon site visible as far afield as the Scottish hills and Holy Island. The hill is designated a Marilyn - any hill or mountain more than 150 metres in relative height.

ELLINGHAM

7 miles N of Alnwick off the A1

Ellingham is a small agricultural village centred on St Maurice's Church, whose Norman details were all but swept away in a restoration of 1862. It features a central tower instead of the more usual west one. Ellingham Hall stands at the end of a quiet lane beyond the village.

CHATHILL

8 miles N of Alnwick off the A1

Close to Chathill is **Preston Tower**, built by Sir Robert Harbottle, Sheriff of Northumberland, in 1392. The outside walls are seven feet thick, whilst inside are fine tunnel-vaulted rooms which have changed little over the centuries. Two turret rooms have been simply furnished in the style of the period and there are displays depicting the Battle of Flodden and life in the Borders at the start of the 15th century.

CRASTER

6 miles NE of Alnwick off the B1339

Craster is a small, unpretentious fishing village with a reputation for the best oak-smoked kippers in the country. At one time, herring were caught around this coast in vast quantities, but a combination of over-fishing and pollution resulted in a decline in numbers, so the fish now have to be imported. During the kipper curing season, visitors can peer into the smoking sheds where the herring are hung over smouldering piles of oak chips. Best known of the smokehouses is L Robson & Sons Ltd, established in 1906.

South of Craster is **Howick Hall**, built in 1782 and long associated with the Grey family whose family lineage includes many famous public figures - most notably the 2nd Earl Grey, the great social reformer and tea enthusiast. The grounds include wonderful herbaceous borders, a bog garden, magnificent spring bulbs and a 65-acre arboretum planted with thousands of trees and shrubs planted in six geographical groups.

Craster Quarry was closed in 1939 and is now a small nature reserve called the Arnold Memorial Site. It was this quarry that supplied London and other large cities with its kerbstones. This is the starting point for a pleasant walk along the coastal footpath to Dunstanburgh Castle, or south to Howick, where you will find the site of a Mesolithic house. A reconstruction of the house stands on the cliffs.

See entry on page 156

See entry on page 156

Howick Hall, Craster

sister of King Oswald, King of Northumbria. This is a delightful stretch of coast, and keen walkers can follow the coastline either by shore path or along the B1340 past St Aidan's Dunes (owned by the National Trust) to Seahouses.

EMBLETON

8 miles NE of Alnwick on the B1339

The dramatic ruins of **Dunstanburgh Castle** stand on a clifftop east of the village, on a site that was originally an Iron Age fort. The fabric of the castle as seen today was built in 1313 by Thomas, Earl of Lancaster, and in the Wars of the Roses it withstood a siege from troops led by Margaret of Anjou, Henry VI's Queen. The damage caused by the siege was never repaired, and the castle remains ruinous to this day.

The castle can't be reached by road, but a path from the village passing through Dunstan Steads, a mile southeast of Embleton, leads to it. The Castle, plus the whole coastline to the north as far as Brunton Burn, is owned by the National Trust. A painting of the Lilburn Tower at sunrise by Turner can be seen in Tate Britain.

To the north of Embleton is the village of Newton-by-the-Sea, where there are some attractive 18th century fishermen's cottages built around three sides of a square.

BEADNELL

10 miles NE of Alnwick on the B1340

Beadnell is a small fishing village with a harbour and some important 18th-century lime kilns that are now owned by the National Trust. Running eastwards from the harbour into the sea is Ebb's Nook, a narrow strip of land with the scant remains of 13th century **St Ebba's Chapel**, dedicated to the

SEAHOUSES

13 miles NE of Alnwick on the B1340

Seahouses is a lively fishing port and small resort with an interesting harbour, magnificent beaches and sand dunes stretching for miles on either side of the town. It is conveniently situated for viewing the Farne Islands, which lie between two and five miles off the coast, and visitors can take a boat trip departing from the harbour to see them at close hand. The Lifeboat Station at Seahouses (formerly known as the North Sunderland) can be visited daily between March and October, and at weekends in November. It has an inshore and an all-weather lifeboat.

BERWICK-UPON-TWEED

England's northernmost town sits midway between Edinburgh and Newcastle. The River Tweed serves as the border between Scotland and Northumberland along much of its length, but a few miles to the west of Berwick, the border takes a curious lurch north, and curls up and over the town to the east before reaching the coast. So, while Berwick is on the north bank of the Tweed, it's well and truly within Northumberland.

For centuries, this former Royal burgh of Scotland was fought over by the Scots and the English, and changed hands no less than 14 times until it finally became part of England in 1482. But even now, Scotland exerts a great influence. The local football team, Berwick Rangers, plays in the Scottish League, and in 1958 the Lord Lyon, who decides on all matters armorial in Scotland, granted the town a coat-of-arms - the only instance of armorial bearings being granted in Scotland for use in England.

But for many years after becoming English, the town was a curious anomaly. In the 16th century Berwick was declared a free burgh, neither in Scotland nor in England, a situation that lasted right up until 1885. Its ambiguous status was such that when war was declared on Russia in 1853, it was done in the name of "Victoria, Queen of Great Britain, Ireland, Berwick-upon-Tweed and all the British Dominions". When peace was announced in 1856, no mention was made of Berwick. So technically, the town remained at war with Russia.

The situation was rectified in 1966, when a Soviet official made a goodwill visit to the town, and a peace treaty was signed. During the ceremony, the Berwick mayor told the Soviet official that the people of Russia could at last sleep easy in their beds.

Berwick's strategic location led it to become an important military town. For many years the garrison soldiers were billeted in local taverns and private houses, but this placed a heavy financial burden on the townspeople. Complaints to the government led to the building of Berwick Barracks between 1717 and 1721. Designed by Nicholas Hawksmoor, they were the first purpose-built barracks in Britain, and within them you'll find the **King's Own Scottish Borderers Museum**. Here visitors will learn about a Scottish regiment that was raised in 1689 by the Earl of Leven, and which is still in existence today, by means of uniforms, badges, medals, weapons, relics, tableaux, dioramas and pictures. Tel: 01289 307426

Housed in the clock tower of the barracks is the **Berwick-upon-Tweed Museum and Art Gallery**, which explores the history of the town. The museum contains a remarkable collection given to the town by Sir William Burrell, who lived in nearby Hutton Castle. Famous for collecting the works of art that can now be seen in the Burrell Art Gallery in Glasgow, Burrell also donated 300 works of art, sculpture and pottery to Berwick. The Gymnasium Gallery, opened in 1993, displays changing exhibitions of contemporary art. Call 01289 301869 for opening times.

Three distinctive bridges linking the town centre with the communities of Tweedmouth and Spittal span the Tweed estuary. The oldest of these is the 17th-century Berwick Bridge, a handsome stone bridge with 15 arches completed in 1626. The Royal Tweed Bridge is the most modern, having been completed in 1928 with a concrete structure built to an iron bridge design. The enormous 126 feet high, 28 arch Royal Border Bridge, carrying the East Coast main-line railway, was built between 1847 and 1850 by Robert Stephenson.

The Berwick skyline is dominated by the imposing **Town Hall** with its clock tower and steeple that rise to 150 feet, and which is

113 BERWICK BARRACKS

Berwick-Upon-Tweed

At Berwick Barracks you and your family can experience military life first hand.

See entry on page 157

114 THISTLE DO NICELY

Berwick-upon-Tweed

Passersby are attracted to this delightful tea room by its fresh home cooked food made with the finest local ingredients.

See entry on page 157

115 THE BARRELS ALE HOUSE

Bewick upon Tweed

Lively pub bursting at the seams with character and atmosphere, serving a great selection of rotating cask ales and hosting quality live entertainment acts.

See entry on page 158

often mistaken for a church. Built between 1754 and 1761, this fine building has a façade as elaborate as its well-documented history. On the ground floor, markets were held in the Exchange and shops and cells existed where now a gift shop and coffee house stand. Guided tours in the summer enable visitors to explore the upper storeys, where there are civic rooms and the former town gaol. A small Cell Block Museum is also located there.

Facing Berwick Barracks is Holy Trinity Church - one of the few Commonwealth churches in England. It was built between 1650 and 1652, during the Commonwealth of Oliver Cromwell, to replace a dilapidated medieval church, which stood on the same site. Berwick's Lifeboat Station, with an all-weather and an inshore boat, is open for visits daily from 9 to 5.

AROUND BERWICK-UPON-TWEED

TWEEDMOUTH

1 mile S of Berwick off the A1

Tweedmouth and Spittal, on the English side of the Tweed estuary, are largely suburbs of Berwick. In mid-July a ceremony is held in Tweedmouth, dating back to 1292, to celebrate the fact that the River Tweed, one of the best salmon rivers in Britain, reaches the sea here. The local schools hold a ballot to elect a Salmon Queen, and her crowning marks the beginning of Feast Week which centres on a church service and involves lots of festivities including a traditional salmon supper.

See entry on page 159

LOWICK

8 miles S of Berwick on the B6353

Lowick is a quiet farming community which contains only a few shops and a couple of pubs. About a mile east of the village are the earthworks of a former castle. The Norman church was replaced by the present St John the Baptist Church.

LINDISFARNE, OR HOLY ISLAND

10 miles SE of Berwick off the A1

Northumberland's northern coastline is dominated by Holy Island, also known by its Celtic name of Lindisfarne. The island is accessible only at low tide, via a 3 mile-long causeway linking it with the mainland at Beal. Tide tables are published locally and are displayed at each end of the road. There are refuges along the way for those who fail to time it correctly.

As you cross, note the 11th-century Pilgrims' Way, marked by stakes, still visible about 200 metres south of the modern causeway. This route was in use until comparatively recent times.

The island was given to St Aidan in AD 635 by Oswald, King of Northumbria. St Aidan and his small community of Irish monks came from Iona to found a base from which to convert northern England to Christianity. This led to the island being called one of the cradles of English Christianity. St Cuthbert came here to teach and the island became a magnet for pilgrims. When he died in AD 687 he was buried in the church. St Cuthbert's island can be reached at low tide from the island and was used by the saint during times of solitude. A cross marks the site of his tiny chapel.

The early monks are remembered for producing some of the finest surviving examples of Celtic art - the richly decorated **Lindisfarne Gospels**, dating from the 7th century. When the island was invaded by Vikings in the 9th century, the monks fled taking their precious gospels with them. These have, miraculously, survived and are now in the safety of the British Museum. Facsimiles are kept on Lindisfarne and can be seen in the 12th century parish church on the island. The monks also took with them St Cuthbert's bones and wandered around for over 100 years with them before eventually finding a safe resting place in Durham.

During the 11th century a group of Benedictine monks settled here, and the ruins of their great sandstone **Lindisfarne Priory** with its Romanesque great pillars can still be explored.

Lindisfarne Castle was established in Tudor times as yet another fortification to protect the exposed flank of Northumbria from invasion by the Scots. In 1902 it was bought by Edward Hudson, the owner of Country Life magazine, who employed the great Edwardian architect Sir Edwin Lutyens to rebuild and restore it as a private house. It is now in the care of the National Trust, and the house and its small walled garden (the work of Gertrude Jekyll) are open to the public during the summer months. Opened in 2009, a green interpretation centre explains composting and records of climatic conditions. Tel: 01289 389244

Holy Island is the finishing point for the 62-mile long **St Cuthbert's Way**, a long distance footpath which opened in 1996. The trail begins at Melrose, across the Scottish border, and along the way passes through the Northumberland National Park and the Cheviot Hills.

Garden based on Lindisfarne Gospels, Lindisfarne

BELFORD

14 miles S of Berwick off the A1

Belford is an attractive village of stone houses whose broad main street contains some interesting old shops and a fine old coaching inn, reflecting the fact that this was once an important town on the Great North Road. Today it is an ideal holiday base, standing on the edge of the Kyloe Hills, where there are some fine walks, and close to the long golden beaches and rocky outcrops of the coast.

St Cuthbert's Cave, to the north of Belford, is only accessible by foot. It is completely natural, and concealed by a great overhanging rock surrounded by woodland. It is believed that the saint's body lay here on its much interrupted journey across Northumbria. From the summit of nearby Greensheen Hill there are superb views of the coast and of the Cheviots to the west.

Lindisfarne Castle

WAREN MILL

15 miles SE of Berwick on the B1342

Waren Mill is a small village situated on Budle Bay, a large inlet of flats and sand where vast numbers of wading birds and wildfowl come to feed. Caution should be taken when walking on the flats, as sections quickly become cut off at high tide.

BAMBURGH

16 miles S of Berwick on the B1340

The seaside village of Bamburgh is dominated by the magnificent **Bamburgh Castle**, epic in scale, even by the standards of this coastline and its abundance of spectacular castles. Situated on a dramatic basalt outcrop on the very edge of the North Sea, it was almost certainly the royal seat of the first kings of Bernicia. The dynasty was founded by the Saxon King Ida in AD 547 and mentioned in the Anglo-Saxon Chronicle. Ida's grandson Ethelfrid united the kingdoms of Bernicia and Deira, and thus created Northumbria, a kingdom that stretched from the Humber to the Forth and was ruled from Bamburgh.

In those days, the castle would have been made of wood - a mighty stockade surrounding a great royal hall, sleeping quarters, stables, workshops and a garrison for troops. Later on, when Northumbria embraced Christianity, chapels would have been added, and the castle would have been an ostentatious declaration of the Northumbrian kings' power and wealth.

The present stone castle covers eight acres and has an imposing 12th century keep around which three baileys were constructed. The castle was extensively rebuilt and restored in the 18th and 19th centuries, latterly by the first Lord Armstrong whose descendants continue to make this their home.

Bamburgh Castle is open to the public, and rooms on display include the Armoury, King's Hall, Court Room, Cross Hall, Bakehouse and Victorian Scullery, with collections of tapestries, ceramics, furniture and paintings. Occupying the former laundry room is an exhibition dedicated to the first Lord Armstrong and his many remarkable engineering inventions in the fields of hydraulics, ships, aircraft and arms. Here, too, are relics of aviation in the Bamburgh Castle Aviation Artefacts Museum. Tel: 01668 214515.

Bamburgh was the birthplace, in 1814, of Grace Darling, whose father was the keeper of Longstone and Brownsman Lighthouses. She was only 22 years old when she became a national heroine, rowing with her father in a small coble to rescue survivors from the paddle steamer *Forfarshire*, wrecked on Big Harcar in a violent storm. Visitors can see her boat and many other reminders of her heroic deeds in the **RNLI Grace Darling Museum**. Grace Darling died of tuberculosis in 1842, aged just 27, and it buried with her parents in St Aidan's churchyard.

Just offshore are the **Farne Islands**. This small group of 28 uninhabited islands of volcanic Whin Sill rock provides a major breeding sanctuary for migratory seabirds including puffins, guillemots, razorbills, artic and sandwich terns and kittiwakes. They are also home to a large colony of Atlantic Grey seals, which can often be seen from the beach on the mainland.

The islands have important Christian links, as it was on Inner Farne that St Cuthbert died in AD 687. A little chapel was built here in his memory and restored in Victorian times. The nearby Tower House was built in medieval times by Prior Castell, according to legend, on the site of Cuthbert's cell. Boat trips to the Farne Islands leave from the harbour in Seahouses. Landings are permitted on Inner Farne and Staple Island, times are restricted for conservation reasons and advance booking is necessary at busy times of the year. In a chapel on Great Farne Island there is a stone monument erected in 1848 in honour of Grace Darling.

Farne Islands

HORNCLIFFE

4 miles W of Berwick off the A698

The village of Horncliffe, five miles upstream of Berwick, can only be reached by one road that leads into and out of the village, making it feel rather remote. Many visitors are unaware of the existence of the river, but there is nothing more pleasant than wandering down one of the paths leading to the banks to watch the salmon fishermen on a summer's evening.

Not far from Horncliffe, the River Tweed is spanned by the Union Suspension Bridge linking Scotland and England, built in 1820 by Sir Samuel Browne, who also invented the wrought-iron chain links used in its construction. The graceful structure, 480 feet long, was Britain's first major suspension bridge to carry vehicular traffic, and although not carrying a major road, it is still possible to drive over it.

NORHAM

6 miles SW of Berwick on the B6470

Norham is a neat village on the banks of the Tweed. Up until 1836 the town was an enclave of the County Palatinate of Durham, surrounded by Northumberland on the south, east and west, and Scotland on the north. **Norham Castle** was built in the 12th century by the Bishop of Durham on a site of great natural strength, guarding a natural ford over the river. It withstood repeated attacks in the 13th and 14th centuries and was thought to be impregnable. However, in 1513 it was stormed by the forces of James IV on his way to Flodden and partially destroyed.

Although it was later rebuilt, the castle was again destroyed by the Scots in 1530, and had lost its importance as a defensive stronghold by the end of the 16th century. The castle is now under the care of English Heritage. Tel: 01289 382329. Norham Station Museum, on the former Tweedmouth-Kelso branch line, features the original signal box, booking office and porters' room. Tel: 01289 382217.

DUDDO

7 miles SW of Berwick on the B6354

Close to the village are the **Duddo Stones**, one of Northumberland's most important ancient monuments. This ancient stone circle, which now consists of five upright stones over seven feet high, dates back to around 2000 BC, and can only be reached from the village by foot.

TILLMOUTH

9 miles SW of Berwick on the A698

The village of Tillmouth lies along the banks of the River Till, a tributary of the Tweed which is crossed by the 15th-century **Twizel Bridge**, although a more modern structure now carries the A698 over the river. Up until the building of the 1727 Causey Arch in County Durham, the old Twizel Bridge, with a span of 90 feet, had the largest span of any bridge in Britain. There are some lovely walks here and a well-signed footpath leads to the ruins of Twizel Castle, and the remains of St Cuthbert's Chapel on the opposite bank, dating from the 18th or 19th centuries, but incorporating some medieval stonework.

117 THE OLD SCHOOL HOUSE

Tillmouth

Luxurious bed and breakfast accommodation situated in a rural location where guests enjoy fantastic home cooked breakfasts made using the finest local produce.

See entry on page 159

Accommodation, Food & Drink and Places to Visit

The establishments featured in this section includes hotels, inns, guest houses, bed & breakfasts, restaurants, cafés, tea and coffee shops, tourist attractions and places to visit. Each establishment has an entry number which can be used to identify its location at the beginning of the relevant county chapter.

In addition full details of all these establishments and many others can be found on the Travel Publishing website - www.findsomewhere.co.uk. This website has a comprehensive database covering the whole of the United Kingdom.

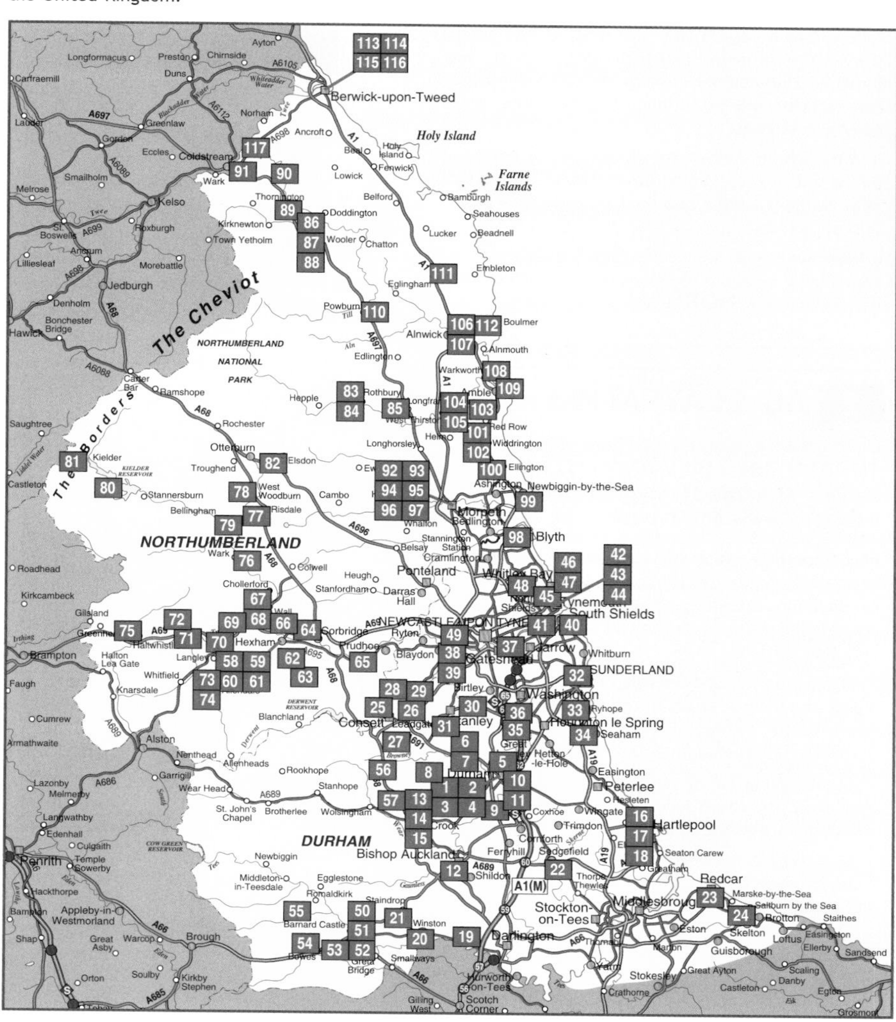

1 MOOR END GUEST HOUSE

7/8 Moor End Terrace, Belmont, Durham DH1 1BJ
Tel: 0191 384 2796

Dating back to 1840 this quality bed & breakfast stands conveniently next door to the village pub. **Moor End Guest House**, which has a four star rating, is owned by Martin and Debbie who have only recently taken over. They are full of enthusiasm for this new venture of theirs and have already welcomed plenty of visitors through their doors.

Open all year round the child-friendly guest house has five en-suite bedrooms that are all located upstairs. The rooms, which vary in size, are traditionally decorated and the very reasonable tariff includes breakfast, available between 7am and 9am. Breakfast can be enjoyed in the pleasant and airy dining area, which has a real homely feel to it.

Although no evening meals are served here, dining out in the evening never proves problematic with Belmont village pub next door and the city of Durham nearby.

Moor End Guest House can be found in the former coal mining village of Belmont off the A690 close to its junction No62 of the A1.

2 66 CLAYPATH

Durham City, County Durham DH1 1QT
Tel: 0191 384 3193 / 07974352372
e-mail: richard@66claypath.co.uk
website: www.66claypath.co.uk

66 Claypath is a fantastic guest house in the heart of Durham City. Though it has only two guest bedrooms they are comfortable, tastefully decorated and well-furnished. Quality breakfasts are served fresh to order in the dining room overlooking a beautiful secluded garden.

This Grade II listed Georgian town house is located on one of the oldest and historic roads in the City; just a short walk from the Market Place, Castle, Cathedral, Gala Theatre and riverside paths. Some of Durham's best restaurants and pubs are within easy walking distance.

Guests can arrive by road rail or air; the main line station is 15 minutes walk away, the A1(M) Junction 62 is 2 miles via the A690 and Newcastle and Durham Teesside Airports are only 40 minutes away by car.

66 Claypath is owned by the Fletcher family. Richard and his wife Paddy provide a home from home whether their guests are away on business or visiting the region on holiday, all are assured of a warm and friendly welcome.

We think **66 Claypath** is perfectly situated for exploring not just the City of Durham but all that the North East has to offer.

3 DURHAM CASTLE

The College, Durham, County Durham DH1 3EH
Tel: 0191 3864266

In 1069, three years after landing in Britain, William the Conqueror finally subdued the North of England. William recognised the defensive potential of the rocky peninsula of Durham and a castle was founded there in 1072. Nine centuries later, **Durham Castle** remains one of England's largest and best-preserved Norman strongholds and one of the grandest Romanesque palaces. Since 1836 it has housed the Foundation College of Durham University, England's third oldest university after Oxford and Cambridge.

4 CROOK HALL AND GARDENS

Sidegate, Durham, County Durham DH1 5SZ
Tel: 01913 848028
e-mail: info@kbacrookhall.co.uk
website: www.crookhallgardens.co.uk

Described by Alan Titchmarsh as 'a tapestry of colourful blooms' Crook Hall is a beautiful medieval manor house surrounded by romantic gardens which include ancient fruit trees and climbing roses.

Visitors are invited to try out the maze, hunt down the ghosts, experience the peace and tranquillity of the walled gardens or simply relax and enjoy a homemade cream tea in the pretty little courtyard café.

The Hall is just a short walk from Durham's bustling market place yet the atmosphere is one of peace and tranquillity. Disabled access is difficult, owing to the historical layout of the site. Please telephone Maggie on 0191 3848028 or email us to discuss individual needs.

Crook Hall is open from 11.00 a.m. to 5.00 p.m.

5 THE SALUTATION

Dryburn View, Framwellgate Moor,
Durham DH1 5AP
Tel: 01913 749185
e-mail: thesalutation@hotmail.co.uk

Just a short distance from the centre of Durham City, **The Salutation** is situated in the village of Framwellgate Moor. This inviting pub is popular for its excellent food, good beer, lively atmosphere and fantastic entertainment at the weekends.

Chris and Racheal are the new owners, having taken over in February 2011. Although young, they have plenty of experience in the trade and they are both genuinely enthusiastic about what they do. They are joined by Chris' brother Daniel who is a professional chef, so you know you're in for a treat when you eat here!

All of the meals are freshly prepared and the menu is constantly changing, although you will find many of your classic pub favourites including steaks, burgers and the Chef's special pies. There is also a children's menu and a great selection of desserts to tempt you. Food is served from 12pm to 9pm seven days a week, and on Sundays there is a carvery roast with generous helpings of all the usual trimmings.

6 THE TRAVELLERS REST

Front Street, Witton Gilbert,
County Durham DH7 6TQ
Tel: 0191 371 0458
e-mail: travellersrest2@btconnect.com
website: www.the-travellers-rest.co.uk

The Travellers Rest, located in the village of Witton Gilbert occupies a pleasant situation in a valley on the road from Durham to Lanchester.

The Travellers Rest restaurant is an impressive and - as befits the name - relaxing destination for a meal out. The menu here comprises a wonderful selection of traditional English dishes, cooked fresh to order using the best local produce where possible. Booking is advised at all times.

The Travellers Rest offers a bespoke menu service. If required the head chef can design a tailored menu specifically for your party or special occasion at a cost to suit you. To compliment the food or to simply quench a thirst, The Travellers Rest stock a wide range of drinks including, Fosters & Kronenbourg Lagers, John Smith's extra cold, as well as three real ales, Marston's Pedigree the regular and two rotating guest ales. There is a good range of wines and spirits available, plus a large range of soft drinks too. Every Tuesday night is quiz night with 50 general knowledge questions including pictures. Entry is £1 per person and this includes a free supper! Prompt 9.00pm start.

8 THE ROYAL OAK

1 Commercial Street, Cornsay Colliery, County Durham DH7 9BN
Tel: 0191 373 4224 Fax: 0191 373 1322

The **Royal** Oak is a fine, traditional pub at Cornsay Colliery by the B6301 Lanchester to Tow Law road, 4 miles south of Lanchester and 8 miles west of Durham City. For 16 years this splendid place has been owned and run by Ian and Sonia Truby; they have made it very much the social hub of the community as well as a popular stopping place for motorist and other visitors. The owners guarantee a warm welcome for all who cross the threshold, whether it's for a drink, a meal or an overnight or longer stay. Sonia is an excellent cook, and her generous home cooking has built up a large and loyal band of happy eaters who come here from all over the region. Chicken dishes appear in many guises on the menu, and on a typical day you might find hunter's chicken, chicken tikka, chicken in black bean sauce, and stir-fried chicken with vegetables or oyster sauce. There's plenty else to choose from, including steaks, seasonal venison pie and a classic cod in parsley sauce. Two rotating real ales head the list of drinks, which include a good variety of wines, spirits and soft drinks. The Royal Oak is open all day, seven days a week, in the summer months, all day Saturday and Sunday throughout the year and from 3pm on winter weekdays. Children are always welcome, and bills can be paid by cash, cheque or the major credit/debit cards.

The pub also provides quiet, comfortable accommodation for both business and leisure guests in 5 well-appointed en suite upstairs bedrooms. The tariff includes a hearty breakfast served at a time to suit guests. There's good walking hereabouts in Weardale, and nearby attractions include Beamish Museum, Hall Hill Farm, a working sheep farm open all year round; the delightful Weardale Railway; the town of Lanchester with houses and a church incorporating parts from the Roman fort at Longovicum; Hamsterley Forest, one of the Forestry Commission's most attractive Forest Parks; and the wonderful City of Durham, with its magnificent Cathedral and Castle and many other sights to see.

The colliery that gave Cornsay Colliery its name stood opposite the Royal Oak in the main Commercial Street. The most prominent building on the street is this pub, which was built, like the whole village, on empty fields and woodland when the colliery started operating (it was in constant use from 1868 to 1953).

7 BROOM HOUSE FARM

nr Witton Gilbert, County Durham DH7 6TR
Tel: 0191 371 9697
e-mail: info@broomhousedurham.co.uk
website: www.broomhousedurham.co.uk

Broom House Farm is a large organic livestock farm just outside Durham City. Mark and Jane Gray sell their home-raised Aberdeen Angus beef, lamb, mutton and Saddleback pork, along with home-produced bacon and sausages and a range of top-quality local produce. The best ingredients find their way into the **Coffee Shop**, which serves delicious cakes and scones, tasty treats and light hot and cold meals as well as Sunday lunches. There's a vast grassy play area and also here is one of the region's most exciting family attractions, the **Woodland Adventure Trail**.

9 COACH AND HORSES

Butchers Race, Croxdale, Durham DH6 5JU
Tel: 01388 814484 Fax: 01388 814484
e-mail: claudemurray@hotmail.co.uk
website: www.coachandhorses.me.uk

Originating back to 1590, this much loved pub well known for its reasonably priced food, inherited its current title **Coach and Horses** in 1801 when it became a popular resting place for many a traveller. Today it is renowned for its fantastic menu offering freshly prepared dishes and has been personally run by Anthony and Tracy for almost three years. Open all day every day Coach and Horses is always frequented by a good mix of people, many who come to sample the traditional fare on offer. Food is available Mon - Fri 12-9.30pm, Sat 12 - 10pm Sunday 12 - 9pm.

10 BRAMBLES COFFEE SHOP

Poplar Tree Garden Centre, Hall Lane,
Shincliffe, Durham DH1 2NG
Tel: 0191 384 7553
e-mail: info@poplartreegardencentre.co.uk
website: www.poplartreegardencentre.co.uk

Brambles Coffee Shop is located within Poplar Tree Garden Centre, which is just one mile from Durham City and has the added benefit of free parking, as well as walks around the acres of open land by The River Wear and beautiful woodlands surrounding Durham's Historic Castle and Cathedral.

Now firmly on the agenda for local shoppers, walkers and thousands of weekly tourists alike, Brambles is the ideal place to go for lunch with a varied menu offering a wonderful range of sandwiches, paninis, jacket potatoes, quiches and salads with "mouth watering" hot or cold toppings. For those with a sweet or savoury tooth there is also a large selection of homemade cakes and scones.

Inside the Coffee Shop is an array of indoor plants to help you relax. When the weather allows there is a patio area outside the coffee shop where you will find wooden tables and chairs with green parasols. Sitting among the most fabulous hanging baskets in full bloom and watching people wandering through the garden centre, will make you feel miles away from Durham City and somewhere much more tropical.

11 THE AVENUE INN

Avenue Street, High Shincliffe,
Durham DH1 2PT
Tel: 0191 386 5954
e-mail: info@theavenue.biz
website: www.theavenue.biz

Located just over a mile from the historic city of Durham **The Avenue Inn** is an outstanding village inn located in the hamlet of High Shincliffe. The inn was taken over six years ago by Geoff and Tracy Wise and their family and they have built up a strong reputation.

Open all day every day The Avenue Inn is extremely popular with locals and visitors and offers three real ales with Black Sheep the regular. Quality food is available 6pm - 9pm Monday - Saturday with a fish & chip special deal every Friday between 12md and 2pm. Roast dinners are served each Sunday between 12md and 3pm.

There are eight well-appointed bedrooms (four en-suite) and the tariff includes a full English breakfast. The friendly inn is an ideal place to stop over for those visiting Durham and the surrounding area as it is within an hour's drive of the moors, beach, places of historical interest and shopping venues.

A general knowledge quiz is held every Monday evening from 9pm and on Tuesday night there is a friendly darts and dominoes league.

12 TIME FOR YOU TEA ROOMS

The Four Clocks, Bishop Auckland,
County Durham DL14 7EH
Tel: 07742 402963
e-mail: timeforyoutearoom@yahoo.co.uk
website: www.fourclockscentre.org.uk

Housed in a de-consecrated church in the centre of Bishop Auckland, is the Four Clocks Centre. It is here, that visitors will find the superb Time For You Tea Rooms.

Created by Francesca in 2008, the building's fantastic architecture with stained glass windows creates a superb setting in which to dine. The menu offers a wide range of freshly prepared snacks and meals such as jacket potatoes, sandwiches, home-made quiche, paninis, breakfasts and plenty more all made with local produce where possible. A range of tempting treats including caramel slice, scones, cakes and biscuits is sure to satisfy a sweet tooth.

Each month an exhibition of local arts and crafts are displayed around the tearooms, all of which are available to purchase. Francesca also offers a book swapping session, whereby visitors can bring a book of their own and exchange it for one of hers. Disabled access is not a problem and baby changing facilities are available.

Open Mon - Fri 8.30 - 4pm and Saturdays 10am - 2pm.

13 THE COLLIERY INN

High Jobs Hill, Crook, County Durham DL15 0UL
Tel: 01388 762511 Mob: 07904 373101 Fax: 01388 764550

On a cold winter's day there's no finer sight for a motorist, a cyclist or a walker than a friendly pub. But the **Colliery Inn** is very much a pub for all seasons, with the warmest of welcomes and excellent service provided by owners Martin and Mark and their staff, come rain or shine. The pub stands on the shadow of Pontop Pike by the A690, on the left leaving Crook in the direction of Willington and Durham City. The interior of the pub is full of charm and character and the outstanding collection of ornaments and bygones provides a talking point for all who visit this lovely old hostelry. Two real ales - Camerons Strongarm and a regularly changing guest - head the list of liquid refreshment, which includes a free-house variety of other draught and bottled beers, lagers, wines, spirits and soft drinks.

The Colliery Inn, once called the Shoulder of Mutton, has earned a fine reputation for the quality and variety of its cooking, which attracts a loyal band of local regulars as well as a growing number of visitors in the know from the surrounding area and beyond. Local suppliers provide the raw materials for dishes that range from classics like steaks, cod & chips and mince with dumplings to spaghetti carbonara and lemon & ginger chicken.

Crook is an old mining town named after its location on a bend on its river. The colliery after which the pub is named was located just behind the pub. Mining declined down the years, here as elsewhere, and Crook's pit was closed down from the 1960s. The town is now regarded as the gateway to the countryside for travellers coming from Durham City; in its heart is a wide square that is filled with flowers in the summertime. There's excellent walking hereabouts - the Weardale Way runs nearby - and good trout fishing is available in the locality. But those with less energy can relax and unwind at the Colliery Inn, enjoying a drink in the beer garden or drinking in the fine views that open out at the front. The pub is closed on Mondays except on Bank Holidays, also closed in the daytime on Tuesday and Wednesday. Food is served lunchtime and evening Thursday and Friday and all day Saturday and Sunday. Tuesday is curry night, Thursday steak night; Sunday brings traditional roasts from 12 to 6, reverting to the main menu in the evening.

14 COTTONS CAFÉ AND RESTAURANT

60/61 Hope Street, Crook, County Durham DL15 9HU
Tel: 01388 767738
e-mail: d.threadgill@btinternet.com

Situated at the heart of the beautiful market town of Crook, **Cottons Café and Restaurant** has a fantastic reputation for its home cooked food and friendly atmosphere. Owner David Threadgill took over the property in April 2010 and created the fully licensed business from scratch. The child-friendly eatery is now well known among food-lovers thanks to David's hard work and the superb food that cook Jackie O'Boyle serves up.

A great mix of diners frequent Cottons Café and Restaurant and senior citizens have the option to eat two courses for £5.95 from a special deal menu that runs Monday - Saturday. There is room to seat 55 diners and the place is always bustling with eager locals and visitors keen to sample the affordable home cooked food on offer. The ingredients and produce used to create each dish are mostly sourced locally to ensure the best quality food is delivered.

The aroma of home baking often attracts passers-by through the doors of this splendid café and restaurant that is open seven days a week between 9am and 5pm. On Friday and Saturday evenings a restaurant style menu is available for diners to choose from, and this menu has proved so popular it is essential for diners to reserve a table for evening dining (as well as Sunday lunchtime when a roast dinner is added to the menu). Steak pie, potatoes & veg, lamb hotpot served with steamed veg, spaghetti bolognase, and chicken curry & rice served with naan bread are all popular choices on the standard menu, where most dishes are priced between £5 and £7. It isn't just the dishes on the main menu that are very reasonably priced, the daily specials offer great variety at credit crunch prices with choices including king prawn, red Thai curry, rice & naan bread, and luxury fish pie with salmon, prawns & steamed veg.

Disabled access is not a problem here and the bathroom facilities are easily accessible.

15 DOWFOLD HOUSE

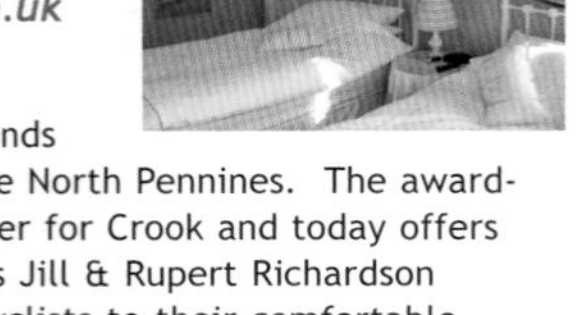

Low Jobs Hill, Crook, County Durham DL15 9AB
Tel: 01388 762473 e-mail: enquiries@dowfoldhouse.co.uk
website: www.dowfoldhouse.co.uk

Dating back to the 1860s, Dowfold House is located in its own grounds and overlooks the bustling market town of Crook and beyond to the North Pennines. The award-winning Bed & Breakfast was once the house of the Colliery Manager for Crook and today offers visitors three superior bedrooms, all with en-suite facilities. Hosts Jill & Rupert Richardson welcome well-behaved children & pets and attracts walkers and cyclists to their comfortable home. Open all year round, a top quality, locally-sourced breakfast is served in the elegant dining room between 7.30am and 9.30am.

16 THE CAUSEWAY

Elwick Road, Stranton, Hartlepool TS24 7QT
Tel: 01429 273954

There is always plenty going on at **The Causeway** in terms of entertainment and it has become a social hub where regulars and visitors can mix freely. Situated in Stranton this impressive public house is always bustling with people sipping real ales such as Camerons Strongarm and Banks Bitter.

Home cooking comprising of old fashioned pub dishes has recently been introduced at The Causeway, which is fast becoming a place to dine out in the area. The child-friendly pub hosts quizzes, themed music nights and live bands, which are well worth checking out.

17 HARTLEPOOL HISTORIC QUAY AND MUSEUM

Jackson Dock, Maritime Avenue, Hartlepool TS24 0XZ
Tel: 01429 860006 Fax: 01429 867332
e-mail: historic.quay@hartlepool.gov.uk
website: www.thisishartlepool.com

Open every day all year round and voted one of the top six Heritage & History attractions in the UK, **Hartlepool Historic Quay and Museum** is a fun day out for all the family. Here you will find a re-creation of an 18th century seaport which tells the story of life at sea at the time of Captain Cook, Nelson and the Battle of Trafalgar. As well as the coffee shop and gift shop, authentic reconstructions of harbour-side shops surround the Quay, including gunsmiths, tailors and instrument makers. A film presentation shows how two brothers were press-ganged into serving aboard ship and 'Fighting Ships' lets you experience the noise and drama of a naval sea battle.

Guided tours are available of HMS Trincomalee, launched in Bombay in 1817. The oldest floating warship in Britain, it has been lovingly restored at Hartlepool Historic Quay.

The Museum tells the story of Hartlepool from prehistoric times to the present day and includes exhibits such as sea monsters, a Celtic 'Roundhouse', the first 'gas illuminated lighthouse', models, computer interactive displays and PSS Wingfield - a fully restored Paddle Steamer.

18 NIP IN CAFÉ

Unit 5, Avenue Road, Hartlepool,
Cleveland TS24 8BB
Tel: 07738227244
e-mail: nipincafe@yahoo.co.uk

Situated at the heart of the vibrant town of Hartlepool, **Nip in Café** has been family owned and run by Andrew and Mihaela since March 2010. They have been ably assisted by Romanian chef Eugen, who has created an English/Romanian menu that includes a varied selection of breakfasts, jacket potatoes, sandwiches, paninis, burgers and dinners.

The team here has enjoyed great success and have built up a great reputation in the area with locals and visitors. They really have made their mark on this town. Children are welcomed warmly to the café and there is a specially adapted children's menu that includes favourites like sausage & chips and chicken nuggets & chips.

Open Monday - Saturday from 9am - 4.30pm, there is room to seat 32 diners inside and a further four outside. There is plenty for customers to choose from off the seasonal menu and there is always a special dish of the day, should you fancy something different.

19 THE CARLBURY ARMS

Piercebridge, County Durham DL2 3SJ
Tel: 01325 374286

The Carlbury Arms is a destination premise for lovers of fine food, well-kept real ales and unbeatable hospitality. The florally decorated pub, personally run by the Parker family has long been well regarded for its excellent freshly prepared cuisine cooked by head chef Nick.

A rack of lamb pan-fried and oven finished with a red wine and rosemary jus served on a spring onion potato mash, and breast of Gressingham duck with a port & wine sauce served with baby roasts are listed on the main menu and the quality of the starters and desserts often have undecided diners opting for a three-course meal. A specially adapted early evening menu is served between 5.45pm and 7.30pm with all dishes, including homemade poultry and ham pie served with mash or chips and vegetables, a very reasonable £8.50.

There is space to seat up to 53 diners with a private dining area seating up to 10 people which is available for small private family dining. There are two real ales to sample at The Carlbury Arms with Black Sheep and Theaksons both from North Yorkshire breweries.

20 THE BRIDGEWATER ARMS

Winston, Teesdale, County Durham DL2 3RN
Tel: 01325 730302
website: www.thebridgewaterarms.com

The picturesque hamlet of Winston may not be a large place, but what it lacks in size, its local pub - **The Bridgewater Arms** - more than makes up for in quality and style. The original Bridgewater Arms stood in a nearby location before it moved into the former village school, where it now operates, more than 51 years ago. Many of the features from the school days are still visible, including class photographs and names of former pupils can even be found inscribed above the bar. It adds to the character of this village pub which has a real fire and a glowing reputation for fine food, well-kept ales and unbeatable hospitality.

Today The Bridgewater Arms is in the capable hands of Paul and Kathryn who have been here now for three years. Paul, who has been a chef for 28 years, cooks alongside chef Richard. The atmospheric restaurant serves some fantastic dishes, which is the main reason why so many people frequent this delightful establishment. The produce used is sourced locally and favourite main dishes include roast confit leg of duck on garlic mashed potato & red wine sauce, monkfish wrapped in bacon with a spicy prawn risotto, and roast venison haunch with dauphinoise potato & port sauce. If it is a three course meal you are after you certainly will not be disappointed. Your main meal can be preceded by a tasty range of starters such as king scallops with black pudding, sweet potato puree & oyster sauce, smoked haddock, prawn & saffron risotto, Laceys mature cheese & spinach soufflé and warm salad of black pudding, roast belly pork, chicken liver & apple. Be sure to leave room for one of the irresistible desserts like jam roly poly & custard, vanilla panna cotta with roast figs, or creamy rice pudding with roast pineapple.

Open Tuesday - Saturday, The Bridgewater Arms seats 35 diners in its restaurant and a further 20 in the bar area. There are two real ales always available and food is served 12md - 2pm and 6pm - 9pm and table reservations are essential on Friday and Saturdays when this place is at its busiest. On Sundays and Mondays, when closed to the general public, this former school building can be hired out for private parties. Ring for details.

21 THE BLACK SWAN

40 Front Street, Staindrop, Darlington, County Durham DL2 3NH Tel: 01338 660749

The Black Swan is a superb village pub that is personally run by Karen and Steven McLoughlin and their children Cavan and Harley. Located in Staindrop, it serves locally brewed ale and traditional hearty food.

Open all day every day, food is served 12md - 8pm Monday - Saturday and 12md - 4pm every Sunday and such is the popularity of this place it is essential to make table reservations on Saturday evenings and Sunday lunchtimes. The Black Swan can be found on the A688 north east of Barnard Castle, close to the famous Raby Castle.

22 CROSS HILL HOTEL AND SALVOS BISTRO

1-2 The Square, Sedgefield, County Durham TS21 2AB Tel: 01740 620153

Standing proudly in the centre of Sedgefield the **Cross Hill Hotel and Salvos Bistro** is a popular venue where locals mix freely with visitors. Salvatore Pinna has owned this fine establishment for almost two years and with more than 20 years as a professional chef in the UK and in his native Sardinia you can be assured to be served high standard cuisine.

The Italian/English evening menu offers a good variety of pizza, antipasti and pasta dishes as well as pollo surf and turf, filleto Rossini, and filletto dolcelatte. The bistro, which seats 50 diners, is always busy with people and many return again and again. A lunch and takeaway menu is available 12md to 6.30pm each day (a part from Monday).

Accommodation is available at the Cross Hill Hotel and Salvos Bistro all year round with six en-suite bedrooms located upstairs comprising of four doubles, one twin and one single room. The reasonable tariff includes a hearty breakfast guaranteed to set you up suitably for a day exploring the area.

23 THE CLARENDON HOTEL

2 High Street, Redcar, Cleveland TS10 3DU
Tel: 01642 484301
e-mail: info@theclarry.co.uk
website: www.theclarry.co.uk

Just a two minute walk from a beautiful sandy beach and esplanade, **The Clarendon Hotel** offers the very best in accommodation, food and drink. The family-run hotel enjoys a central location in Redcar and is open all day every day.

Formerly called The Railway Station Hotel, today The Clarendon is personally run by Russell and Sarah Clark, who have been here since December 2009. Having collectively brought 30 years' experience in the trade to their new venture, the hotel is professionally run and is already building a positive reputation.

With ten en-suite guest rooms available, The Clarendon Hotel provides the ideal base for those visiting the area as it is within walking distance of the beach, racecourse and Cleveland Golf Club. The rooms, which vary in size, are available all year round and guests can stay on a B&B rate or B&B and evening meal rate.

Delicious food is available 11am-8pm Monday - Friday, 11am - 3.30pm on Saturday and 12md - 3.30pm on Sunday. The extensive bar menu offers a varied section of sandwiches, baguettes and jacket potatoes as well as hearty meals such as homemade lasagne, chicken curry and rump steak. A special menu offers two meals at a discounted rate and the tasty dessert menu tempts diners with chocolate fudge cake, jam roly poly and apple pie.

With a separate function room The Clarendon caters for private functions such as wedding receptions and birthday parties. The room is often available for business meetings or conferences, which is ideal because of the overnight accommodation located upstairs.

Discounts can be offered for large parties going to either Redcar Races or Cleveland Golf Club, but if neither of those takes your fancy there are plenty of other things to do. The hotel is surrounded by places of interest including various museums, small mining villages, busy town centres and shopping retail parks.

The hotel hosts entertainment most days of the week with weekly quizzes, comedy nights, discos and live music. Ring for details.

24 RAPPS CAFÉ & THE KINGS GRILL

11-13 Milton Street, Saltburn by the Sea, Cleveland TS12 1DH
Tel: 01287 625354
website: www.thekingsgrill.co.uk

Behind its floor-to-ceiling window **Rapps Café** is a bright, relaxed spot for enjoying a snack or a meal daily between 9am in the morning and 9pm in the evening. Just a short walk from the promenade and beach, the licensed café is a popular place with locals and tourists, the latter including walkers and cyclists on the Cleveland Way. The menu offers an excellent variety of wholesome, straightforward fare, from panini and jacket potatoes to cakes, pastries and cream teas. Lunch specials include homemade old spot pork burger, fish cakes, and braised beef and root vegetable stew. The stone baked pizzas cooked in the café's own oven are extremely popular with the many people that visit this place, which include families with children.

The café is owned by business partners Greg Beaty and Fraser Lloyd-Scott who have recently taken over the adjoining property and created **The Kings Grill**. The restaurant seats around 40 diners with an additional private dining area for up to ten people and its popularity is such that table reservations are essential for Friday and Saturday dining to avoid disappointment.

Fine dining here goes hand in hand with fine wine and diners can choose from the a la carte menu or the changing daily specials. Starters include confit duck served with shredded vegetables and Chinese pancakes, smoked and cured fish platter, and Yorkshire black pudding and scallops. The selection of steaks on the main menu are always very popular as well as dishes like lamb loin with puy lentils, wilted greens, sweet potato puree and a redcurrant jus; poached locally smoked haddock with Yorkshire black pudding, parsley mash and a pancetta cream; and grilled vegetable polenta with a roast vegetable and bean cassoulet. The desserts often prove too irresistible for diners so be sure to leave room. Choices include sticky toffee pudding served with stem ginger ice cream, selection of English farmhouse and continental cheeses, and Kirsch cherry and coconut tart served with vanilla pod ice cream.

The Kings Grill is open Tuesday - Saturday 6pm - late.

25 THE SCOTCH ARMS

48 Derwent Street, Blackhill, Consett, Co Durham DH8 8LZ
Tel: 01207 593709
e-mail: grahamaford@hotmail.co.uk

The Scotch Arms is a real hidden gem that many locals and visitors to Blackhill have become extremely fond of. Graham and Louise have built up a superb reputation since they took over in September 2008. There are two rotating guest ales available, which are all brewed locally. Each February a real ale festival is held here when seven real ales and three ciders are added to the standard beverage menu. Although no main meals are served at The Scotch Arms, bar snacks are available daily. A popular quiz is hosted every Thursday from 9pm followed by Play Your Cards Right and occasional bands play of a Saturday night.

26 THE JOLLY DROVERS

Redwellhills, Leadgate, Consett, Co Durham DH8 6RR
Tel: 01207 503994

The **Jolly Drovers** is a popular, unpretentious pub in the shadow of Pontop Pike, on the roundabout where the A691, A692 and A693 meet. It's very much a family affair, with Ronnie Kay at the helm, and a friendly welcome is guaranteed in the traditionally appointed bar. Open all day, every day, the bar stocks a good range of keg bitters and lagers, enhanced by real ales in the summer months. The cooking is as traditional as the surroundings, with generous platefuls of classic pub dishes served from 11.30 to 9 Monday to Saturday and from 11.30 to 7 on Sunday, when roasts are the popular centrepiece. Wednesday is quiz night, with the questions starting at 8.45pm.

28 THE MANOR HOUSE INN

Caterway Heads, Shotley Bridge,
Northumberland DH8 9LX
Tel: 01207 255268
e-mail: info@themanorhouseinn.com
website: www.themanorhouseinn.com

A small family-run business mid-way between Edinburgh and Leeds, **The Manor House Inn** is situated on the A68 overlooking the stunning Derwent valley. Here you can expect a warm welcome, real ales, good food, log fires in winter and comfortable accommodation, Four Diamond plus Silver Award standard (English Tourism Council).

The main emphasis has been to establish a successful country pub atmosphere with restaurant-quality food. Walk into the bar area and you will be shown the definition of 'country pub', the roaring coal fire and traditional wood flooring make it even easier to relax with a pint of real ale and a bite to eat. Perfect for catching up with friends or catching the match.

Being 30 minutes from both Newcastle and the historic city of Durham makes the Inn a good base for exploring the region, with a wide range of tourist attractions, i.e. Hadrian's Wall, within easy driving distance. They also offer *free* wi-fi access and are open all day everyday.

27 THE OLD MILL - KNITSLEY

Knitsley, County Durham DH8 9EL
Tel: 01207 581642
website: www.knitsleymill.com

Offering outstanding accommodation in a very eye-catching location, **The Old Mill - Knitsley** stands secluded within the hamlet after which it takes its name. The property is undoubtedly one of the most impressive of its kind in Northumberland and Durham and is set within 100 acres of beautiful countryside.

This privately owned business provides visitors and locals the very best in facilities, food and drink. It has become a well-known venue for wedding receptions and its grounds provide a lovely setting for wedding photographs. On entry to the grounds your eyes are attracted to the superb working water wheel which stands to your right and a herd of red deer to your left. The interior does not disappoint either. It is full of character, atmosphere and style. These characteristics extend to the six en-suite guest rooms that are situated in a converted farmhouse. Each was renovated in 2010 and provides a comfortable place to stay overnight if you are visiting the area, be it on business or holiday. The rooms vary in size and several are located on the ground floor, making them suitable for wheelchair-bound or disabled guests. A hearty breakfast is included in the excellent tariff, which attracts plenty of overnight guests through the doors of this picturesque guest house.

Guests and members of the public can enjoy quality home cooking and real ales across the courtyard in the spacious dining area. Delicious homemade food is available daily between 12pm and 9pm and diners can choose from the printed menu or specials board. Steak nights are held every Monday and Wednesday and favourites include trio of local sausage, chive mash & onion gravy, and braised lamb shank, root vegetables & herb mash. A tasty range of roast dinners are added to the menu each Sunday and a sandwich menu is available every day for those with a lighter appetite. Sixty diners can be seated in the dining area and it is definitely advisable to make table reservations on Friday and Saturday evenings as well as Sunday lunchtimes.

All in all, The Old Mill - Knitsley is a fantastic find and guests can partake in a spot of fly fishing on three separate lakes within the grounds should it take their fancy.

29 THE MINERS ARMS

41 Manor Road, Medomsley,
County Durham DH8 6QN
Tel: 01207 560428
website: www.theminersarmsmedomsley.co.uk

Taking its name from the many pits in the area and the brave men who worked in them, **The Miners Arms** dates back to the early 19th century. Situated in the village of Medomsley, the pub has plenty of character throughout with many prints of the bygone mining age displayed in the bar area.

Johan and Polly are your hosts here, and despite only taking charge in January 2010 have already given this place a real boost. Open every other session and all day on Sundays, The Miners Arms is fast becoming well-known in the area for its tasty traditional pub fayre. Homemade steak & ale pie and fish & chips always please hungry bellies and the Sunday lunch, with a choice of four roast dinners, always attracts plenty of diners. Food from the printed menu and daily specials board is served Tuesday - Saturday between 12md and 2.30pm and 6pm - 9pm; on Sundays food is available from 12md until 3.30pm. It is rare to see a table empty here on weekends, so it is definitely advisable to make a table reservation if you are planning to eat here on a Friday, Saturday, or Sunday, to avoid being turned away.

The weekly Tuesday quiz from 9pm is always a crowd-pleaser too. Well worth checking out.

30 BEAMISH MARY INN

No Place, Beamish, Stanley, County Durham DH9 0QH
Tel: 0191 3700237

Found close to the famous Beamish Museum, **Beamish Mary Inn** can be found in the hamlet of No Place. The historic inn is owned by business partners George and Simon and they are ably assisted by general manager Sally Crowther. The new team has only recently taken over here, but regulars are already very pleased with how it is run, which is why so many of them choose to spend their free time socialising with friends here.

Open all day every day there are eight real ales for punters to sample with all of them coming from local micro breweries. Regulars include White Hot, Red Dust, Lamplight and No Place Bitter, which is specially brewed for the Beamish Mary Inn. If you are not fond of real ale there are plenty of other beverages available from the well-stocked bar, including a selection of wines, spirits and soft drinks.

The child-friendly inn has accommodation available all year round in the form of four comfortable upstairs guest rooms, three of which are en-suite. Guests stay on a B&B basis and are treated to a delicious breakfast, ideal for setting visitors to the area up for a day of exploring.

The olde worlde inn is full of character, with open fires eagerly welcomed by hungry customers when they come in from the cold on a winter's day. Many come here to warm their bellies with the tasty cuisine available. This charming establishment serves a superb array of dishes, with daily specials such as tuna steak on a bed of roasted peppers with a ginger and lime sauce and tender pork fillet with a honey & mustard sauce among the most popular dishes. George and Simon employ a professional chef who aims to use as much local produce as possible to create delicious food of the highest standard. All dishes are cooked fresh to order to ensure customers are indulging in some of the best quality pub food in Northumberland. Meals are served Monday - Saturday between 12noon and 2pm and 5pm - 9pm. Bookings are required for Sunday lunch, which is served between 12noon and 3pm.

31 MR CRUSTY'S CAFÉ

202 Park Road, South Moor, Stanley, Co. Durham DH9 7AL
Tel: 01207 230023

A bright orange sign on a cheerful blue background tells you that you've arrived at **Mr Crusty's Café**. Heart daytime eating is what's in store at this friendly place, which is owned and personally run in fine style by Wendy and Amin Moshangai and their son Graeme. Located on the ground floor of a two-storey redbrick building, it's a neat, up-to-date 20-seat café on the main street of South moor, a semi-rural community standing between Oxhill and Quaking Houses southwest of the former important colliery town of Stanley on the northern slope of the Craghead Valley (South Moor was in fact once called West Stanley). Mr Crusty's is a great place to pause for a bite to eat on the way to work, a lunch break or a rest from shopping, and it's also a popular spot for motorists, walkers and cyclists (the Sustrans C2C cycle route from Whitehaven to Sunderland passes quite close by). The main menu and daily specials offer plenty of choice and most of the items are available to take away. Breakfast can be as light or hearty as you like, from a bacon sandwich to a mighty plateful that should provide fuel for even the most energetic day's walking or cycling - 3 rashers of bacon, 3 sausages, 2 eggs, black pudding, beans, tomatoes, hash browns, mushrooms and toast! Sandwiches come with an impressively wide variety of fillings, from ham & pease pudding and tuna sweetcorn mayo to hot roast beef or pork. Popular orders among the hot main-course options include chicken fajitas, cottage pie, quiche, burgers, omelettes, bacon hot pot, mince with dumplings and juicy beef or gammon steaks. And, as the owners say: "If it's not on the menu please ask. We will make it for you". Teas, coffees and cold drinks accompany the generously served food.

If driving to South Moor from the Consett direction, turn off the main A693 before Stanley at the road signposted to South Moor. If coming from the east, leave the A1(M) at J63 or the the A167 and take the A693, turning off just past Oxhill.

South Moor Park, a short walk from Mr Crusty's, is a pleasant place to spend an hour or two, with woodland walks, a bowls pitch and a tennis court. One of the region's most popular visitor attractions, the North of England Open Air Museum at Beamish, is a short drive away from South Moor.

32 SUNDERLAND MUSEUM AND WINTER GARDENS

Burdon Road, Sunderland, Tyne and Wear SR1 1PP
Tel: 0191 553 2323 Fax: 0191 553 7828
website: www.twmuseums.org.uk/sunderland

Sunderland Museum & Winter Gardens combines a museum, art gallery, exhibition space and Winter Gardens to create a stunning visitor attraction in the heart of the city centre.

In the Museum, discover the history of the city from its prehistoric past to the present day. Exciting displays interpret the wide variety of collections, using hands-on exhibits, computer interactives and video presentations.

The Art Gallery features paintings by L S Lowry together with Victorian masterpieces and artefacts from the four corners of the world.

The stunning Winter Gardens stimulate the senses with over 2,000 flowers and plants brought together in a spectacular showcase of the world's natural beauty.

The museum holds an exiting programme of temporary exhibitions which are accompanied by activities and events for all ages.

33 THE ALBION

The Village, Ryhope, Sunderland SR2 0NH
Tel: 0191 521 0293

Situated in the village of Ryhope, found south of Sunderland on the A1018 is where you will find the much loved The Albion. With 10 years experience in the trade friendly couple Robert and Natalie took over the premises in 2010 and since that time it has gone from strength to strength.

The food here is the responsibility of Robert and his team of chefs, and together they create some mouthwatering dishes using as much local produce as possible. Main meals include; Whitby scampi, home-made chicken and mushroom pie; home-made chicken kiev, grilled lamb chops and vegetarian options. There is also a choice of paninis and jacket potatoes for those looking for a lighter option. Food is available Monday - Saturday 12 - 9pm. On Sunday, the carvery goes down a treat and is available from 12 - 4pm, booking is essential.

The bar offers plenty of beverages to accompany your meal with one real ale in Black Sheep and plenty of wines, spirits and soft drinks as well.

There are good disabled facilities and all types of payment are taken.

34 FEATHERBED ROCK CAFÉ

19 - 20 North Terrace, Seaham,
County Durham SR7 7EU
Tel: 0191 513 0099

Overlooking Seaham's famous historic harbour, **Featherbed Rock Café** has gone from strength to strength since the Ramshaw family took ownership of this establishment in September 2010. Since then they have refurbished and improved the café attracting plenty of locals and visitors through its doors.

Open seven days a week Featherbed Rock Café offers a warm welcome to passers-by who are drawn in by the aroma of home cooking. There is a tasty selection of sandwiches, paninis and jacket potatoes as well as traditional meals such as sausage & mash, fish & chips, and vegetable lasagne. Local produce is a strong focus of the menu, which has been created by the professional chef employed here.

The premise is licensed and the function room provides an ideal space for wedding receptions and private parties. It is located above the café and seats around 45 people. Ring for details. The café also hosts entertainment every Friday and Saturday evening with the well-regarded DJ Vinyl Ritchie. It is always really packed, so make sure you get there early.

36 THE DUN COW

Primrose Hill, Bournmoor, Houghton-le-Spring,
Tyne and Wear DH4 6DY
Tel: 0191 385 2631
e-mail: theduncowbournmoor@yahoo.co.uk
website: www.theduncowbournoor.co.uk

Well known for its hospitality, fine food and ale **The Dun Cow** is a superb public house located in the village of Bournmoor, a short drive from Houghton-le-Spring. Experienced licensee Roger Dale, his wife Janice and their children Alex and Katy have been here for the past five years.

They offer a fine selection of malt whiskies and three rotating guest ales from local breweries which go down well with the people who frequent this much loved pub. Son Alex is in charge of the kitchen and he creates some fantastic mouth-watering dishes, using as much local produce as possible. Customers can choose to dine in the bar area that seats 35 or in the beautiful Lambton Conservatory Restaurant that overlooks the well-kept garden and seats 48 diners.

There are plenty of dishes listed on the printed menu and the specials board and a delicious three course Sunday lunch is available. There are plenty of special offers to be had throughout the week and there are two quizzes each week, that help make this place the social hub that it is. There is a function room available at The Dun Cow. Ring for details.

35 THE FLOATERS MILL

Woodstone Village, Haughton-le-Spring, County Durham DH4 6BQ
Tel: 0191 385 6695
e-mail: pauljones2127@hotmail.co.uk
website: www.thefloatersmill.co.uk

Proudly billed as: "The Nearly Famous Floaters Mill", the evergreen country pub and restaurant between Woodstone Village and Bournmoor is deserving of a visit. It may be deliberately downplaying its place in the Durham/Wearside restaurant stakes, but the "Floaters", as known by many locals, is well worth a look.

The extensive menus cater for all ages and tastes; the comfortable and spacious dining areas ensure that you can enjoy your meal in comfort and style. Choose from the full main menu, grill menu, a-la-carte menu, and the daily carvery or from the weekly specials board. The draw for many is the Sunday carvery, which is served between 11.30 and 7pm and booking is advisable. Typical dishes you can expect from across all the menus, include: the traditional pub staples like steak & ale pie, scampi & chips, every kind of steak imaginable, rump, sirloin, rib-eye and even a 12oz horseshoe gammon. Or for those with something to celebrate or looking for a real treat, then turn your attention to the a-la-carte menu, with choices such as, medallions of pork fillet with a cider and apricot cream or the red deer haunch steak with roasted celery, leek and red onion with a chocolate demi-glaze, you will surely find something to tempt your pallet. And then there's the dessert list features all home-made treats, such as sticky toffee pudding with toffee sauce, strawberry meringues, apple & rhubarb crumble plus many more.

The pub is very picturesque, with beautiful tress and flowers surrounding it, making it a great place to relax in the beer garden with a refreshing drink. Outside there is a large kids play area, a large BBQ area as well as a patio area.

With the very friendly staff and fantastic atmosphere this makes it the perfect place to go for a quiet drink with friends and family. There are disabled facilities throughout the premises, as well as a car park, which makes it easily accessible for all. For those sports fanatics in the pub, the two bars have SKY TV, and every Wednesday they hold fantastic Quiz nights.

So whatever your looking for, whether a place for bite to eat, a casual drink, a day out with the family or a place to hold any function or party, The Floaters Mill is your number one choice.

37 GATESHEAD MILLENIUM BRIDGE

Gateshead, Tyne and Wear NE8 3QW
Tel: 0191 433 3000 (Gateshead Council)

See one of the world's most stunning riverside landmarks - the **Gateshead Millenium Bridge**. The world's only tilting bridge opens to allow shipping to pass underneath its graceful arches. Don't forget to catch the bridge in the evening, when it is lit by a high-tech light display, able to create dazzling patterns in millions of colours.

It uses a tilting mechanism to open, turning on pivots on both sides of the river to form a spectacular gateway arch. Two concrete piers hide the massive hydraulic rams, pivots and motors which open the bridge. Each opening or closing takes four minutes, powered by eight electric motors totalling 440 kilowatts or 589 horse power - more power than the fastest sports cars like a Ferrari F50. The main arch rises to 50 metres and is 126 metres wide - but precisely made to a tolerance of 3mm. The weight is over 850 tonnes - enough steel to make 64 double decker buses.

The bridge was designed by Wilkinson Eyre Architects/Gifford & Partners, and built by Gateshead based construction company Harbour & General at a cost of £22 million - almost half of which was paid for by Lottery money through the Millenium Commission.

38 L G COFFEE BAR

Church Chare, Whickham,
Tyne and Wear NE16 4SH
Tel: 0191 488 0420

Tucked away in Church Chare but just yards off the main road in Whickham, you'll find the sheer delight of **L G Coffee Bar**, providing a great place to meet up with friends, or simply to enjoy a bit of 'me' time.

Established over 15 years ago, owner Linda Goodrick offers a great selection of home-made comfort food. If you fancy a delicious panini, quiche, toastie or a traditional breakfast, L G Coffee Bar is the best place to be. For those with a sweet or savoury tooth there is also a large selection of home-made, fresh cakes and scones.

The interior oozes class and local art adorns the walls. The coffee bar also sells a range of arts and crafts including a good selection of greeting and birthday cards.

Open Monday to Saturday, 9.30-3.30pm Monday-Friday and 9.30-1.30pm on Saturdays.

39 POACHERS POCKET

Market Lane, Whickham,
Newcastle-upon-Tyne NE16 4TJ
Tel: 0191 488 7128
e-mail: info@1812pubsandrestaurants.com

Since the arrival of experience licensee Dave Holden in October 2010, **Poachers Pocket** is re-emerging as one of the better pubs in Whickham. Having been in the trade for 18 years, Dave has definitely used his experience to make this place a real success.

Open seven days a week Poachers Pocket offers quality food and two real ales, with Marstons Pedigree the regular. Food, made from locally sourced ingredients, is available daily from 12md to 9pm and it is advisable to book on Sundays to avoid disappointment.

The extensive menu offers a good range of pies, grills, burgers, wraps, sandwiches, jacket potatoes and sizzling dishes as well as favourites such as spaghetti Bolognese, local Cumberland sausage, and Thai green chicken curry. For younger diners there is a specially adapted children's menu, which includes penne pasta and tomato sauce and homemade chicken nuggets and fries.

Plenty of entertainment is held at Poachers Pocket with a quiz held every Wednesday from 8.30pm and live acoustic music from 8.30pm every Saturday that is well worth checking out.

40 SOUTH SHIELDS MUSEUM & ART GALLERY

Ocean Road, South Shields, Tyne and Wear NE33 2JA
Tel: 0191 456 8740 Fax: 0191 456 7850
website: www.twmuseums.org.ik/southshields

South Shields Museum & Art Gallery explores the story of South Tyneside through sensational displays, hands-on exhibits and stunning art. The Museum has three main displays: Tales of South Tyneside, which explores the local and social history of the area during the twentieth century together with the lifetime achievement of the successful local author Catherine Cookson. Art Adventure takes a fresh approach to the interpretation of many of the Museum's paintings. Land, River and Sea looks at how the natural environment has influenced the history and look of the area from prehistoric times to the present day.

41 THE SPREAD EAGLE

1 Front Street, Preston, North Shields NE29 9LB
Tel: 0191 257 7111

Dating back to the 18th century, this premises is full of character and has long been providing rest and refreshment to village locals and those passing through Preston Village. As time has seen the village merge with the surrounding towns, this haven of hospitality has retained its status as a country pub, upholding tradition and maintaining rural charms. Fine hosts, Jill and Dave provide a friendly welcome as you enter the cosy bar, warmed by lovely open fires and typified by the gaggle of gossiping locals stood at the bar. With the combination of the couple's personalities, the excellent facilities available and Jill's tremendous cooking, they both have many years of experience in the trade, which makes this business a wonderful one to visit.

Here, patrons can select from four real ales, three regulars - Deuchars IPA, Theakstons, Olde Peculier and an additional guest ale, or indulge in a double of something stronger. A Chef of 17 years, Jill entices customers with fresh, locally sourced ingredients and offers a weekly changing selection of dishes with a real leaning toward tradition. Expect dishes like the ever-popular fish and chips served with lashings of proper mushy peas, heart-warming pie, lasagne, beef chilli and even a roast of the day. Food is served from 12-2pm Tuesday to Saturday, 4-8pm Tuesday to Friday and 12-4pm on Sundays. Due to its popularity booking is essential on Sundays and advisable at all times during the high season.

Being a pub with everything, the entertainment that regularly takes place is well attended and extremely popular with the locals. There is a quiz night every Thursday evening and live music every Saturday evening.

The Spread Eagle is everything that you could possibly want in a local - good food and good beer at reasonable prices, with good conversation thrown in for free.

42 COUNTRY HOUSE TEA ROOMS

14 Percy Park Road, Tynemouth NE30 2EP
Tel: 01912 574449

A Tea Rooms like no other!

Tasteful decor, ornate antiques, friendly staff and delicious home-made treats, is what guests will find at the Country House Tea Rooms.

This fantastic tea rooms is family run by attentive owners Marina and William, their daughter April and sister-in-law June. The premises oozes class and the fine decor and furnishings running throughout, go hand in hand with the delicious smell of homecooking and unbeatable hospitality. The tea rooms seats 21 downstairs, 12 upstairs and 10 outside, with both levels offering individual decor and unique antiques.

With home-made delights including, scones, a selection of cakes and choice of sweet waffles, guests will be left spoilt for choice when indulging a sweet tooth. For those looking for something savoury to fill a hole, the menu offers a range of triangle cut sandwiches, soup of the day; chill beef cheesy chips, beef lasagne, beef burgers; bacon and tomato penne pasta, the very popular Welsh rarebit and plenty more, all of which are once again home-made. There is also a specials board which means even the most regular of visitors have something new to try.

The couple's daughter April is a talented pianist and singer and often performs her own compositions in the tea rooms. So why not sit back, enjoy a cream tea and relax to the sound of some live music? Open Tuesday - Friday 10am - 4pm and Saturday/Sunday 10am - 5pm.

Great food, friendly staff and a warm welcome!

43 GINGERSNAPS VICTORIAN TEAROOMS

Land of Green Ginger Shopping Mall, Tynemouth, Tyne and Wear NE30 4BP Tel: 01912 572051

If you want a tearoom with a difference then this is for you. Brimming in character the building in which it is housed was once the town's main church. Inside there are many other individual little shops that offer something different and more personal.

The tearoom is a good spot to pause, put your shopping down and enjoy a delicious home baked dessert and hot drink. The tearoom also offers a variety of excellent sandwiches and hot food. Open 7 days a week and payments are to be made in cash only.

44 MARTINEAU GUEST HOUSE

57 Front Street, Tynemouth NE30 4BX
Tel: 01912 579038
e-mail: martineauhouse@gmail.com
website: www.martineau-house.co.uk

The first female journalist in England, Harriet Martineau was a 19th Century reformer and early feminist, it is after her that the Martineau Guest House takes its name.

Dating from 1790, this magnificent Georgian Town House has been offering quality bed and breakfast accommodation for the past 10 years. There are four tastefully decorated en-suite bedrooms to choose from, two benefiting from spectacular views of the coastline, the other two enjoying picturesque views of the village.

Guests can start their day with a wide choice of hearty breakfasts cooked to order by Sally, including the delicious Martineau sausage made exclusively for the guest house by an award winning Northumbrian butcher and Sally's own homemade organic bread.

The guest house has been included in the 2011 Michelin guide and has also been presented 4 **** and a Silver Award.

With rooms offering every comfort for a relaxing stay, guests are sure to find Martineau Guest House the perfect choice whether for business or pleasure.

45 QUEENS HEAD

6 Front Street, Cullercoats, North Shields NE30 4QB
Tel: 01912 536970
website: www.queenshead-cullercoats.co.uk

Situated in the village of Cullercoats with fine views over the seafront, is the **Queens Head**. Central to the vibrant Cullercoats community, this well established pub offers a perfect place to drink and dine with friends and loved ones. With leaseholder Andrew having been a chef for over 7 years, it comes as no surprise that the menu here is second to none. Delectable delights such as lamb shank, chicken and gammon pie; trio of Cumberland sausages, and plenty more adorn the menu. The bar offers two real ales with draught Bass the regular, along with a choice of wines, spirits and soft drinks. Food is served Mon-Sat 11.30am-2.45pm & 5pm-8.45pm, Sun 12-8.15pm.

46 THE CORNERSTONE

96 Oxford Street, Whitley Bay NE26 1AD
Tel: 01912 891445
e-mail: info@cornerstone.co.uk
website: www.cornerstonecafe.co.uk

With a beautiful crescent of golden sand stretching northwards from Cullercoats to St. Mary's Island, it is no wonder visitors return year after year to enjoy Whitley Bay. It is here that Cornerstone has made it's home.

Run by a friendly local family; this delightful café has made it's mark as a popular place in which to dine. Lyn and her daughter Lucy present a superb menu of home-made dishes including breakfasts, pancakes, paninis; pasta dishes, and plenty more; all created using local produce as much as possible. There is also a range of cake and scones to satisfy those who wish to indulge in something sweet. Lyn always aims to please and is always on hand to discuss individual dietary requirements, for example gluten free pasta, bread and cakes are available. Children's portions of all the meals are available upon request.

Although the café does not sell alcohol, diners are welcome to bring their own to evening functions for a small corkage fee. Opening hours are Monday - Saturday 9am - 4.30pm. Opening evenings as a Bistro in the summer.

47 BARNACLE CAFE/BISTRO

7 Lower Central Prom, Whitley Bay NE26 1AN
Tel: 01912 533876
e-mail: info@thebarnacle.co.uk
website: www.facebook/thebarnaclewhitleybay
or www.thebarnacle.co.uk

Located on the beach front, the Barnacle Cafe/Bistro offers an ideal place to drink and dine, accompanied by a warm welcome and spectacular sea views. Attentive owner Cathryn, took over the premises in April 2010 and along with her team of helpful staff, the Barnacle has become a well established place to eat.

A beach cafe by day, the Barnacle serves a range of delicious lunches such as beer battered fish and hand-cut chips, range of baguettes, wraps and salads along with a specials board. All sauces from the Tartar to the onion marmalade are all made in house so you can taste the difference. There is a scrumptious selection of home-made cakes, scones and cupcakes all of which can be enjoyed with a cup of tea, coffee or hot chocolate.

By evening the cafe takes on an alternative role as a bistro. Guests can enjoy a range of tasty dishes and fresh seasonal produce is used as much as possible, therefore the menu changes regularly and is small but great in taste. It offers a range of dishes from ribeye steak accompanied by creamy parsnip dauphinoise to seabass with lyonnaise potato drizzled with salsa verde and a side of rocket to name but a few, along with vegetarian options. After your mains the temptation to have puddings is overwhelming as they are all home-made. The Barnacle is available for private functions and children's parties. Please call for the opening times.

48 BROWN SUGAR LOUNGE

Unit 5, Platform 2, Monkseaton Metro Station,
Monkseaton NE26 3NR
Tel: 01912 520202
e-mail: ianrutteruk@hotmail.co.uk
website: www.brownsugarlounge.co.uk

Set within Monkseaton Metro Station, **The Brown Sugar Lounge** offers a fantastic place to share a bite to eat with friends or enjoy a hot beverage before setting off on a journey.

Patty & Ian Rutter took over The Brown Sugar Lounge in January 2009 and completed an extensive internal refurbishment to offer local people a convenient, chic and relaxing place to enjoy good home cooked food.

Ian has been a qualified chef for over 25 years and the menu displays his passion for good honest food. Visitors can expect to see dishes such as baked quiche, chilli cheese wedges; corned beef and crushed potato pie, home-made soup; a range of breakfast options, sandwiches and salads. The dessert menu is equally as tempting, and presents the perfect way to indulge a sweet tooth.

This superb cafe bistro is open 8am-4pm Tuesday - Saturday (closed on Sunday and Monday). The premises is also available to hire for private functions, please call for more details.

49 THE BOATHOUSE

Water Row, Newburn,
Newcastle upon Tyne NE15 8NL
Tel: 0191 229 0326
e-mail: newburn.boathouse@hotmail.co.uk

Boasting an outstanding location, **The Boathouse** has quality facilities and can be found adjacent to the River Tyne. Since she took over in January 2011 owner Alison Kappen has offered a warm welcome to a wide range of people including a lot of walkers who attempt the Hadrians Wall walk at Newburn.

Alison has given The Boathouse a new lease of life and has attracted plenty of new faces through the doors as well as all the regulars. Open all day every day, there are two rotating real ales to enjoy as well as a fabulous selection of home cooked meals. All of the dishes are created using as much local produce as possible and there is plenty to suit all tastes on the daily blackboard menu. Sunday lunch is becoming more popular each week, so much so that it is definitely advisable to book to avoid disappointment.

The Boathouse benefits from a really incredible riverside location and there are some fantastic views to be enjoyed at this child-friendly pub.

50 BARNARD CASTLE

Barnard Castle, County Durham DL12 8PR
Tel: 01833 638212 website: www.english-heritage.org.uk

Set on a high rock above the River Tees, imposing Barnard Castle was the stronghold of the Balliol family. Taking its name from Bernard de Balliol, who rebuilt it in the 12th century, it includes a fine great hall and a dominating round-towered keep. Unsuccessfully besieged by the Scots in 1216, it was confiscated when John de Balliol, briefly king of Scotland, was deposed by Edward 1. It last saw action during the Northern Rising against Queen Elizabeth in 1569, surrendering to 5000 rebels, and was partly dismantled in 1630 to furnish materials for Sir Henry Vane's new Raby Castle.

51 CAFÉ NEST

25 Newgate, Barnard Castle, County Durham DL12 8NG
Tel: 01833 631529
e-mail: becky@barnardcastlenest.org.uk
website: www.barnardcastlenest.org.uk

With its relaxed and informal atmosphere **Café Nest** is an outstanding property that stands yards from Barnard Castle's main street. It provides the ideal meeting place for work or pleasure with a selection of bespoke seating inside and out.

The café has been owned by business partners Clare Dixon and Sue Black since August 2010 and the day-to-day running is managed by Becky Errington. Since this successful team took over they have attracted plenty of customers through its doors including a lot of walking enthusiasts and cyclists.

Situated in Newgate, just a few yards from the Market Cross, Café Nest houses a superb café, gallery, studio space and digital hub and is well worth the extra minute walk from the main street.

Open 9am - 5pm Monday - Saturday and 10am - 3.30pm on Sunday, there is some really tasty food to be enjoyed. Locally sourced ingredients are incorporated into the menu wherever possible and a children's menu is available. There is a delicious and varied selection of freshly prepared jacket potatoes, salads, sandwiches, wraps and paninis to be sampled as well as homemade soup and pate of the day. Homemade cakes and scones can be enjoyed alongside a range of hot and cold beverages including Pumphery's coffee and Madhatters tea.

The food really is delicious and this place has built up a real loyal following of regular diners and is continuing to attract a steady stream of new faces too. With space to seat 30 diners inside and a further 30 outside larger parties are advised to book to avoid disappointment.

Customer Comments:

"Fabulous Cafe, Gorgeous Food, Very Welcoming and Brilliant Service"

"A Superb Addition to the Town" "Excellent Food, Cake and Service"

52 BOWES MUSEUM

Barnard Castle, County Durham DL12 8NP
Tel: 01833 690606 Fax: 01833 637163
e-mail: info@bowesmuseum.org.uk
website: www.bowesmuseum.org.uk

The Bowes Museum is one of County Durham's great surprises - a beautiful and grand French chateau-style museum on the outskirts of the historic town of Barnard Castle. It was built by John Bowes, illegitimate son of the 10th Earl of Strathmore, and his Parisian actress wife, Josephine, Countess of Montalbo, between 1862 and 1875. They wanted to house the vast collection of works of art they had amassed from all corners of Europe so that people from all walks of life could see and enjoy them, but unfortunately they died before their dream was realised.

But realised it eventually was, and today it has an outstanding collection that will take your breath away. Here the visitor can admire a vast range objets d'arts and paintings, including what is acknowledged to be the most important collection of Spanish paintings in Britain. But John and Josephine Bowes didn't just restrict themselves to the grand and the prestigious. There is also a wonderful display of toys, including the world's first toy train set.

The Museum's most famous exhibit is undoubtedly the Silver Swan. The life-sized bird, with its exquisite silver plumage, is an automaton and musical box, set in a stream made from twisted glass rods with small fish "swimming" among them. When it is wound up, the glass rods rotate, a tinkling tune is played, and the swan preens itself before lowering its head towards the water and seemingly picking up a fish. It then raises its head once more and appears to swallows it.

53 THE GEORGE & DRAGON INN

Boldron, Barnard Castle, County Durham DL12 9RF
Tel: 01833 638215
e-mail: georgeanddragon_boldron@yahoo.com
website: www.thegeorgeanddragoninn.co.uk

Providing locals and passers-by with well-kept real ales, tasty home cooked food, and even a place to stay for the night, **The George and Dragon Inn** can be found in the picturesque village of Boldron. Located close to the historic market town of Barnard Castle, the inn is an ideal resting spot for those exploring the beautiful countryside that surrounds the area.

Business partners Sarah and Kevin (who both cook) have totally refurbished the inn since they took over at the end of August 2010. After a short period of closure, The George and Dragon Inn was reopened with a new lease of life in mid-September 2010 and is now a designated free house.

The interior has been carefully thought out and tastefully decorated throughout with the two guest en-suite bedrooms providing a comfortable place to rest your head. Both are spacious and modern and are available all year round on a B&B tariff, which includes an unforgettable Full Yorkshire Breakfast, hot baked morning scones and real coffee & teas served in their own private parlour.
The George & Dragon Inn is open all day every day (apart from Tuesday) and serves a selection of real ales from local breweries and a fine choice of delicious home cooked food that is cooked to order using fresh and seasonal local produce. Before your main course, why not try one of the fine starters such as homemade sliced gravlax of organic Scottish salmon with crispy fennel & pomegranate salad, soy & herb dressing, or fish cakes with lemon grass, pink pepper & herbs, crunchy salad, fresh yoghurt & mayonnaise green sauce. There is a good variety of main meals to choose from, all at reasonable prices. Slow braised blade of beef in a rich red wine & tomato gravy, red lentil curried dal & crunchy greens, and grilled fresh fillet of North Sea cod, parmesan crust, warm char grilled vegetables, wilted greens, white balsamic, basil & spring onion dressing are among the options.

To accompany each dish, the wine list has been carefully chosen to offer an eclectic mix of old school and new origin. They have been sourced and carefully chosen by people who love great food and wine.

54 THE ANCIENT UNICORN

High Street, Bowes, nr Barnard Castle, County Durham DL12 9HL
Tel: 01833 628321
e-mail: ancient.unicorn@virgin.net
website: www.ancient-unicorn.com

Located in an Area of Outstanding Natural Beauty, **The Ancient Unicorn** is a real pub-lover's pub. The 16th century stone building has enormous character and is everything a proper pub should be. When Joanne and Ian took over in the summer of 2006 they brought with them a wealth of experience in the licensed trade and added the finishing touches of knowledge and outstanding hospitality to the pub's other assets.

The three-storey building is impressive in its own right, and the expectations created by the exterior are fully realised in the public rooms, where 2ft-thick walls, beams and a huge fire create an irresistible ambience for locals, walkers, hikers, families and tourists. For centuries, this place has been a popular resting stop for travellers who journey across the Pennines and today it remains a fantastic place to stay.

This is wonderful walking country, and The Ancient Unicorn offers a very comfortable, civilised base with four immaculate en suite bedrooms - including a family room - in a courtyard-style annexe. Families are very welcome here and there is always a warm friendly welcome awaiting visitors here, many who develop a real fondness for this former coaching inn, its low beamed bar and roaring fire.

As well as offering suitable accommodation, The Ancient Unicorn is a superb place to enjoy a spot of lunch or dine out in the evening following a day of exploration. So whether you are hoping to visit the nearby Bowes Museum, Barnard Castle or simply take a walk or cycle through the beautiful countryside which surrounds the inn, be sure to stop off for some refreshments or a bite to eat.

The main menu, served lunchtime and evening, highlights prime local produce in dishes such as deep-fried Cotherstone cheese fritters; warm salad of black pudding with mushrooms and a poached egg; Cumberland sausage; and slow-roasted Teesdale lamb shank. Black Bull and Shepherd Neame Spitfire are the resident cask ales, but before the urge to sample the beer the pub serves morning coffee from 10 o'clock in the morning.

55 CLOVE LODGE

Baldersdale, Barnard Castle, County Durham DL12 9UP
Tel: 01833 650030
e-mail: carolinecarter69@aol.com
website: www.clovelodge.co.uk

Caroline Carter had always had a yen to own a farm, and she chose a wonderful part of the world when she acquired a twenty-acre livestock farm on the edge of the fells. **Clove Lodge**, which stands next to the farmhouse, is a Victorian stone-built, slate-roofed cottage with accommodation on two floors. New for 2011, and aside from the cottage, is a completely refurbished barn, which can accommodate up to six guests. Situated just yards from the main house, it is ideal for a group of walkers of cyclists.

The picturesque cottage is run both as a self-catering property and as bed & breakfast, depending on what you prefer. It has attracted a wide range of guests over the years, with many of them returning year on year to soak up all that it and its scenic location has to offer. On the ground floor are an en-suite double/twin bedroom, a large, comfortable sitting room, a well-equipped kitchen and a cosy dining room. Upstairs is a double bedroom with its own bath/shower room. The two rooms at Clove Lodge can be let separately or the cottage let as a whole, for either Bed & Breakfast (with evening meals by arrangement) or self-catering; for the latter, fresh eggs and lamb from the farm can be supplied.

The breakfasts that Caroline serves up are absolutely superb and are sure to set up any visitor to the area for a day of exploration. Barnard Castle is a short drive away, and other places of interest in the vicinity include high and Low Force waterfalls, Raby Castle and the villages of Romaldkirk and Cotherstone.

Peace, solitude and the dramatic scenery of the North Pennines attract a wide cross-section of visitors, including tourists, walkers, cyclists, anglers (there's excellent fishing on nearby reservoirs) and wedding guests at the wonderful Bowes Museum. The cottage has an attractive south-facing area with tables, chairs and a small barbecue overlooking a wooded bank, waterfall and stream. In the summer months guests often make the most of this area, which enjoys views across rolling countryside. No credit cards.

56 THE PANTRY

43 High Street, Tow Law, Bishop Auckland, County Durham DL13 4DH
Tel: 01388 730033

Frequented by locals and visitors alike, **The Pantry** offers delicious home cooked food, which is all freshly prepared on site. The hospitality at the tea rooms is friendly and efficient and this place really has gone from strength to strength since owner Leanne Parkin created the business two years ago.

Having been a chef for more than ten years, Leanne has plenty of culinary skills and her experience is evident in the tasty and popular food served here. Traditional favourites such as cottage pie, mince & cheese cobbler, and roast pork can be enjoyed at very reasonable prices. Among the most popular dishes is the selection of breakfasts, which can be ordered throughout the day alongside a wide variety of other dishes from soup to scrambled eggs on toast.

The dining area itself is light, modern and spacious and is usually bustling with eager diners, many who have become familiar faces to Leanne and staff members Andrea and Jason.

The Pantry is open 8am - 3.30pm Monday - Saturday and is child and wheelchair friendly, which ensures a homely mix of people pass through its doors.

58 KNIGHTS CAFE

3 Old Church, Hexham, Northumberland NE46 1NG
Tel: 01434 605454

Situated at the heart of Hexham, **Knights Cafe** is one of the longest-running cafes in the town. Owner Ian has been welcoming hungry passersby for that past 34 years and has been ably assisted by manageress Paula for 25 years.

The child-friendly cafe is located upstairs and is well-known among the locals. The breakfasts are particularly popular, although if they don't take your fancy there is plenty more to choose from off the blackboard menu and there is always a daily special. There is a delicious selection of filled sandwiches, jacket potatoes and burgers as well as a good range of light snacks and beverages available throughout the day.

Open Monday - Saturday between 8am and 3pm, Knights Cafe seats 40 diners and is always bustling with friendly people keen to sample the delights on offer. The service is just as pleasant and Ian and Paula are always welcoming back familiar faces as well as new customers.

Only cash is accepted.

57 HELME PARK HALL HOTEL

Fir Tree Village, Bishop Auckland, County Durham DL13 4NW
Tel: 01388 730970 Fax: 01388 731799
e-mail: post@helmeparkhotel.co.uk
website: www.helmeparkhallhotel.co.uk

Situated in two acres of beautifully landscaped gardens, **Helme Park Hall Hotel** offers quality accommodation with easy access to both country and town. This charming property is privately owned, but managed by Heather Main who ensures the needs of each guest are suitably met.

Built in 1643, The Hall has had various occupants and been used for different purposes over the years and was once a distinguished family home. Today it offers fine accommodation, quality dining and a lovely bar area, which serves a good variety of real ales, and the best selection of vintage Scotch Whiskies in the county.

Helme Park Hall Hotel has an impeccable reputation for providing guests with unrivalled quality, service and superb attention to detail. There are 14 en-suite guest rooms located upstairs, which are all tastefully decorated and vary in size. Guests can stay on a B&B rate or B&B and dinner.

Bar and restaurant meals are available at the hotel, with the excellent cuisine a major attraction to guests who choose to stay here. The child-friendly hotel is renowned locally for its Sunday Lunch, which is served between 12md until 3pm. Head Chef David Harvey will always supply the restaurant with excellent value meals and every item on the menu bears his own hallmark of quality and are locally sourced were possible. Food is served Monday - Friday between 12md and 2.30pm and 6pm - 9pm, all day Saturday 12md - 9pm and 12md - 8pm on Sundays. Such is the popularity of this place with food lovers it is advisable to book at all times to avoid disappointment.
Be it business or pleasure, the hotel aims to provide its guests with genuine northern hospitality, good food and above all an incredible and memorable stay.

The hotel can be found adjacent to the main A68, just over a mile north of the A68's junction with the A689. It is an extremely popular venue in the area and caters for all occasions including short breaks, civil weddings and conferences.

59 THE GARDEN COFFEE HOUSE (FORMERLY PHAT KATZ)

20 Hallgate, Hexham, Northumberland NE46 1XD
Tel: 01434 606656
e-mail: thegardencoffeehouse@gmail.com
website: www.thegardencoffeehouse.com

The Garden Coffee House has only been open to the public for a few months, but if its current trade is anything to go by it is well on its way to being a total success. Formerly Phat Katz, the establishment has been completely refurbished by new owners Lindsay and Austin Birney.

Its new title forms part of the transformation that has taken place, which has pleasantly surprised the locals, who now come here to enjoy homemade lunches, cakes and locally produced ice cream. Located at the heart of Hexham, next to the old jail, The Garden Coffee House is already rather popular with residents and visitors to the town. Families are always welcomed at this child-friendly cafe and there are plans to build a children's play area and terrace later in the year.

The coffee house is open seven days a week between 10am and 4pm and provides seating for 40 customers inside and a further 60 in the delightful courtyard garden. It can be found a 12 minute drive away from the village of Matfen, where the Birney family has run the Matfen Village Store and Coffee Shop for many years.

60 UPPER TEAS CAFE

13A Cattlemarket, Hexham, Northumberland NE46 1NJ
e-mail: sisterson@hotmail.com

Regarded as one of the best places to dine in Hexham, **Upper Teas Cafe** offers homemade cakes and lunches Monday - Saturday between 9am and 5pm. As well as delicious food you can be assured of a pleasant and friendly service.

Owned by Debra Sisterson, the child-friendly cafe that seats 29 diners is located above Grants the Bakers in Cattlemarket, which is one of the town's main roads. Fresh homemade sandwiches, daily homemade soup and home baked scones are just some of the tasty options available from the printed menu, which offers a lot of local produce. Fair trade, gluten free and low fat options are also available.

61 IN THE CHARE

19a St Marys Chare, Hexham,
Northumberland NE46 1NQ
Tel: 01434 608558

Located at the heart of Hexham, **In the Chare** offers the very best in hospitality and home cooking. The cafe changed hands in August 2010 and is currently owned by Angela and Geoff, who have done a fantastic job, and really enjoy their new way of living.

The aroma of home cooking attracts plenty of passersby to this delightful cafe, which seats 20 diners inside and a further 32 in the courtyard area. It is Angela who is in charge of the kitchen here and she ensures that all dishes are freshly prepared and cooked on the premises. Children are very welcome at In the Chare and many families take advantage of a superb children's offer every day after school.

The plan for 2011 is to create a separate business in the courtyard called The Courtyard 2 Go, which will offer a fantastic take-away service that will run alongside the main business and create more inside seating. In the Chare is open Monday - Saturday between 9am and 4.30pm in winter months and 9am - 5pm in summer months.

62 LOUGHBROW HOUSE

Hexham, Northumberland NE46 1RS
Tel: 01434 603351
e-mail: patriciaclark351@btinternet.com
website: www.loughbrowhouse.co.uk

Dating back to the 18th century, **Loughbrow House** is an impressive guest house which overlooks Hexham to the North Tyne Valley. Standing 600ft above the River Tyne, the establishment offers some breathtaking views across the surrounding countryside and provides the ideal base for visitors wanting to explore Northumberland.

Owner Mrs Clark personally runs the charming Loughbrow House, which has five comfortable guest rooms available all year round. There is a twin and double room with en-suite facilities, a twin room with private bathroom and two single rooms with a shared bedroom. The reasonably tariff includes a full English breakfast.

If the guests of 4 or more prearrange to have diner at Loughbrow House they will be treated to a 3 course meal by candle light in the formal dinning room, for a very reasonable additional cost. All guest have the use of the Drawing Room, which is beautifully furnished with antique furniture.

The guest house is within easy reach of the Lake District, Durham and several National Trust properties. The surrounding area offers spectacular views and there are three golf courses nearby.

63 TRAVELLERS REST

Slaley, Hexham, Northumberland NE46 1TT
Tel: 01434 673231
e-mail: info@travellersrestslaley.com
website: www.travellersrestslaley.com

Dating back to the 16th century, the **Travellers Rest** offers quality accommodation and fine food in an isolated scenic location. Locals Ian and Darren have personally run this popular establishment for the past three years and have built up a fantastic reputation both as a B&B and a place to dine out.

The inn has provided a place to rest for weary travellers for more than 150 years and it continues to be just as well received today. There are three en-suite guest rooms available at the Travellers Rest, which have recently undergone a wonderful refurbishment. The rooms are modern and light and offer all the home comforts one could wish for when away from home. The rooms (one double, one twin, and a king size room with a four poster bed) are available all year around and the reasonable tariff includes a super breakfast that is available between 7.30am and 9am.

Fine food and drink can be enjoyed in the bar or cosy restaurant, where local produce is used at all times to ensure the best quality food is served. All dishes are cooked fresh to order and it is this attention to detail that attracts so many diners through the doors of the Travellers Rest. Food is available every lunch time and evening (except Sunday evening) and there are separate menus for each session. The dining area seats 22 people, but this place is so well-regarded for its food, that table reservations are required at all times.

Open all day every day, there are four real ales available with Black Sheep the regular and several rotating guest ales, which are all kept in tip top condition. The gardens here are very beautiful and there is an outstanding children's play area, which is always proves very popular with the youngsters who also have their own specialised menu.

64 THE RAT INN

Anick, nr Hexham, Northumberland NE46 4LN
Tel: 01434 602814
e-mail: info@theratinn.com
website: www.theratinn.com

Situated in the picturesque hamlet of Anick, **The Rat Inn** boasts spectacular views over Hexham and across the Tyne Valley. Experienced owners Karen and Phil took over the Rat in September 2007 and due to Phil's expertise in the kitchen the inn has been featured in the Michelin Eating out in Pubs 2009, as well as the Good Pub Guide 2008 and the Good Beer Guide 2008.

The dining area offers a hint at the locally-sourced, award-winning food that Phil creates. Dishes include braised local beef in Allendale ale and North Sea fish pie topped with creamy mash and Berwick Edge cheese. Drinks can be enjoyed in the welcoming bar or cosy lounge area, which have period fireplaces, wooden flooring and various pub paraphernalia decorating the walls.

The stone building was built in the 18th century but there has been an alehouse on the site for hundreds of years. No-one is quite sure as to the exact origin of the inn's curious name, the most popular theory is that the then ale-keeper passed information to the Crown during the Jacobite uprisings of 1715 and 1745 and thus became known as 'The Rat'.

66 THE SUN INN

Main Street, Acomb, Northumberland NE46 4PW
Tel: 01434 602934
e-mail: info@thesuninnacomb.co.uk
website: www.thesuninn-acomb.co.uk

Brian Dodd, a member of the British Institute of Innkeepers, and his wife Lorraine, put their experience to excellent use at **The Sun Inn**, where a cheerful, relaxed ambience and fine home cooking attract a loyal clientele from Acomb and the nearby towns and villages.

It's much more than a popular local, with a good choice of beers served in the cosy bar and a games room with pool and satellite TV for the big sporting events. It's also a great choice for a meal, with a menu of traditional British comfort food that keeps all the patrons content and well fed. Food is served 12md - 2pm and 6.30pm - 9pm from Wednesday to Sunday (except Sunday evenings).

The Sun is located in an area that's rich in history and scenic splendour, and for visitors touring this lovely part of Northumberland the Sun has comfortable, well-priced guest accommodation - two en-suite rooms and two with shared facilities. Nearby Hexham is a town with plenty to see and do, and Hadrian's Wall, the best known Roman monument in Britain, is very close by.

Acomb is situated just off the A6079 a couple of miles from Hexham.

65 THE BLUEBELL INN

17 Mount Pleasant, Stocksfield, Northumberland NE43 7LP
Tel: 01661 843146
website: www.bluebell-stocksfield.co.uk

The Bluebell Inn has plenty of character and charm, with beamed ceilings and open fires. This superb scenic village inn can be found just up from the main A695 Prudhoe to Stocksfield Road.

Personally run by Judith and Michael Kindleyside for the last two years, the pub serves delicious wholesome home cooked food, which uses locally sourced produce.

With professionally employed chefs taking charge of the kitchen, every dish that it serves is of a high standard. All dishes available are listed on the blackboard and are cooked fresh to order. Whether it is a three course meal you are after or a relaxed pub meal, a visit to The Bluebell Inn can be highly recommended.

Starters include soup of the day, deep fried Camembert and garlic prawns. All of the dishes are very reasonably priced and main meals listed on the relatively traditional menu include steak & ale pie, haddock & spring onion fish cakes, and lasagne. Daily desserts are listed on the blackboard and often prove too tempting for diners here. Closed on Monday, food is served Tuesday - Saturday between 12md and 3pm and 6.30pm - 9pm. On Sunday, when a succulent roast dinner is added to the menu, food is served between 12md and 3pm.

Food can be enjoyed in the cosy dining area or, on sunnier days, in one of the most spectacular beer gardens in the region. The hidden garden to the rear of the pub is beautiful and has colourful seasonal shrubs and flowers throughout most of the year. If not at the bar, it is here you will find many regulars and visitors to The Bluebell sipping on one of three-four rotating real ales.

This child-friendly pub welcomes people of all ages and is usually bustling with a steady stream of regulars and visitors to the area. There is a large off-road car park opposite the pub, so parking is rarely a problem.

67 THE HADRIAN HOTEL

Wall, nr Hexham, Northumberland NE46 4EE
Tel: 01434 681232
e-mail: david.lindsay13@btinternet.com
website: www.hadrianhotel.com

Nestled in the unspoilt territory of the ancient Hadrian's Wall, you will find **The Hadrian Hotel.** The country hotel in the Tyne Valley serves food all day in the main bar and in the restaurant area at lunch and dinner time.

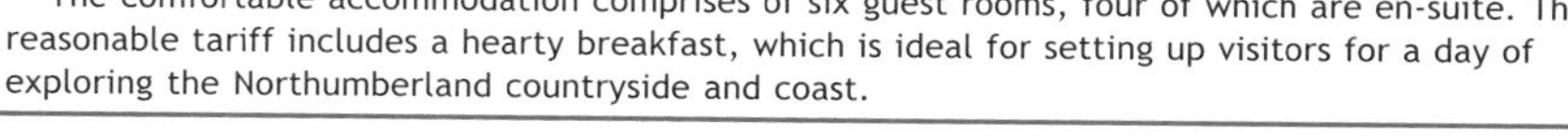

The comfortable accommodation comprises of six guest rooms, four of which are en-suite. The reasonable tariff includes a hearty breakfast, which is ideal for setting up visitors for a day of exploring the Northumberland countryside and coast.

68 HADRIAN'S WALL

Hexham, Northumberland NE46 4BQ
Tel: 01912 691600
Tel: 01434 322002 (English Heritage)
Tel: 01434 652220 (Hadrian's Wall Country)

Welcome to the unspoilt beauty of Hadrian's Wall Country, where the rugged countryside hides a wealth of activities and attractions.

The area preserves some of the most spectacular sections of Hadrian's Wall. Nearly 2,000 years ago this wall defined the northern frontier of Rome's mighty Empire. Today it is a World Heritage Site, with the surrounding countryside forming a stunning background and offering mile upon mile of exhilarating walks.

But there is much more to see than the Wall. To the north, the Northumberland National Park leads to the vast forest and lake at Kielder. Here, lakeside and forest trails provide a wealth of surprises and things to do. In the south of the area the hills and moors of the North Pennines shelter secluded dales and a rich heritage.

In the valleys between lie towns and villages, each with its own character and charm. Hexham is the centre and main market town for the district; its beautiful and historic face contrasts with its modern shopping, arts and leisure facilities. All around are villages: picturesque Corbridge on the banks of the Tyne, Bellingham and Allendale, quaint capitals of their respective valleys, Haltwhistle, gateway to Hadrian's Wall, and Blanchland, a hidden gem in its secluded Pennine Dale.

69 RED LION

Newbrough, Northumberland NE47 5AR
Tel: 01434 674226
website: www.redlionnewbrough.co.uk

Red Lion is an outstanding village inn, which enjoys a scenic location in the picturesque village of Newbrough. Andrew and Susan Smith have been in charge since May 2010 and through their hard work and experience this former coaching inn is once again becoming a destination venue for lovers of fine cuisine.

Dating back to the 12th century, the Red Lion, which is named after the Red Lion of Scotland, has been brought back into the 21st Century, whilst maintaining all the charm of a countryside bed & breakfast. The four comfortable guest bedrooms are all located upstairs and three have en-suite facilities, with a private bathroom for the fourth room.

Offering a wide selection of freshly made food with a twist, The Red Lion prides itself on providing very high quality, delicious food. The menu is seasonal and the produce is locally sourced with home grown vegetables. The food is absolutely mouth-watering with starters including homemade duck liver pate with tomato chutney with stottie cake, twice baked cheese soufflé with creamy cheese sauce, and king prawns with parsley and pine nut salsa and roast cherry tomato and lemon.

Grilled fillet of fresh mackerel horseradish crust with beetroot and ginger salad, and pot roast shank of lamb with redcurrant and mint jus on mash are among the main meal options. Andrew has been a professional chef for more than 20 years and as the head chef at a nearby exclusive country castle hotel you can be sure of the highest quality food and service here.

The tempting desserts such as sticky toffee pudding with butterscotch sauce and vanilla icecream, apple and sultana crumble and custard, and summer fruit pudding with mixed berry coulis are hard to resist, so be sure to leave room to sample one.

With its original wood and stone work, open log fires and comfortable chairs, the bar area is often busy with locals and visitors relaxing and enjoying one of the locally sourced ales, fine wines or other beverages available from the well-stocked bar.

If you are after some form of entertainment, the popular games room has darts and snooker, and there is a large beer garden to the rear of the pub with decking and an outside smoking area.

70 ANCHOR HOTEL

Haydon Bridge, Hexham, Northumberland NE47 6AB
Tel: 01434 688121
e-mail: theanchorhotelhaydonbridge@hotmail.co.uk

The quality **Anchor Hotel** enjoys a superb location next to the South River Tyne at Haydon Bridge, which is now by-passed by the main A69. The hotel has witnessed a real revival since current owners Steve and Lindsay took charge in October 2010.

With a lot of hard work in the short time they have been here the couple has really put this place back on the map and it is fast becoming a popular place to sleep, eat and drink. It offers visitors to Northumberland a wonderful mix of rural tranquillity and easy access to the cities of Newcastle and Carlisle. There is plenty to explore in the surrounding area including Hadrian's Wall and Northumberland National Park. Nearby activities such as tennis, golf and swimming can be enjoyed as well as walks or cycles through the rural landscape, which includes the John Martin Trail.

Steve has been a chef for many years and so only the finest quality food is served here. A good variety of dishes adorn the printed menu, which changes frequently depending on what produce is available. Food is served between 12md and 9pm everyday and as word spreads about this wonderful dining establishments it is becoming more and more popular.

Accommodation is available all year round in the form of nine guest bedrooms, which are all located upstairs. Eight of the rooms have en-suite facilities and the ninth has its own private facilities. The rooms vary in size and are all comfortable and well-presented. Guests are welcomed on a B&B or dinner and B&B rate and with off-road parking there should be no concerns about where to leave your vehicle overnight.

Open from 12md every day until late and in the summer months from 10am for morning coffee, there are always two rotating real ales available, with at least one of them guaranteed to be from a local micro brewery.

71 BOWES HOTEL

Bardon Mill, Hexham,
Northumberland NE47 7HU
Tel: 01434 344237 Mob: 07860213159
e-mail: info@theboweshotel.com
website: www.theboweshotel.com

Formerly an old coaching inn, when the main Carlisle-Newcastle road ran in front of it, **Bowes Hotel** is a fine establishment found at the heart of Hadrian Wall country. Tommy Yeats is the man in charge here and has been since July 2009. He offers a professional and friendly service and personally runs the hotel himself to ensure the highest of standards.

Tommy offers superb accommodation and delicious food Tuesday - Sunday lunchtimes between 12md and 3pm and Wednesday - Saturday 6pm - 9pm. There are four quality en-suite rooms available, all of which are located upstairs. There are three double rooms and one family room and guests are welcomed on a bed & breakfast or room only basis. The breakfasts, however, can be highly recommended so it might be worth your while to book B&B as many returning guests do.

Yates Real Ale is available all year round as well as a rotating guest ale in the summer months. Bowes Hotel is open from 3pm on Mondays and Tuesday - Sunday from 12md - close.

72 VINDOLANDA AND ROMAN ARMY MUSEUM

The Vindolanda Trust, Chesterholme Museum, Bardon Mill,
Hexham, Northumberland NE47 7JN
Vindolanda Tel: 01434 344277 Roman Army Museum Tel: 016977 47485
e-mail: info@vindolanda.com website: www.vindolanda.com

Vindolanda was once a Roman frontier military and civilian site. Substantial remains are visible and on display are rare and fascinating objects from the past, including Roman boots and shoes, jewellery, tools, locks and textiles. Special photographs of rare ink on wood letters, written nearly 2000 years ago, are also on show. The Open Air Museum has full sized replicas of a Roman Temple, a Roman shop, a Roman house, as well as a Northumbrian croft, all set in relaxing gardens.

The **Roman Army Museum** is located next to the superb Walltown Crags section of Hadrian's Wall and gives a fascinating insight into life as a Roman soldier, garrisoned along the forts and milecastles of the Wall. Here you can find out about the weapons, uniforms, pay, training and off duty activities. The Museum has reconstructions, life sized figures, Roman objects, films and much more.

Both sites are open daily form 10am and have good facilities. Both have coffee shops serving light snacks and a gift shop selling a range of gifts and souvenirs. Both have toilets, picnic sites, free parking and disabled access.

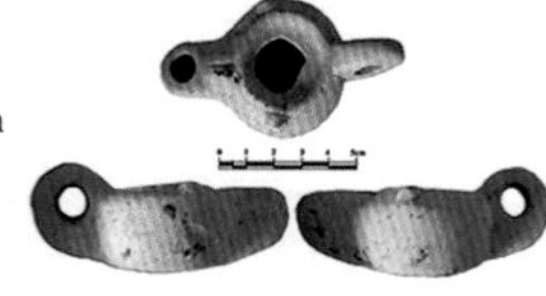

73 THE GOLDEN LION

The Market Place, Allendale, Hexham,
Northumberland NE46 9BD
Tel: 01434 683225

A fine old traditional hostelry, **The Golden Lion** has been dispensing hospitality since 1660. The interior is full of charm and character, especially when the open fires are blazing away. Owner Les Elliott took charge here in 2009 and serves no fewer than five real ales on tap including Black Sheep and locally brewed Wylam Gold Tankord and Timothy Taylors Landlord.

The pub is well-known for its appetising home-cooked food with old favourites such as steak & ale pie popular with regulars who come here to enjoy meals, which have been created using the finest local produce. Food is available everyday from 12md - 3pm and the upstairs restaurant, which seats 40 diners, is open Thursday, Friday and Saturday evenings between 6pm and 9pm. Such is the popularity of this place, especially in the summer months, it is advisable to book to avoid disappointment. Themed evenings on the last Friday of each month are also very popular and require reservations.

The Golden Lion is very much the social centre of Allendale. It has its own pool teams and on the last Wednesday of every month hosts traditional music/jamming from 8.30pm, with live entertainment once a month on a Saturday. Ring for details.

74 ALLENDALE TEA ROOMS AND BED & BREAKFAST

Market Place, Allendale, Hexham,
Northumberland NE47 9BD
Tel: 01434 683575
e-mail: allendaletearooms@hotmail.co.uk
website: www.allendaletearooms.co.uk

The aroma of home cooking welcomes visitors to the **Allendale Tea Rooms and Bed & Breakfast**, which has been given a real lease of life by new owners Graeme and Wendy Pearson. The couple took charge here in August 2010 and since then have transformed the premises, which enjoys a scenic location on the edge of the Northumberland and Cumbrian borders.

The tea rooms offer a wonderful and relaxing area to sit and enjoy refreshments or a light lunch. Homemade cakes and soups are often irresistible to diners and once you pay a visit here you will understand why. Local produce is used wherever possible and if the printed menu or specials board doesn't offer something you will fancy Graeme and Wendy are more than happy to make what you would like providing they have the ingredients. It is this friendly and accommodating nature that has made this place a real hit with locals and visitors.

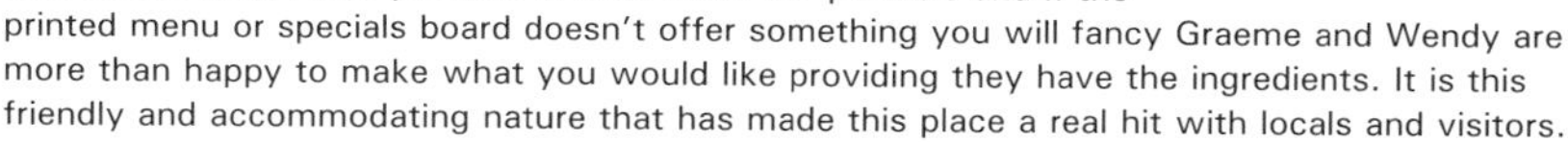

The Grade II listed building stands overlooking Market Square and is home to two comfortable en-suite guest rooms, which are available on a B&B basis. There is a king-size room and a twin room and the reasonable tariff includes a hearty and delicious breakfast.

75 THE MANOR HOUSE INN

Main Street, Haltwhistle, Northumberland NE49 0BS
Tel: 01434 322588 Fax: 01434 320975
e-mail: manorhouseinn@orangehome.co.uk
website: www.themanorhousehaltwhistle.com

Offering a fantastic base from which to explore the Northumberland countryside and coast, **The Manor House Inn** serves real ale and delicious meals daily. The inn, which recently changed its name from The Manor House Hotel, has been family run by Raymond and Kathleen Nicholson and their son Earl for the past 11 years.

The inn has six en-suite guest rooms available all year round, all of which are located on the first or second floor. Double and twin rooms are available and the reasonable tariff includes a hearty breakfast that can be enjoyed between 8am and 9.30am.

The Manor House Inn is located in what is geographically known as 'the centre of Britain' and is close to the historical Hadrian's Wall. The inn attracts plenty of overnight guests, many who are eager to join locals and other visitors in the restaurant and bar area.

The restaurant seats 36 and is away from the public bar and dining area if an enjoyable quiet evening meal is what you are after; the dining area itself seats a further 38. Both areas serve a variety of tasty home cooked food and real ales as well as other beverages from the well-stocked bar.

76 THE BLACK BULL

Main Street, Wark, Northumberland NE48 3LG
Tel: 01434 230239
e-mail: granticus2@msm.com
website: www.blackbullwark.co.uk

Located in the picturesque village of Wark, **The Black Bull** is a destination property for lovers of homemade food and well-kept ales. Grant and Mel Charlton have personally run this wonderful inn since June 2010 and their hard work is definitely paying off.

The inn now attracts plenty of people through its doors, many who come here to enjoy the fine pub food on offer. Local produce is used wherever possible in the reasonably priced traditional dishes that make up this menu such as steak & ale pie and fish & chips. Diners here often welcome the option to sample one of the two real ales from the well-stocked bar, which is open all day every day.

Accommodation is available at The Black Bull all year round in the form of seven en-suite guest bedrooms. The rooms, which are all located upstairs, vary in size but are all extremely comfortable, providing the ideal place for an overnight stop if you are visiting the area. The affordable tariff includes a hearty breakfast that is guaranteed to set you up for a day of relaxation or exploring the beautiful countryside Northumberland has to offer.

77 THE GUN INN

Ridsdale, Northumberland NE48 2TF
Tel: 01434 270223
e-mail: stayatguninn@yahoo.co.uk
website: www.guninn.co.uk

Dating back to 1840, this isolated village inn offers tourists and locals the very best in hospitality and facilities. **The Gun Inn** offers the weary traveller rest, food and ale and is open all day every day in the summer months, all day Saturday and Sunday in winter and from 4pm Monday - Friday.

Liz and Michael are in charge here and offer a very warm welcome to all who pass through its doors. The picturesque inn is surrounded by countryside and is very popular with walkers and cyclists.

Food is available at all times and Liz cooks all of the meals fresh to order, using local produce. The restaurant area boasts spectacular panoramic views and it is here where you can enjoy a meal from the printed menu, specials board or one of Liz' scrumptious traditional Sunday roast dinners.

The Gun Inn has three guest bedrooms available all year round. All of them are located upstairs and two have en-suite facilities, while the third has its own private bathroom.

78 THE BAY HORSE INN

West Woodburn, Northumberland NE48 2RX
Tel: 01434 270218 Fax: 01434 270274
e-mail: enquiry@bayhorseinn.org
website: www.bayhorseinn.org

The Bay Horse Inn is a late-18th century mellow sandstone hostelry standing in the heart of the Cheviot Hills, by a stone bridge on the main A68 Darlington-Edinburgh road. Hilda Wright, who was first associated with the inn more than 20 years ago, is an admirable host along with her husband Johnny and their immaculate inn is a delightful place to pause for a drink, relax over a leisurely meal or enjoy a break in a picturesque setting.

There is a strong focus on home-cooked food at The Bay Horse Inn, with prime local produce very much a feature of the extensive and varied menus. Among the perennial favourites are beer-battered haddock, lasagne, chilli con carne, mince with dumplings, lamb chops, chicken tikka masala and specials featuring seafood caught off the nearby Northumberland coast.

To accompany the food there's a good choice of real ales, beers, lagers, wines and soft drinks. Food is served throughout the day and it is definitely advisable to book for Sunday lunch, when they do a hog roast and carvery. Children have their own menu, or small portions are available from the main menu.

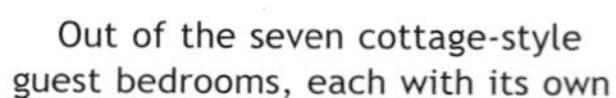

Out of the seven cottage-style guest bedrooms, each with its own individual character, all have en suite facilities. They provide an ideal base for tourists, cyclists and walkers - the Pennine Way passes close by. The inn can arrange a number of outdoor activities, or guests can just relax and unwind - the gardens running down to the river have a grassed play area and tables and chairs for enjoying sunny days. Guests come here on a bed & breakfast basis and all major credit cards are taken.

The Bay Horse Inn, which hosts occasional live music nights and a weekly Thursday quiz, can also cater for barbecues, parties, weddings and other special occasions. Hilda and her team can cater for any number of people and serves a fantastic hog roast for private parties. There are absolutely delicious and well worth checking out as they offer outside catering and bars too.

Disabled access is not a problem, although all of the guest bedrooms are located upstairs.

79 THE CHEVIOT HOTEL

Bellingham, Northumberland NE48 2AU
Tel: 01434 220696
e-mail: enquiry@thecheviothotel.co.uk
website: www.thecheviothotel.co.uk

Standing in the picturesque village of Bellingham at the heart of the Northumberland National Park, **The Cheviot Hotel** is fast-growing in popularity. David and his wife Anne took over here in November 2010 and offer visitors to the area fine accommodation and tasty food made with locally-sourced produce.

Thai chicken patties served on a bed of egg noodles, and fruit salad with a Kirsch and blackcurrant sorbet are among the starters listed on the extensive menu. All of the dishes on the menu are reasonably priced and mains include a good selection of dishes comprising of traditional favourites such as steak & ale pie, beer battered fish & chips, and homemade chilli with rice. Northumbrian lamb casserole, Sunday roast dinner, and locally reared lamb chops with a rich gravy are also very popular. All main meals are served with chips or potatoes, and salad or vegetables unless stated otherwise.

There is always a daily selection of homemade sweets on offer, all at a very affordable £4, so be sure to leave room for dessert. Food is available daily from 12md-2pm and 6pm-10pm and in the height of season is served from 11am 'til 10pm.

The Cheviot Hotel has recently undergone a fairly major refurbishment and is already enticing new faces through its doors. Six comfortable guest bedrooms are available all year round at this lovely hotel nestled deep in the North Tyne Valley. They offer visitors to the area the ideal base to explore the Northumbrian countryside and heritage sites. The rooms, which vary in size, are all en-suite and are located upstairs.
Open every day from 10am 'til late, real ale is always available, with a choice depending on the time of year.

Whether you want to spend time relaxing in the countryside or take advantage of the activities the surrounding area has to offer, The Cheviot Hotel is waiting to welcome you.

80 KIELDER WATER BIRDS OF PREY CENTRE

Leaplish Waterside Park, Kielder, Northumberland NE48 1AX
Tel: 01434 250500
website: www.discoverit.co.uk/falconry

The **Birds of Prey Centre** is located within the magnificent forest lakeside surroundings of Kielder Water at Leaplish Waterside Park. The centre contains one of the largest and most fascinating collections of Birds of prey in the north of England.

At the birds of Prey Centre you will discover a vast variety of species and find out about their essential role within the ecology of the natural world.

Experience the thrills and excitement of handling some of these beautiful and extraordinary birds. Learn about the valuable work of the Keilder Water Bird of Prey Centre's Captive Breeding Programme, which has been established to further the awareness of conservation, propagation and rehabilitation of Birds of Prey.

Falconry is one of the oldest and most aristocratic sports and form many centuries has been regarded as the sport of Kings with the falcon as a symbol of high birth and society. Hunting with birds of prey or raptors was practiced in China as long ago as 2000 B.C. Later, falconry developed as a sport practiced by members of Royal households, with each rank of nobility permitted to use only certain species of birds.

Today, falconry is widely pursued in most European countries and in the United States, although the Arabian peninsula remains the area where the sport is held in highest regard.

As well as being able to get close to birds of prey there are daily demonstrations (weather permitting). This is a fantastic opportunity to see birds of prey in actions. Watch a Peregrine Falcon stoop down from the skies at over 100 mph, see the grace and speed of a Russian eagle.

The Birds of Prey Centre offers our visitors an opportunity to share in a direct 'hands on' experience during which they will meet all the northern region's indigenous Owls as well as birds of prey from around the world - all within a professionally supervised environment.

81 THE ANGLERS ARMS

Kielder, Hexham, Northumberland NE48 1ER
Tel: 01434 250072
e-mail: anglers123@hotmail.co.uk
website: www.anglers-arms.com

New hosts Christine and Dave offer a warm welcome to **The Anglers Arms,** a traditional pub and restaurant that has gone from strength to strength and grown in popularity since this friendly couple took ownership. Situated within a tranquil village, away from the hustle and bustle, the cosy atmosphere and comfortable furnishings inside make this the perfect place to relax and re-energise before once more embarking on your exploration of the surrounding natural beauty of this area.

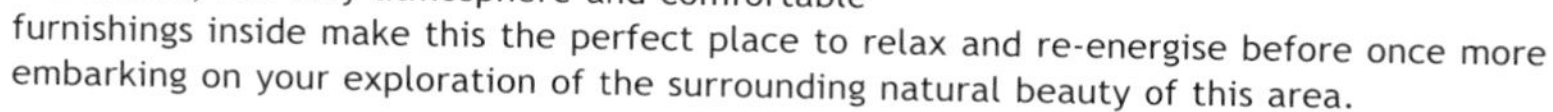

At the bar there is a wide variety of fine wines and real ales which are rotated and often feature locally brewed cask ales from micro breweries. In the restaurant all appetites are catered for and you will find many classic British pub favourites feature on the printed menu and the specials board. All dishes are freshly cooked and prepared using locally sourced and seasonal ingredients wherever possible. The temping dishes include the popular Kielder Cobbler, tender pieces of lakeland steak cooked with mushrooms in a brown ale gravy and served with chips and seasonal vegetables. There is also home cooked Wiltshire ham served alongside organic egg, chips and peas or, to make your taste buds tingle, sample the tasty Chinese style chicken curry served with rice or chips or both and a poppadom.

As its name suggests, The Anglers Arms is perfectly placed for those keen on fishing. This is because it is situated in a scenic location on the edge of Kielder Water which has more than 26 miles of shoreline. Plump salmon also thrive in the nearby rivers of the border country. This is also a great part of the country to visit if you enjoy walking, bike riding or simply soaking up the spectacular scenery.

Well behaved dogs and children are welcome and there is good disabled access. During the summer food is served daily from 12pm to 9pm. In the winter food is served from 12pm to 4pm from Tuesday to Friday and from 12pm to 9pm at weekends. Faultless customer service is of utmost importance to Christine, Dave and their efficient team of staff and this means that customers from near and far return here time and time again.

82 THE COACH HOUSE TEA ROOM

Elsdon, Northumberland NE19 1AA
Tel: 01830 520061
e-mail: info@thecoachhouseelsdon.co.uk
website: www.thecoachhouseelsdon.co.uk

Overlooking one of the largest village greens in England, **The Coach House Tea Room** is situated in the historic and picturesque village of Elsdon in the heart of Northumberland National Park. This wonderful tea room was opened in July 2009 by Rita and Alan Colby who present each and every visitor with a warm and friendly welcome.

Serving a range of traditional refreshments including Twinings teas, freshly brewed Taylor's coffees, soft drinks and Doddington's ice cream, there is also as a delicious selection of home-made soups, sandwiches, scrumptious cakes and melt in your mouth scones. Where possible, ingredients are sourced locally and seasonal produce is used. Customers can relax on squishy sofas or sit and enjoy their food and drink at a table inside or outside.

As well as refreshments there is a range of quirky and classic gifts on sale and a small gallery featuring the work of local artists. Alan and Rita also host a number of ad-hoc events throughout the year, including Artist of the Month, Whisky/Chocolate tasting, and Knit2Together.

The Coach House Tea Room is open from 11am to 4:30pm every day except Mondays and Fridays. Please book for parties over 6 people.

83 NEWCASTLE HOUSE HOTEL

Front Street, Rothbury,
Northumberland NE65 7UT
Tel: 01669 620334
e-mail: rothburynewcastlehouse@gmail.com

Situated at the heart of the well-known town of Rothbury, the **Newcastle House Hotel** stands on the banks of the River Coquet. Surrounded by thousands of acres of countryside, this quality premise is owned and personally run by business partners Chris Poulter and Sarah Bertram. Since their arrival, the establishment has gone from strength to strength because of their fine hospitality and the food they serve.

Accommodation is available all year round in the form of eight comfortable upstairs rooms, which vary in size. Four of the rooms have en-suite facilities and the reasonable tariff includes a hearty breakfast. The hotel is the ideal resting spot for walkers especially because of its rural and scenic location.

The dining area seats 30 people and guests are more than welcome to dine in the lounge or public bar areas. Chris is in charge of the kitchen and serves a good selection of quality dishes created using only the freshest local ingredients. Favourites include pan-fried chicken breast wrapped in bacon with a mushroom sauce, and pie of the day.

The Newcastle House Hotel is open all day every day and always has two real ales to enjoy, with Greene King IPA the regular and a rotating guest ale.

84 VALE CAFE

Coquetdale House, High Street, Rothbury, Northumberland NE65 7TE
Tel: 01669 620461

Sisters Faith and Anne have been running the very successful **Vale Cafe** for almost twenty years. Along with their loyal team of staff, they offer an excellent service and the cafe is adored by locals and visitors alike. This popular cafe is a delightful place to enjoy a fantastic range of quality home cooked food and delicious baked goods and it is certainly not to be missed.

The cafe can be found on the main High Street in the heart of the attractive and picturesque town of Rothbury, which was once the setting of an important livestock market. The town is a perfect base for exploring the valley of the River Coquet and it is also very close to Rothbury forest.

First impressions count here and from the street Vale Cafe has a very traditional appearance with its blue and white striped awning and traditional cafe curtains hung from the centre of the window. Inside the atmosphere doesn't disappoint, it is friendly and welcoming with classic wooden booths providing privacy for diners whilst adding to the olde-worlde ambience.

Once inside the smell of home baking is overwhelmingly tempting and you will soon realise why when you spot the large glass counter displaying a delicious selection of home made cakes and other sweet treats. There is also a selection of savouries to choose from, including home made quiches, pies and pastries. The specials board displays a great selection of freshly cooked dishes on offer to suit all appetites. The very reasonably priced All Day Breakfast is hugely popular among visitors, old and new. There is a selection of burgers, sandwiches, toasties, paninis, and jacket potatoes with various tasty fillings alongside a home made soup of the day and classic favourites including egg and chips and pie and chips. Local produce is used where possible and all of the food served and displayed here is cooked and baked freshly on the premises. At the counter you can also order from a good selection of hot and cold beverages.

Open 7 days a week, the cafe seats approximately 35 people and there is good disabled access. The opening hours are usually between 10am and 4pm. Children are welcome and only cash payments are accepted. This cafe is a great place to take a break from shopping and exploring the town, or to relax and unwind after a bracing walk in the beautiful surrounding countryside.

85 EMBLETON HALL

Longframlington, Morpeth, Northumberland NE65 8DT
Tel: 01665 570249 / 570206 Fax: 01665 570056
e-mail: embletonhall@btinternet.com
website: www.embletonhallmorpeth.co.uk

Embleton Hall is one of the most renowned hotels in Northumberland and stands impressively in five acres of its own grounds. The country house hotel is one of the grandest in the county and is well-regarded with locals and visitors for its luxury accommodation and top of the range cuisine.

Owners Trevor and Judy Thorne have personally run this spectacular establishment for the past 25 years and have loyal cliental who return year on year. There are 13 individually styled en-suite guest rooms, including three on the ground floor, of which one is suitable for disabled guests.

Dating back to the 18th century, Embleton Hall offers the ideal base for visitors to explore the surrounding area. The house was built in 1730 by Thomas Embleton and purchased by the Fenwick family in 1780. Since then it has been extended in size and now has a large Victorian south wing.

The restaurant offers some of the finest hotel cuisine in Northumberland, which is available daily between 12md-2pm and 7pm-9.30pm. It is essential for non-residents to book due to its popularity. Diners can choose from a variety of delicious meals from the excellent table d'hote menu as well as a wide selection of bar snacks and lighter meals.

The landscaped gardens here are absolutely stunning and guests often spend time walking around them and the surrounding woodland. The walled gardens are well kept and produce much fruit and vegetables in season. A grass tennis court is available for guests to use and the surrounding area offers plenty of other activities for visitors to partake in.

Trevor and Judy are friendly hosts and are more than happy to help guests plan their stay here. There are an abundance of places to visit nearby including the ancient market town of Morpeth and more than six miles of unspoilt beaches.

Whether you are choosing Embleton Hall as a holiday destination, short break, business function or to enjoy the most memorable of wedding venues, you are assured of exceptional service, outstanding scenery, modern facilities blended with old world charm and service that is second to none.

Embleton Hall can be found in Longframlington, which is on the main A697 road from Morpeth to Coldstream, just 30 minutes from Newcastle and one and a half hours from Edinburgh by car.

86 THE ANCHOR INN

2 Cheviot Street, Wooler, Northumberland NE71 6LN
Tel: 01668 281412
e-mail: mcvicker35@gmail.com
website: www.anchorinn-wooler.co.uk

Wooler is a small town set in great walking country at the northern end of the Cheviots. One of the most pleasant and popular meeting places in the town is **The Anchor Inn**, which has been personally run by Tony and Abby since December 2010.

Open from 6.30pm on Mondays and all day throughout the rest of the week, the inn is well-regarded in the area. In recent years the whole place has been smartly refurbished, from the bar/lounge to the dining room, the pool room, the terrace and the beer garden.

There are two rotating real ales served in the bars and these are among the most popular drinks with the regulars that frequent here. The Anchor Inn is always bustling with people and attracts a lot of locals, walkers, cyclists, bikers, motorists and holidaymakers.

If you are visiting Northumberland The Anchor's three well-equipped en suite guest bedrooms (one twin, one double and one family room) provide an ideal base for discovering the scenic and historic delights of the countryside, coast and Border country. The accommodation is available all year round and children are welcome. The tariff includes a hearty breakfast and once you have tasted the food here you are sure to be back of a lunch time or evening to sample one of the many traditional dishes listed on the extensive menu.

With generous helpings of value-for-money food, this place is always busy with people wanting to dine. Whether it is a light snack, sandwich or a pub classic you are after, The Anchor is bound to have something to satisfy your requirements. On Sundays a two-course lunch is available, which includes a delicious roast dinner. They are very popular with diners and so it might be an idea to book in advance to ensure you get yourself a table.

Food is available from 12md - 2pm Tuesday to Sunday, and evening meals are served 6.30pm - 9pm Monday to Saturday. There are no evening meals on Sunday.

87 BREEZE

29 High Street, Wooler,
Northumberland NE71 6BU
Tel: 01668 283333
e-mail: info@breezewooler.com
website: www.breezewooler.com

Situated in the delightful town of Wooler at the heart of walking country, **Breeze** offers locals and visitors fine homemade food, beverages and an array of arts, crafts and gifts. Owned by Pauline Aitchison and her mum Jenny for the past three and a half years, this place is well-known in the area for all of the right reasons.

The duo created this business from scratch and tastefully decorated and furnished the building themselves. The child-friendly cafe has an individual twist in that it doubles as an independent shop selling paintings, textiles, ceramic, glass, sculptures, jewellery and gifts. The shop displays original and limited edition pieces and exhibits work by local artists.

Pauline and Jenny both cook and their homemade meals are absolutely delicious. The printed menu lists a tasty selection of baguettes, platters, baked potatoes and home-baked cakes and scones. Each day there is also a homemade soup, pate, and a special hot meal of the day.

During the winter months Breeze is open from 10am until 4.30pm and in the summer months between 10am-5pm (4pm on Saturdays). Closed on Sundays.

88 THE BLACK BULL HOTEL

2 High Street, Wooler,
Northumberland NE71 6BY
Tel: 01668 281309
e-mail: theblackbullhotel@hotmail.com
website: www.theblackbullhotel.co.uk

Popular with walkers, golfers and fishermen who visit the area, **The Black Bull Hotel** is a two star hotel. Dating back to the 17th century, this former coaching inn now offers everything you would expect from a well-regarded modern inn.

Owned by Christine Clow since September 2008, The Black Bull Hotel is located at the heart of Wooler and offers comfortable all-year-round accommodation, food and locally brewed ales. It provides an ideal base for visitors to Northumberland who want to explore the picturesque surroundings and nearby towns of Berwick upon Tweed and Alnwick.

The inn has 13 rooms, all with en-suite facilities, and the reasonable tariff includes a full English breakfast. Ten of the rooms are available within the main building and a further three are located in the annex, one of which is a ground floor room. Guests can enjoy the hotel's very own gym and facilities, ideal for those wanting a relaxing break away in Northumberland. Room prices are from £50 based on two people sharing.

The hotel is fully licensed and good homemade food is served every evening and lunch time in the restaurant or bar areas. Two real ales, brewed locally, are available from the well-stocked bar and food is served Monday - Sunday between 12md and 2.30pm and Monday - Saturday between 7pm and 8.30pm. Sunday lunches are always very popular and so diners need to book at all times in the summer period.

The onsite separate Milan Restaurant serves the very best in Italian and contemporary cuisine and caters for all occasions from romantic dinners to family get-togethers. The menu focuses on freshly prepared classic and modern Italian dishes with plenty of pizza, pasta, seafood and meats to enjoy. Booking is essential.

The Black Bull Hotel is located in one of the most spectacular parts of North Northumberland and there is plenty of countryside and coastline to explore. Overnight guests tend to comprise of businessmen and women and visitors to the area.

89 THE RED LION INN

Milfield, Northumberland NE71 6JD
Tel: 01668 216224
e-mail: redlioninn@fsmail.net
website: www.redlionmilfield.co.uk

The Red Lion Inn is a classic windstone building dating from the middle of the 18th century. Once providing rest and refreshment for sheep-drovers, and later a stop for passengers and horses on the London-Edinburgh coaching run, it is now a cosy, welcoming inn with outstanding hosts in Iain and Clare Burn. They extend a traditional welcome and unbeatable hospitality to all who pass through the door, from locals to walkers, cyclists, anglers (there are several good fishing rivers nearby) and gliders.

The inn's three en suite bedrooms (a double, a triple and a family room) provide an ideal base for pausing on a journey to Scotland or for exploring the rich history and beautiful scenery of the region. The Northumberland National Park is just down the road; the coast and Holy Island are an easy drive away and other attractions in the vicinity include the Battlefield of Flodden and the estate villages of Ford and Etal.

The bar is a great place for enjoying a glass or two of real ale (Scottish & Newcastle brews and regularly changing guest ales) with great conversation. Iain prides himself on the quality and value for money his menu provides. He uses fresh seasonal ingredients from the region whenever possible for his wholesome dishes, which include daily fish specials and a signature dish of honey-roast belly pork with bubble & squeak mash and crispy bacon. Starters and lite bites also feature on the extensive menu with choices such as wild mushroom bruschetta with poached egg, poached salmon fishcakes served with caper mayonnaise, and bacon, black pudding & poached egg salad. After such a delicious meal, it will be hard to resist the list of tempting desserts, so make sure you leave room. Warm baked almond tart with vanilla ice-cream, Bramley apple crumble with custard and lemon cheesecake with lemon meringue ice-cream are among the favourites.

The village of Milfield, which grew around the inn, lies on the A697 between Wooler and Cornhill-on-Tweed.

90 THE BLACK BULL

Etal Village, Cornhill-on-Tweed,
Northumberland TD12 4TL
Tel: 01890 820200
e-mail: karenwtchyp@aol.com

As pretty as a picture, **The Black Bull** is a whitewashed, thatch-roofed village inn with a history going back eight centuries. This charming exterior, adorned by hanging baskets in spring and summer, is matched by the interior with its beams, thick walls and a unique decorative feature of hundreds of witch dolls from all round the world.

Over the past seven years resident owner Karen Hunter has built up a strong and loyal local following with her warm welcome and genuine hospitality. Her chef Stephen Percival enjoys an ever-widening reputation with his honest, generous cooking based on prime Northumberland produce (his pies are definitely not to be missed). As well as being a great place for a drink and a meal, the Black Bull is also the social hub of the local community, with regular events throughout the year. The child-friendly pub is closed on Tuesdays.

In the same ownership as the Black Bull is The Witchery, down the A697 in the village of Thropton, near Rothbury, close to the River Coquet on the edge of the Northumberland National Park. This mid-terrace cottage for four provides an idyllic self-catering base for exploring the unspoilt countryside and discovering the wealth of local history.

91 THE COLLINGWOOD ARMS HOTEL

Main Street, Cornhill-on-Tweed,
Northumberland TD12 4UH
Tel: 01890 882424
e-mail: enquiries@collingwoodarms.com
website: www.collingwoodarms.com

The Collingwood Arms Hotel has long been a predominant feature of the delightful village of Cornhill-on-Tweed. For centuries visitors to the Borders have often frequented this establishment, which is a former coaching inn.

The hotel underwent a major transformation in 2007, which really brought it up to modern standards. Award-winning architects collaborated with historians and local craftsmen to refurbish and re-instate period details; restoring this Grade II Listed, Georgian building to its glorious best.

There are 15 bedrooms awaiting guests to the hotel, which take their names from the 15 ships in Collingwood's division at the Battle of Trafalgar. The Collingwood Arms takes its name from the local merchant family which owned it up until 1955. It has strong ties with Northumberland's 19th Century naval hero, Vice Admiral Cuthbert Collingwood.

The Collingwood Arms Hotel offers the ideal base for visitors wanting to explore the unrivalled landscapes of north Northumberland and the Scottish Borders. The hotel has its own dog kennels, so your pooch need not miss out.

92 OLD RED BULL INN

Dark Lane, Morpeth, Northumberland NE61 1ST
Tel: 01670 513306

The Old Red Bull Inn is a well-known pub in Northumberland and can be found a short walk away from the centre of Morpeth. It has been family-run and owned since 1989 by the Henderson family, with Dean and Lindsey now at the helm. The premise, which dates back to 1907, is well-regarded in the area for its well-kept ales, friendly atmosphere and tasty toasted sandwiches. There are three rotating real ales to enjoy, all from local breweries, and they are popular with locals and visitors. Children are welcome here until 6pm.

93 SOUR GRAPES WINE BAR

86 Newgate Street, Morpeth,
Northumberland NE61 1BU
Tel: 01670 519069
e-mail: stewarttodd@todd21.freeserve.co.uk

Sour Grapes Wine Bar has been owned by Susan and Stewart for some time now and it is an absolutely fantastic place to dine out, enjoy a relaxing drink, or catch up with friends.

All meals are cooked fresh to order by Susan and it is highly recommended that if you are planning on dining here to book ahead to avoid disappointment. This place is extremely popular especially on a Tuesday when a special steak night is held. An evening spent at Sour Grapes is a great way to socialise as there is a special nibbles menu, ideal for sharing with friends. Options include chilli olives with cheese straws, duck spring rolls with ginger sauce, and prawns in hot and spicy batter with dipping sauce. If it is a three-course meal you are after however, you will not be disappointed. Grilled goats cheese with sweet tomato chutney is among the choice from the concise, but mouth-watering menu. Mains include rib-eye steak with vine tomato and potato wedges, and for dessert why not try sticky toffee pudding with lashings of toffee sauce.

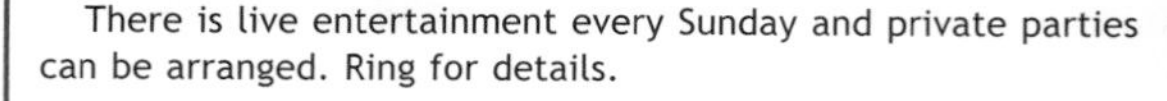

There is live entertainment every Sunday and private parties can be arranged. Ring for details.

94 PEPPERPOT CAFE-BISTRO

5 Oldgate, Morpeth, Northumberland NE61 1PY
Tel: 01670 514666
website: www.pepper-pots.co.uk

Open since December 2010, **PepperPot Cafe-Bistro** has already become a destination venue for lovers of fine food and hospitality. Experienced chef Brian Scott secured ownership of the building at the end of November 2010 and since then has totally renovated it, creating PepperPot Cafe-Bistro.

The delightful establishment can be found at the heart of the historic town of Morpeth by the clock tower. It offers a cosy, warm and friendly place to enjoy tea (it is the only place in Morpeth to serve teapigs real tea) and coffee as well as home baking and fresh locally sourced food cooked in a modern Mediterranean style.

Having been in the catering industry for 20 years, this is the first time that Brian has owned his own business and the first signs are very positive. PepperPot is Morpeth's only bistro with Bring Your Own wine or beer to consume with a meal and is open Monday - Saturday 9.00am - 7pm and seats around 32 diners. The menu offers a fine selection of pizzas and pasta dishes, which are only £4.75 as an early evening offer. Other meals include garlic and rosemary tiger prawns, honey and black pepper duck, and warm Northumberland goats cheese.

The child-friendly cafe/bistro is available for private hire during the evenings and on Sundays.

95 LANSDOWN HOUSE

90 Newgate Street, Morpeth, Northumberland NE61 1BU
Tel: 01670 511129 Mob: 07919314812
website: www.lansdownhouse.co.uk

Dating back to the 18th century, this superb bed & breakfast can be found at the heart of the market town of Morpeth. **Lansdown House** has been owned by Lesley Mamamtel for six years and she has been running her property as a guest house for the last three years.

There are four en-suite guest bedrooms available in a separate building attached to the main house. Three of the rooms are doubles, with the fourth a twin room. They are all clean, fresh and modern and offer the ideal place to rest overnight if you are visiting Morpeth or the surrounding area. Guests are made to feel very welcome and they stay on a bed & breakfast basis.

Lesley's cooked breakfasts are absolutely delicious. She uses local produce and freshly laid eggs from her own hens to ensure the best quality meals are served.

On sunnier days guests can enjoy sitting outside and a refreshing drink sat in the patio area, which overlooks the beautiful enclosed garden.

The bed and breakfast is within easy walking distance of several pubs and a selection of restaurants including Thai, Chinese, Indian and Italian. It is also close to idyllic beaches and historical castles.

96 THE JOINERS ARMS

7 Wansbeck Street, Morpeth,
Northumberland NE61 1XZ
Tel: 01670 513540

Located next to the River Wansbeck, **The Joiners Arms** is a superb free house, which has been personally run by George Hall for the past 23 years. As the longest standing licensee in Morpeth, George is well known in the area and he attracts a lot of locals and visitors through the pub's doors.

Although no food is served at The Joiners, there is a selection of up to seven real ales to be enjoyed, with Black Sheep and Deuchas IPA the regulars. The other five real ales rotate, with a mixture of local and national breweries.

Above the bar there is an impressive encased display of stuffed animals, which include a Russian Eagle, wild cat and even the pet dog and puppy of a past landlord. The display is frequently a conversation starter between locals and visitors in this child friendly pub.

Open all day every day The Joiners can be found on Wansbeck Street, which is now a minor thoroughfare, but once a section of the Great North Road from London to Edinburgh.

Tuesday evenings are always popular because that is when the weekly quiz is held from 8.30pm.

97 BEETROOT GRILL AND CAFE

42 Bridge Street, Morpeth, Northumberland NE61 1NL
Tel: 01670 511846
e-mail: info@beetrootgrillandcafe.com
website: www.beetrootgrillandcafe.com

Situated at the heart of Morpeth, **Beetroot Grill and Cafe** is a modern business created from scratch in October 2010 by owners and business partners Neville King and Kate Hannaford. The cafe and restaurant are already a great success and the place is fast becoming one of the area's must visit dining establishments.

The downstairs restaurant is closed on Sunday and Mondays, but is open every other day from 5pm until late. The restaurant seats 42 diners and it is definitely an advantage to book to avoid disappointment. Starters include ham hock terrine and Craster smoked salmon. Roast rump of lamb with garlic roast potatoes, swede puree & black pudding beignets; loin of venison with butternut squash and roast salsify, dauphinoise potatoes & a bitter chocolate sauce are among the main meals listed on the extensive menu. As well as the printed menu there is also a daily specials board.

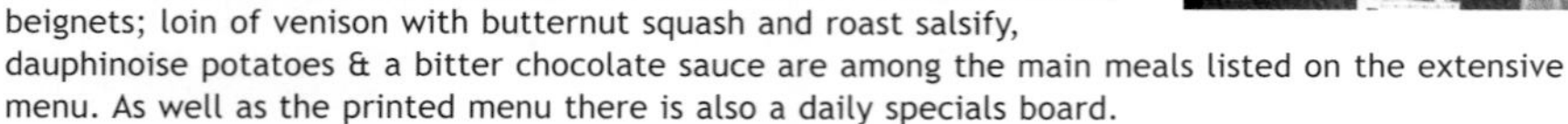

On Tuesdays Beetroot Grill and Cafe hosts a gourmet burger night. From 5pm diners can choose from a selection of succulent homemade burgers, which are all served with homemade chunky chips & beetroot salad.

The cafe upstairs is open seven days a week between 8am and 5pm (Monday and Saturday) on Sundays. The cafe seats around 45 diners.

99 THE NEW SHIP INN

42 Gibson Street, Newbiggin-By-The-Sea, Northumberland NE64 6UW
Tel: 01670 850337
e-mail: wharton434@btinternet.com
website: www.newship-newbiggin.co.uk

The New Ship Inn situated at Newbiggin-By-The-Sea is the ideal public house to call to if you are visiting the north east coast of the UK. Dating back to 1865, this free house has always had the same name and has been owned by Yvonne and Bobby for the past 18 months. Offering all year accommodation and home cooked food, this place is in an ideal base for those wanting to explore the area.

Open every day from 12md-12mn there is always one real ale from the Farne Island Brewery to be enjoyed with most regulars fond of draught John Smiths Smooth, Carling and Fosters.

Home cooked food is served daily at The New Ship Inn and it is advisable to book in advance for Sunday lunches as they are extremely popular. The food menu changes regularly, but current daily dishes, at affordable prices, include Cumberland pie, meatball melt, and barbecue belly pork, which are all served with chips or vegetables.

Food is available every lunch time between 12md and 3pm and is cooked by head chef Liz or Yvonne, who use as much local produce as possible in the tasty dishes on offer. A separate restaurant seating 40 will soon be opening on Tuesday and Thursday evenings from 7pm and will definitely be worth checking out.

There are six guest bedrooms, all located upstairs, with shared bathrooms. Guests stay on a room only basis, although breakfast is available by request.
The bar has darts, pool, poker and dominoes, and all of the big sporting events and weekly football is televised live on a big screen.

Customers can win a cash jackpot during the Tuesday night quiz, which starts at around 9pm. On a Saturday night punters take to the stage in the weekly karaoke session, which is very popular, especially with pub regulars and visitors to the two caravan sites at Newbiggin. Private parties can be catered for at this child-friendly public.

98 WINDMILL INN

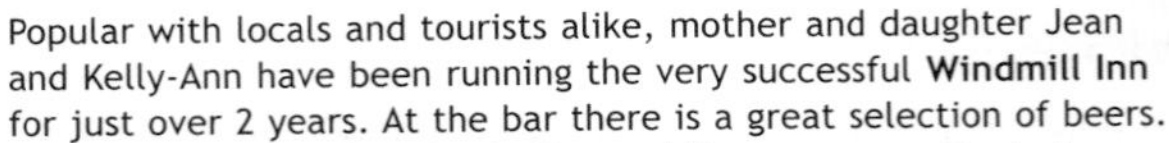

Cowpen Road, Blyth, Northumberland NE24 5JP
Tel: 01670 359580

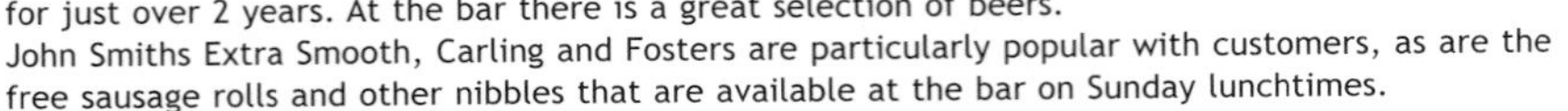

Popular with locals and tourists alike, mother and daughter Jean and Kelly-Ann have been running the very successful **Windmill Inn** for just over 2 years. At the bar there is a great selection of beers. John Smiths Extra Smooth, Carling and Fosters are particularly popular with customers, as are the free sausage rolls and other nibbles that are available at the bar on Sunday lunchtimes.

Entertainment at the weekends includes Karaoke from 8pm on Friday nights and live music on Saturday from 9pm. A function room for up to 80 people is available for hire. Children are welcome and there is good disabled access. Only cash payment is accepted.

100 THE PLOUGH INN

Ellington, Northumberland NE61 5JB
Tel: 01670 860340 Mob: 07957795215
e-mail: plough_inn@yahoo.co.uk
website: www.theploughinn-ellington.co.uk

For lovers of good food, real ale and fine hospitality, **The Plough Inn** is a real destination hot spot in the Ellington area. Situated a short distance east of the A1068 coastal road, the inn is personally run by Katrina Robinson. Katrina has been in the trade for many years and since her arrival here in 2009 she has given this place a new lease of life.

Open all day every day food is served between 12md and 8pm Monday - Saturday and 12md - 3pm on Sundays. All of the dishes are homemade and freshly prepared to order. Local produce is used where possible and roast dinners are definitely a favourite on Sundays, so booking is essential. Diners can choose from the printed menu or the specials board and there are plenty of tasty dishes to choose from.

Quality accommodation, in the form of four en-suite guest rooms, is available all year round and there is free WiFi throughout the premise. The reasonable tariff includes a hearty breakfast, which is sure to set you up for a day of exploring the area.

Entertainment is hosted occasionally - ring for details.

102 THE COUNTRY BARN FARM & COFFEE SHOP

Widdrington Farm, Widdrington Village, Morpeth, Northumberland NE61 5EA
Tel: 01670 760181
e-mail: info@thecountrybarn.co.uk
website: www.thecountrybarn.co.uk

Nestled in a wonderful location overlooking the picturesque coastal area of Druridge Bay, **The Country Barn Farm & Coffee Shop** offers quality local produce (including meat from its own farm) and a fantastic selection of homemade treats.

Owners Hugh and Sarah Annett take great pride in their work and are very hands on when it comes to the business front of house and behind the scenes. The farm has been in the Annett family since 1515 and both Hugh and Sarah are very passionate about what they do, offering all customers a warm welcome.

There is a wonderful family atmosphere here, with staff members clearly enjoying their roles and customers seen more as friends at times, creating a lovely relaxing ambience to this place. The child-friendly coffee shop is splendid and can be found on the ground floor, with a gift shop selling a wide range of gifts and cards for all occasions on the first floor.

Tempting homemade treats for lunch or afternoon tea are very popular with diners here, many who also think highly of the special coffee available. The coffee has been created especially by Pumphreys for the coffee shop and is known as the Country Barn blend.

There is a homemade traditional Sunday lunch served weekly 12 - 2pm with fresh, hand-peeled vegetables. The only frozen vegetable used is peas. The premises are fully licensed and there is a range of spirits, beers and wines on offer.

There is room to seat 80 customers. The Country Barn Farm & Coffee Shop is open 9am - 5pm Tuesday, Wednesday and Thursday; 9am - 5.30pm Friday and Saturday; and 10am - 4pm on Sunday.

101 WIDDRINGTON INN

Widdrington Village, Morpeth,
Northumberland NE61 5DY
Tel: 01670 760260 Fax: 01670 760166
e-mail: widdin@hotmail.co.uk
website: www.thewiddringtoninn.co.uk

Lovers of fine food in Morpeth regard **Widdrington Inn** very highly. It is undoubtedly one of the destination establishments in this area for those who enjoy dining out. Billy and Julia have been here for 11 years and their success is evident in the fantastic reputation the inn has.

Open all day every day, this place is always bustling with locals and visitors, who come here to drink, eat and socialise. There are always two to three real ales available from the well-stocked bar with Old Speckled Hen the regular.

Food wise, it is an advantage to book at all times to avoid disappointment. If you do manage to reserve a table the food definitely will not disappoint. The extensive menu includes a fine range of grills such as grilled pork chops, mixed grill and grilled gammon steak. Traditional favourites like fresh battered cod, homemade lasagne and homemade steak pie are also available.

On Sundays there is no food served in the evening, although of a lunchtime diners can indulge in a succulent roast dinner. No bookings are taken for Sunday lunch, so make sure you arrive early as it is a first come, first serve basis.

104 THE NORTHUMBERLAND ARMS HOTEL

West Thirston, Mopeth, Northumberland NE65 9EE
Tel: 01670 787370
e-mail: info@northumberlandarmshotel.co.uk

A former coaching inn, **The Northumberland Arms Hotel** is situated in the village of West Thirston across the road from the Rover Coquet, which splits this village from Felton. Licensees Tony and Gill Elliott took over here in August 2010 and are enjoying real success.

The magnificent building dates back to the 18th century and is full of charm throughout. The guest accommodation comprises of five rooms, two of which are en-suite. They are available all year round and the affordable tariff includes a delicious breakfast.

A professional chef is employed in the hotel's kitchen and he uses as much local produce as possible to ensure the best quality meals are served. Locally reared meat and locally caught fish all add flair to the splendid menu and daily specials board. Food themed evenings are very popular, including the steak nights held every Thursday in the attractive restaurant/dining area.

The family friendly hotel is open all day every day and serves two real ales with Black Sheep and a brew from the local Wylam Brewery available. Quality food is served 12md-2.30pm and 5.30pm-9pm daily and 12md-3pm and 6pm-8pm on Sundays.

103 THE TRAP INN

Main Street, North Broomhill, Morpeth, Northumberland NE65 9UT
Tel: 01670 761672 Mobile: 07770 922579
e-mail: dickinsonsandyd@aol.com
website: www.trapinn.co.uk

Situated in the charming village of North Broomhill, **The Trap Inn** is surrounded by beautiful countryside and is only a short drive from some spectacular coastline. Owners Sandra and Mike Dickinson, their son Scott and daughter Gemma have been here for the past 8 years. They clearly take immense pride in running this fantastic Inn, which dates back to the 1780s and is situated within close proximity to RAF Boulmer where Mike himself had his last posting as a member of the RAF.

Open all day, every day, a warm welcome is guaranteed. At the bar you will find a choice of three hand pulled real ales featuring two guest ales on a rotating basis. Delicious home cooked food is prepared by the family and the menu features classic pub favourites including gammon steak, lasagne and scampi and chips. On Sunday there is a fantastic carvery serving the finest quality British beef, lamb, pork or turkey alongside hand peeled vegetables, roast potatoes, delicious homemade Yorkshire puddings and real gravy.

There is a large and comfortably furnished dining room at the rear of the pub and the main bar also offers excellent surroundings in which to enjoy your meal, with comfortable furniture and attractive wooden and slate flooring. There is good access for wheelchair users with a ramp at the side of the building and there is also a disabled toilet.

Excellent guest accommodation is available all year round with five upstairs rooms to choose from, all of varying sizes and with en suite facilities. Included in the price is a superb breakfast to set you up for the day ahead.

The Trap Inn has excellent facilities, including a pool table and two snooker tables, as well as a function room for up to 80 people. Wednesday is busker's night and musicians congregate with their instruments to sing along and jam the night away. On Thursdays everyone is welcome to join in a pub quiz and you can even join in a game of Poker on Sunday and Tuesday evenings from 6pm.

Weddings held in the grand Northumbria Suite always run without a hitch as delighted guests are welcomed with a glass of fizz and excellent hot and cold buffets and sit-down meals are served. To round off a perfect day the happy couple can book to stay in the Honeymoon Suite, which can be prepared with flowers and champagne.

105 STAGS HEAD

45 Main Street, Felton, Northumberland NE65 9PP
Tel: 01670 787207 e-mail: stagsheadfelton@aol.com

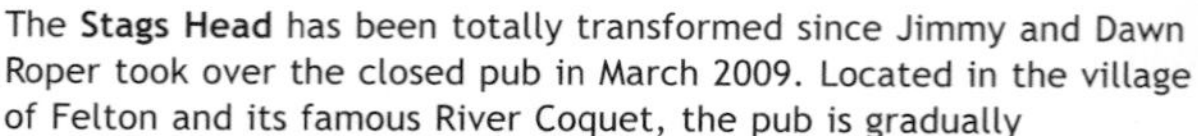

The **Stags Head** has been totally transformed since Jimmy and Dawn Roper took over the closed pub in March 2009. Located in the village of Felton and its famous River Coquet, the pub is gradually becoming a popular place to drink and dine with locals and visitors. Open all day every day, there are three rotating real ales available as well as delicious meals cooked freshly to order. Jimmy is a professional chef and specialises in English and Indian cuisine.

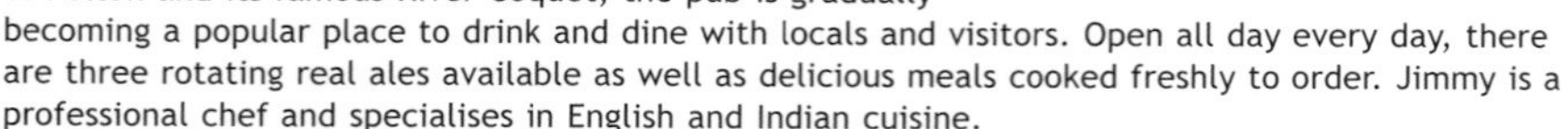

Accommodation comprises of three quality bunk rooms, which each sleep up to eight people. There is also a small guest room, which sleeps four.

106 ALNWICK CASTLE

Alnwick, Northumberland NE66 1NQ
Tel: 01665 510777
e-mail: enquiries@alnwickcastle.com
website: www.alnwickcastle.com

Owned by the Percy family since 1309, **Alnwick** is one of the finest castles in the British Isles. Originally built to defend England's northern border from the Scottish armies, the castle is the family home of the Duke and Duchess of Northumberland. With magnificent views over the River Aln and surrounding countryside, the castle is a few minutes walk from the centre of the historic market town of Alnwick.

Within the massive stone walls, the beautifully kept grounds contain fascinating exhibitions. Discover the history of the Northumberland Fusiliers since 1674 in the Abbot's Tower. Marvel at the richness of Northumberland's archaeological past in the Postern Tower and listen to life as a member of the Percy Tenantry Volunteers (1798-1814) in the Constable's Tower.

At the heart of the castle is the keep. Pass through the medieval towers and enter a wonderful family home. State Rooms, refurbished in the mid 19th century by the Fourth Duke, contain paintings by Canaletto, Van Dyck and Titian. Finely carved wooden panels adorn the walls, windows and ceilings. Children's quiz helps your family learn about Alnwick Castle.

There are various events held throughout the spring and summer, including Birds of Prey displays, horse driving trials and an International Music Festival. Noted as a location for 'Harry Potter', 'Elizabeth' and 'Robin Hood, Prince of Thieves', Alnwick Castle is open daily from 1st April to 31st October.

107 ALNWICK CASTLE GARDEN

The Alnwick Garden, Denwick Lane, Alnwick, Northumberland NE66 2NJ
Tel: 01665 511350
website: www.alnwickgarden.com

The vision is to create a beautiful public space accessible to everyone. A garden which is a place of contemplation, a place of fun, a place of inspiration and education. The Alnwick Garden in Northumberland is one of the most exciting contemporary gardens to be developed in the last century, a magical landscape created from a unique idea.

The Duchess of Northumberland's vision was to create a beautiful public space accessible to everyone: a garden for contemplation, fun, inspiration and education. The Alnwick Garden was officially opened in October 2002 by its patron HRH The Prince of Wales, as the first phase of development was complete. The Garden is now halfway to completion and features spectacular water displays, wonderful gardens and one of the largest tree houses in the world.

The world renowned Belgian designer Jacques Wirtz and his son Peter were chosen to create The Garden, interpreting the Duchess's vision for the 12-acre walled site which was a forgotten and derelict plot before The Alnwick Garden project began work in 2000. Wirtz International's design has transformed it into an exciting scene, dancing with water and ringing with the sounds of life. The Garden is a sequence of busy and quiet spaces, with the gentle and introspective Rose Garden feeling far remote from the children playing in the water jets of the Grand Cascade. An important element of the Wirtz design is the strong green structure which unifies The Garden's diverse themes, visible in the beech hedges, clipped hornbeams and yew. In winter, this structure is evident and visitors are able to see the bones of The Garden, while in summer it provides the backdrop for exuberant flower displays.

Sir Michael Hopkins, recognised as a leading international architect, has designed The Garden's Pavilion and Visitor Centre which will open in 2006. These stunning contemporary buildings will house excellent visitor facilities for eating, shopping, learning and relaxing, and places to find out more about other things to do in the region.

However The Garden is more than a garden, and in a relatively short space of time has become recognised not only for gardening excellence but also as a transformational project using its resources to provide real, measurable benefit for people. The vision is being taken forward by The Alnwick Garden Trust who continue to fundraise to complete The Garden by 2009. The Garden is contributing to the regeneration of a rural community as tourism takes on a new level of importance, and as well as being a meeting place for local people provides an opportunity for people of all ages and abilities to experience the arts, enjoy learning new skills and get outdoors for activity or relaxation, and for families to play together. All surplus revenue is channelled back into the project, helping The Trust go from vision to reality.

108 HERMITAGE INN

23 Castle Street, Warkworth, Northumberland NE65 OUL
Tel: 01665 711258
website: www.hermitageinn.co.uk

Dating back to the 18th century, this wonderful former coaching inn is now a fantastic family run inn located at the heart of the historic town of Warkworth. **Hermitage Inn** has been personally run by Steve and Liz Proud, and their daughter Emma, for the past five years. In that time they have built up a strong local following and attract plenty of visitors through its doors, many who come here to enjoy the wide variety of delicious meals on offer.

The a la carte menu is very popular as is the special Sunday menu and so it is essential that table reservations are made if you are planning to dine here in the summer months. Traditional favourites can be found on the starters menu such as prawn salad and garlic mushroom alongside more unusual dishes like wild boar pate, asparagus wrapped in an omelette, and chilli garlic spare ribs. Fish, steak, lamb and poultry dishes are all available from the superb a la carte menu. Fillet steak Rossini, roast duck, trio of lamb chops, and king prawns are all popular with diners to the Hermitage Inn. Vegetarians are well catered for with a selection of delicious meals on offer including deep fried vegetable patties, vegetable stir fry, and vegetable curry. For those with a lighter appetite there is a good range of lite bites to choose from too.

The Hermitage Inn is well-regarded for its carvery, which is available Friday, Saturday and Sunday between 12md and 2.15pm and Friday and Saturday evenings 6pm - 9pm.

Open all day every day, there are four real ales to choose from the Jennings Brewery Range; Butler, Cumberland Ale, Sneck Hitter and a guest ale.

Accommodation is available all year round in the form of five upstairs traditional guest rooms (two with en-suite facilities). There is also a ground floor self catering flat available for weekly stays only, which sleeps two people. Ring for details.

109 THE SCHOONER

Lime Street, Amble, Northumberland NE65 0AD
Tel: 01665 712391 Mob: 07968436823
e-mail: susanstraker@aol.com
website: www.schoonerhotelamble.co.uk

Nestled in the delightful fishing town of Amble, **The Schooner** is a wonderful bed & breakfast, which dates back to the late 19th century. Susan and Derrick have personally run the B&B for the past eight years, in which time they have built up a good reputation and loyal clientele.

There are seven en-suite guest rooms available, which vary in size and are all located upstairs. The reasonable tariff includes a hearty Northumberland cooked breakfast and breakfast times are flexible.

Former fisherman Derrick is a local man and a massive Newcastle United fan, which you will soon realise when you enter the bar area as there is an array of Newcastle United football shirts displayed on the ceiling. Open all day every day, the bar is well-stocked and offers a good selection of draught drinks. It is always bustling with locals and visitors who come here to enjoy a relaxing drink, games room and large beer garden.

The B&B is close to the town's bustling harbour, where there are yachting, sailing, boating and canoeing clubs, as well as regular daily fishing trips. There is plenty to do in the area with Warkworth Castle close by and the market town of Alnwick and its world famous garden and castle just 15 minutes away.

110 CRAWLEY FARMHOUSE & CRAWLEY TOWER COTTAGE

Powburn, Alnwick, Northumberland NE66 4JA
Tel: 01665 578413
e-mail: crawleyfarmhouse@hotmail.co.uk
website: www.crawley-farmhouse.co.uk and www.crawleytowercottage.co.uk

Dating back to 1820, **Crawley Farmhouse** offers fantastic bed and breakfast accommodation which welcoming owner Noreen has been running for the past 8 years. Located on the edge of Northumberland National Park, this is the perfect base for exploring the stunning surrounding countryside and historic attractions, including the famous Alnwick Castle and Gardens.

The three star accommodation comprises one double bedroom with en-suite facilities, two twin rooms and a single room. A home cooked traditional farmhouse breakfast is included.

Located just a short distance away and nestled under a hillside, **Crawley Tower Cottage** is a four star self catering holiday home. The spacious accommodation is laid across one level and the cottage can comfortably sleep three people. There is a well equipped kitchen, sitting room with log burner and a conservatory leading to a private garden and ample parking. The cottage is ideal for weekly lets or short breaks with a minimum stay of three nights.

111 COACH HOUSE

Brownieside, Alnwick, Northumberland NE67 5HW
Tel: 01665 579488
e-mail: info@coachhouse-brownieside.co.uk
website: www.coachhouse-bownieside.co.uk

Boasting a rural location in the beautiful hamlet of Brownieside, **Coach House** is a splendid B&B, which provides the ideal place for visitors to explore Northumberland's various attractions. Dating back in parts more than 250 years, the B&B is housed within what was the old Masons Arms and has been owned and personally run by Tracey and Neil Sprigg for 1 ½ years.

Inside, you will find three en-suite guest rooms which have been furnished to a high standard. One of these rooms is situated on the ground floor and there is also a family room available. The reasonable tariff includes a hearty breakfast and evening meals can be arranged on request.

The dining room is delightful and its walls have been decorated with original paintings, created by Neil's father Charlie who is a well-known local artist. They help add character to the building, which in its lifetime has been a granary, coach house, and for more than 100 years a pub.

Coach House is very popular with visitors to the area and with its high quality accommodation and proximity to the Northumberland countryside and coast it isn't hard to figure out why.

112 THE FISHING BOAT INN

Boulmer Village, Alnwick, Northumberland NE66 3BP
Tel: 01665 577750
website: www.thefishingboatinn.co.uk

The Fishing Boat Inn enjoys a spectacular location alongside the beach and North Sea in Boulmer, which 200 years ago was the gin smuggling capital of England. In those days the inn itself was a smuggler's haunt, where pirates used to meet and plan their next jobs.

Today, it remains just as popular (just not with pirates), and has been in the very capable hands of Mike and Margaret Boyle for the past six years. With around 20 years in the pub/restaurant business, a passion for good food and a real fondness for the surrounding area the couple have done a fantastic job here.

During the summer months the inn is open all day every day and serve three real ales, with Black Sheep the regular. The food is absolutely delicious and the speciality here is seafood caught from the North Sea. Lobster, crabs and salmon are caught locally in season and delivered daily. They make up some of the dishes on the extensive printed menu and daily specials board.

There is dining room for 40 people at The Fishing Boat Inn and it is definitely an advantage to book at all times during the summer months due to its popularity with lovers of fine food.

113 BERWICK BARRACKS

Berwick Barricks & Borough Museum, The Parade, Berwick-upon-Tweed, Northumberland TD15 1DF

Here, you and your family can experience military life first hand. Berwick is one of the outstanding fortified towns of Europe and a visit to our 'Beat of the Drum' Exhibition at these 18th century barracks recreates the detail and tradition of days in the barrack room. Come into the Gymnasium Gallery - there are art exhibitions in the summer. See the museum dedicated to the King's Own Scottish Borderers - and don't miss the Clock Block, it houses part of the famous Burrell Collection with further lively and imaginative exhibitions.

114 THISTLE DO NICELY

8 Walkergate, Berwick-upon-Tweed TD15 1DB
Tel: 01289 332442

Fresh home cooked food made with the finest local ingredients is a big draw to visitors of **Thistle Do Nicely**, which can be found just off the main street in Berwick-upon-Tweed. The tea rooms are family owned and run by Carol and Allan Mackay and their children Feidh, Mairi and Ruairidh. The family has been in charge here for the last four years and created this business from scratch after taking ownership of the former dry cleaners that stood here.

Diners can choose a great variety of dishes from the printed menu or specials board. All of the dishes here are made on the premises, with the only thing bought in being the bread and teacakes. Homemade cakes and scones are very popular with locals and visitors, along with homemade jam, marmalade and chutney. Daily soups and home cooked breakfasts are among the most frequently ordered meals.

The dining area seats around 40 customers and is always bustling with hungry passersby and regulars. A lovely friendly atmosphere surrounds this delightful tea room, which is open Monday-Saturday from 8am - 4pm.

115 THE BARRELS ALE HOUSE

59/61 Bridge Street, Berwick-upon-Tweed, Northumberland TD15 1ES
Tel: 01289 308013
website: www.thebarrels.co.uk

Included in the Good Beer Guide for many years, **The Barrels Ale House** is what you might call a real old fashioned boozer. This fantastic pub is well worth a visit for anyone who enjoys great beer, a lively atmosphere and quality live entertainment. Situated in a prominent location within the town of Berwick upon Tweed, you will find The Barrels Ale House occupying a distinctive curved stone building adjacent to the Quay and the old one way road bridge over the River Tweed.

Experienced and welcoming landlord Martin has run this pub alongside his right hand Jaki for the past 16 years and its popularity among locals and visitors alike has gone from strength to strength. They take their real ales very seriously here, with 5 constantly changing cask ales available including regulars Timothy Talyor Land Lord, Stewart Brewing Pentland IPA and Shepard Neame Spit Fire. Many other firm favourites are available on rotation from both local and national breweries. Martin is keen to offer as many real ales from small local breweries as he can. There is also a great selection of other alcoholic and non-alcoholic drinks to choose from alongside a range of bar snacks.

The interior is full of character and style, with something interesting to look at and admire in every direction. From the old fashioned dentist's or barber's chair at the bar, to the numerous signed photographs and album covers adorning the walls. Downstairs there is an atmospheric stone walled area which was once at street level but is now underground and this is where amazing live entertainment can be experienced.

On Friday night live bands entertain the punters, including a variety of well known international acts, local bands and up-and-coming talent. All gigs start at 9pm and entry costs £4 unless otherwise stated. You can sign up on their website to receive the latest gig listings as well as some great promotional offers on drinks. Saturday night is all about underground music with guest DJs playing Funk, Soul, House, Hip and RnB from 9pm.

The Barrels Ale House is open all day everyday from 12pm to midnight on Sunday to Thursday and for an extra half an hour past midnight on Fridays and Saturdays. From Monday to Friday between 2nd January and 1st April there are slightly reduced hours, opening from 3pm. Only payment by cash or card is accepted.

116 THE CAT INN

Great North Road, Berwick-upon-Tweed,
Northumberland TD15 2RL
Tel: 01289 387251
e-mail: marionandjenny@tiscali.co.uk

Named after a Galleon from the Napoleonic Wars 200 year ago, Marion and Paul took the helm of **The Cat Inn** in October 2009 and they have successfully put this historic pub back on the map. Easily accessed along the Great North Road (the A1) a short drive south of Berwick upon Tweed, this pub enjoys a scenic location with upstairs rooms enjoying stunning views towards Holy Island.

Excellent food is freshly cooked by Marion using only the finest ingredients, sourced locally where possible. The menu features succulent sirloin and ribeye steaks, beer battered haddock, poached wild salmon, homemade meatballs and a delicious vegetarian curry. Meal times are Mon - Sat 12 - 2.30pm and 5pm - 8.30pm and Sunday 12 - 3pm (residents only Sunday evening). Traditional roast dinners with all the trimmings are served from midday to 3pm on Sundays, with residents only dining on Sunday evenings. It is advisable to book during the summer months to avoid disappointment. Children are welcome and there is good disabled access.

Guest accommodation is situated on the first floor with seven comfortably furnished and well equipped en-suite bedrooms of varying sizes, some enjoying fantastic views. A hearty home cooked breakfast is included in the price.

117 THE OLD SCHOOL HOUSE

Tillmouth, Cornhill-on-Tweed,
Northumberland TD12 4UT
Tel: 01890 882463
e-mail: noelhodgson@btinternet.com
website: www.tillmouthschoolhouse.co.uk

Originally built in 1867 as a school and headmaster's residence, **The Old School House** was sympathetically converted into a private dwelling in 1965. Now owned by the Hodgson family, they happily share their beautiful home by offering bed and breakfast accommodation in this tranquil rural location. This is the perfect base from which to explore the stunning countryside and beaches of Northumberland and the Scottish Borders and is within easy reach of many historic attractions including castles, battle sites and historic towns.

The house is set within mature gardens and is full of character features. A friendly and warm welcome awaits with complimentary afternoon tea and home baking on arrival. Before setting out to explore the countryside, guests can enjoy a delicious breakfast made using locally sourced produce. Special dietary requirements can be catered for and guests should ask about this when booking. Guests can relax in luxurious comfort when they stay in The Tillmouth Suite, which has its own private staircase and bathroom. The suite is tastefully decorated and furnished to a high standard, with a king-size bed and comfortable chairs. The Podmore Room, of same standard is a large ensuite room with 3/4 bed, situated on the ground floor.

TOURIST INFORMATION CENTRES

AMBLE

Queen Street Car Park, Amble, Northumberland NE65 0DQ

e-mail: amble.tic@northumberland.gov.uk

Tel: 0166 571 2313

BARNARD CASTLE

Woodleigh, Flatts Road, Barnard Castle, County Durham DL12 8AA

e-mail: tourism@teesdale.gov.uk

Tel: 01833 690909

BELLINGHAM

Station Yard, Woodburn Road, Bellingham, Northumberland NE48 2DF

e-mail: bellinghamtic@btconnect.com

Tel: 01434 220616

BERWICK-UPON-TWEED

106 Marygate, Berwick upon Tweed, Northumberland TD15 1BN

e-mail: berwick.tic@northumberland.gov.uk

Tel: 01289 330733

BISHOP AUCKLAND

Town Hall, Ground Floor, Market Place, Bishop Auckland, County Durham DL14 7NP

e-mail: bishopauckland.touristinfo@durham.gov.uk

Tel: 01388 604922

CORBRIDGE

Hill Street, Corbridge, Northumberland NE45 5AA

e-mail: corbridgetic@btconnect.com

Tel: 01434 632815

CRASTER

Craster Car Park, Craster, Alnwick, Northumberland NE66 3TW

e-mail: crastertic@alnwick.gov.uk

Tel: 01665 576007

DARLINGTON

Address:The Dolphin Centre, Horsemarket, Darlington DL1 5RP

e-mail: tic@darlington.gov.uk

Tel: 01325 388666

DURHAM

2 Millennium Place, Durham City DH1 1WA

e-mail: touristinfo@durhamcity.gov.uk

Tel: 0191 384 3720

GATESHEAD CENTRAL LIBRARY

Central Library, Prince Consort Road, Gateshead NE8 4LN

e-mail: tic@gateshead.gov.uk

Tel: 0191 433 8420

GATESHEAD AT THE SAGE

St. Mary's Square, Gateshead Quays NE8 2JR

e-mail: tourism@gateshead.gov.uk

Tel: 0191 478 4222

GUISBOROUGH

Priory Grounds, Church Street, Guisborough TS14 6HG

e-mail: guisborough_tic@redcar-cleveland.gov.uk

Tel: 01287 633801

HALTWHISTLE

Railway Station, Station Road, Haltwhistle NE49 9HN

e-mail: haltwhistletic@btconnect.com

Tel: 01434 322002

HARTLEPOOL

Hartlepool Art Gallery, Church Square, Hartlepool TS24 7EQ

e-mail: hpooltic@hartlepool.gov.uk

Tel: 01429 869706

TOURIST INFORMATION CENTRES

HEXHAM

Wentworth Car Park, Hexham, Northumberland NE46 1QE

e-mail: hexham.tic@northumberland.gov.uk

Tel: 01434 652220

MIDDLESBROUGH

(PO Box 69), Middlesbrough Info. Centre & Box Office, Albert Road, Middlesbrough TS1 2QQ

e-mail: tic@middlesbrough.gov.uk

Tel: 01642 729700

MIDDLETON-IN-TEESDALE

10 Market Place, Middleton-in-Teesdale, County Durham DL12 0QG

e-mail: middletonplus@compuserve.com

Tel: 01833 641001

MORPETH

The Chantry, Bridge Street, Morpeth, Northumberland NE61 1PD

e-mail: morpeth.tic@northumberland.gov.uk

Tel: 01670 500700

NEWCASTLE-UPON-TYNE GRAINGER STREET

Newcastle Information Centre, 8-9 Central Arcade, Newcastle upon Tyne, Tyne & Wear NE1 5BQ

e-mail: tourist.info@newcastle.gov.uk

Tel: 0191 277 8000

NEWCASTLE AIRPORT

Tourist Information Desk, Newcastle Airport, Newcastle upon Tyne, Tyne & Wear NE13 8BZ

e-mail: niatic@hotmail.com

Tel: 0191 214 4422

NORTH SHIELDS

Unit 18, Royal Quays Outlet Shopping, North Shields, Tyne & Wear NE29 6DW

e-mail: ticns@northtyneside.gov.uk

Tel: 0191 2005895

ONCE BREWED

Address:Northumberland National Park Centre, Military Road, Bardon Mill, Hexham, Northumberland NE47 7AN

e-mail: tic.oncebrewed@nnpa.org.uk

Tel: 01434 344396

OTTERBURN

Otterburn Mill, Otterburn, Northumberland NE19 1JT

e-mail:tic@otterburnmill.co.uk

Tel: 01830 520093

PETERLEE

4 Upper Yoden Way, Peterlee, County Durham SR8 1AX

e-mail: touristinfo@peterlee.gov.uk

Tel: 0191 586 4450

REDCAR

West Terrace, Esplanade, Redcar, Cleveland TS10 3AE

e-mail: redcar_tic@redcar-cleveland.gov.uk

Tel: 01642 471921

ROTHBURY

Northumberland National Park Centre, Church House, Church Street, Rothbury, Northumberland NE65 7UP

e-mail: tic.rothbury@nnpa.org.uk

Tel: 01669 620887

TOURIST INFORMATION CENTRES

SALTBURN-BY-SEA

3 Station Buildings, Station Square, Saltburn-by-Sea, Cleveland TS12 1AQ

e-mail: saltburn_tic@redcar-cleveland.gov.uk

Tel: 01287 622422

SEAHOUSES

Seafield Car Park, Seafield Road, Seahouses, Northumberland NE68 7SW

e-mail: seahouses.tic@northumberland.gov.uk

Tel: 01665 720884

SOUTH SHEILDS

South Shields Museum & Gallery, Ocean Road, South Shields, Tyne & Wear NE33 2HZ

e-mail: museum.tic@southtyneside.gov.uk

Tel: 0191 454 6612

SOUTH SHIELDS (AMPHITHEATRE)

Sea Road, South Shields NE33 2LD

e-mail: foreshore.tic@southtyneside.gov.uk

Tel: 0191 455 7411

STANHOPE

Durham Dales Centre, Castle Gardens, Stanhope, County Durham DL13 2FJ

e-mail: durham.dales.centre@durham.gov.uk

Tel: 01388 527650

STOCKTON-ON-TEES

The Shambles, High Street, Stockton-on-Tees TS18 1AU

e-mail: touristinformation@stockton.gov.uk

Tel: 01642 528130

SUNDERLAND

50 Fawcett Street, Sunderland, Tyne & Wear SR1 1RF

e-mail: tourist.info@sunderland.gov.uk

Tel: 0191 553 2000

WOOLER

Wooler TIC, The Cheviot Centre, 12 Padgepool Place, Wooler, Northumberland NE71 6BL

e-mail: wooler.tic@northumberland.gov.uk

Tel: 01668 282123

IMAGE COPYRIGHT HOLDERS

Some images in this book have been supplied by **http://www.geograph.org.uk** and licensed under the Creative Commons Attribution-Share Alike 2.0 Generic License. To view a copy of this license, visit **http://creativecommons.org/licenses/by-sa/2.0/** or send a letter to Creative Commons, 171 Second Street, Suite 300, San Francisco, California, 94105, USA.

COPYRIGHT HOLDERS ARE AS FOLLOWS:

River Wear, Durham City © Russel Wills *pg 4*
Durham Cathedral, Durham City © John Illingworth *pg 5*
Durham Botanical Gardens, Durham City © Rob Bishop *pg 7*
Castle, Bishop Auckland © Paul Buckingham *pg 9*
Hartlepool Marina, Hartlepool © Des Howard *pg 11*
Country Park, Billingham © Mick Garratt *pg 12*
A Sunny Day, Darlington © J Spencer *pg 13*
Raby Castle, Staindrop © Carol Walker *pg 15*
Hardwick Hall, Sedgefield © Stanley Howe *pg 16*
Preston Hall, Stockton-on-Tees © Chris Allen *pg 17*
Priory, Guisborough © Alison Stamp *pg 18*
Pier and Tramway, Saltburn-by-the-Sea © Carol Walker *pg 19*
Terris Novalis, Consett © Alex Mcgregor *pg 22*
Lumley Castle, Chester-le-Street © Rob Bishop *pg 23*
Tanfield Railway, Beamish © Stephen Daglish *pg 24*
Light Transformer, Sunderland © Andrew Curtis *pg 25*
Windmill, Fullwell © Simon Broder *pg 26*
Penshaw Monument, Penshaw © Kev Murley *pg 27*
Angel of the North, Gateshead © Paul Robson *pg 29*
Bede's World, Jarrow © Andrew Curtis *pg 31*
Tyne Bridges, Newcastle-upon-Tyne © Carol Walker *pg 32*
Grey's Monument, Gateshead © Andrew Curtis *pg 33*
Castle, Prudhoe © Chris Tweedy *pg 37*
Bowes Museum, Barnard Castle © Dave Bailey *pg 41*
Eggleston Hall Gardens, Egglestone © Bill Henderson *pg 42*
Low Force, Middleton-in-Teesdale © Andy Stephenson *pg 43*
Stanhope Old Hall, Stanhope © Andrew Curtis *pg 44*
Weardale Railway, Stanhope © Dennis Lovett *pg 44*
Tunstall Reservoir, Wolsingham © George Hurrell *pg 45*
Pow Hill Country Park, Edmundbyers © David Brown *pg 46*
Killhope Lead Mining Museum, Killhope © Gordon Hatton *pg 47*
River Wear, Ireshopeburn © Andrew Curtis *pg 47*
Northumberland National Park, Ingram © Walter Baxter *pg 50*
Hexham Abbey, Hexham © Wfmillar *pg 51*
St Mungo's Church, Simonburn © Wfmillar *pg 52*
Chesters Walled Garden, Walwick © Mike Quinn *pg 54*
Walltown Quarry, Haltwhistle © Matt Offer *pg 56*
Kielder Water, Falstone © Wfmillar *pg 58*
Cragside House, Rothbury © Paul Buckinhham *pg 60*
Humbleton Hill, Wooler © Gordon Mellor *pg 62*
Flodden Battlefiend Memorial, Branxton © Andrew Curtis *pg 63*
Morpeth Castle, Morpeth © Sarah Clarke *pg 66*
Clock Tower, Morpeth © Nicholas Mutton *pg 67*
Riverside Park, Ashington © Willie Duffin *pg 68*
Alnwick Gardens, Alnwick © David Clarke *pg 71*
Warkworth Castle, Warkworth © Jthomas *pg 72*
Chillingham Castle, Chillingham © Andrew Curtis *pg 73*
Howick Hall, Howick © Les Hull *pg 75*
Gospel Gardens, Lindisfarne © Lisa Jarvis *pg 78*
Lindisfarne Castle, Lindisfarne © Nigel Chadwick *pg 78*
Farne Islands, Bamburgh © Nigel Mykura *pg 79*

ORDER FORM

To order any of our publications just fill in the payment details below and complete the order form. For orders of less than 4 copies please add £1 per book for postage and packing. Orders over 4 copies are P & P free.

Please Complete Either:

I enclose a cheque for £ ______ made payable to Travel Publishing Ltd

Or:

CARD NO: ______ EXPIRY DATE: ______

SIGNATURE: ______

NAME: ______

ADDRESS: ______

TEL NO: ______

Please either send, telephone, fax or e-mail your order to:

Travel Publishing Ltd, Airport Business Centre, 10 Thornbury Road, Estover, Plymouth PL6 7PP
Tel: 01752 697280 Fax: 01752 697299 e-mail: info@travelpublishing.co.uk

	Price	Quantity
Hidden Places Regional Titles		
Cornwall	£8.99	....
Devon	£8.99	....
Dorset, Hants & Isle of Wight	£8.99	....
East Anglia	£8.99	....
Lake District & Cumbria	£8.99	....
Lancashire & Cheshire	£8.99	....
Northumberland & Durham	£8.99	....
Peak District and Derbyshire	£8.99	....
Yorkshire	£8.99	....
Hidden Places National Titles		
England	£11.99	....
Ireland	£11.99	....
Scotland	£11.99	....
Wales	£11.99	....
Other Titles		
Off The Motorway	£11.99	....
Garden Centres and Nurseries of Britain	£11.99	....

	Price	Quantity
Country Living Rural Guides		
East Anglia	£10.99	....
Heart of England	£10.99	....
Ireland	£11.99	....
North East of England	£10.99	....
North West of England	£10.99	....
Scotland	£11.99	....
South of England	£10.99	....
South East of England	£10.99	....
Wales	£11.99	....
West Country	£10.99	....

TOTAL QUANTITY ______

TOTAL VALUE ______

READER REACTION FORM

The *Travel Publishing* research team would like to receive readers' comments on any visitor attractions or places reviewed in the book and also recommendations for suitable entries to be included in the next edition. This will help ensure that the ***Hidden Places series of Travel Guides*** continues to provide its readers with useful information on the more interesting, unusual or unique features of each attraction or place ensuring that their visit to the local area is an enjoyable and stimulating experience. To provide your comments or recommendations would you please complete the forms below and overleaf as indicated and send to:

The Research Department, Travel Publishing Ltd, Airport Business Centre, 10 Thornbury Road, Estover, Plymouth PL6 7PP

YOUR NAME:

YOUR ADDRESS:

YOUR TEL NO:

Please tick as appropriate: COMMENTS ☐ RECOMMENDATION ☐

ESTABLISHMENT:

ADDRESS:

TEL NO:

CONTACT NAME:

PLEASE COMPLETE FORM OVERLEAF

READER REACTION FORM

COMMENT OR REASON FOR RECOMMENDATION:

....

....

....

....

....

....

....

....

....

....

....

....

....

....

....

....

INDEX OF TOWNS, VILLAGES AND PLACES OF INTEREST

INDEX OF TOWNS, VILLAGES AND PLACES OF INTEREST

INDEX OF TOWNS, VILLAGES AND PLACES OF INTEREST

O

P

R

S

T

W

Y

ADVERTISERS

ACCOMMODATION

FOOD AND DRINK

ADVERTISERS

ADVERTISERS

PLACES OF INTEREST